PROVINCE OF REASON

🌷 PROVINCE OF REASON

Sam Bass Warner, Jr.

THE BELKNAP PRESS OF
HARVARD UNIVERSITY PRESS
CAMBRIDGE, MASSACHUSETTS
AND LONDON, ENGLAND
1984

Copyright © 1984 by the President and Fellows of Harvard College
All rights reserved
Printed in the United States of America
10 9 8 7 6 5 4 3 2 1

This book is printed on acid-free paper, and its binding materials
have been chosen for strength and durability.

Designed by Marianne Perlak

Library of Congress Cataloging in Publication Data
Warner, Sam Bass, 1928–
    Province of reason.
    Includes bibliographical references and index.
    1. Boston Region (Mass.)—Biography.   2. Boston
Region (Mass.)—Civilization.   3. United States—
Civilization—20th century.   4. United States—
Biography.   I. Title.
F73.25.W37   1984   974.4′61   84-7653
ISBN 0-674-71956-5 (alk. paper)

The credits on page 290 constitute an extension of the copyright page.

To Rebecca, William, Kate, and Alice
A part of this history is theirs as well as mine

ACKNOWLEDGMENTS

This book has taken me many years to work out, and during that time I have attempted several preliminary versions, two of which have been published as *The Way We Really Live: Social Change in Metropolitan Boston Since 1920* (Boston, 1978), and "Listening for the Dead," in *The Public Historian*, 5 (Fall 1983), 63-70. I am grateful to the John Simon Guggenheim Foundation, the Rockefeller Foundation, and the National Endowment for the Humanities for grants that financed a sabbatical and later a term's leave, which enabled me to find time for research and writing.

While I was writing the early drafts of this book, many friends and scholars offered valuable ideas, suggestions, criticisms, and letters of support. I wish to thank Daniel Aaron, David E. Berndt, Joseph Boskin, John Coolidge, Peter Davison, Michael Frisch, Patricia A. Graham, Mason Hammond, Oscar Handlin, Dolores Hayden, Everett W. Mendelsohn, Richard Rabinowitz, and Robert Shaplen.

Because the subjects touched upon in this book are so various, I depended upon the assistance of a number of librarians and researchers: Margaret DePopolo and Micheline Jedrey of the Rotch Library at MIT, Wallace Dailey of the Theodore Roosevelt Collection of the Harvard University Library, Nancy Pellini of the Technical Information Center of Stone & Webster, Helen Slotkin of the MIT Archives, and the archivists of the Swarthmore College Peace Collection, Rachel Ablow for her Brookline research, Michael Steinlauf for his translations from Yiddish, and the many librarians of Bates Hall, Boston Public Library, where this book was written.

Once the text began to take shape, a number of friends and scholars gave me careful readings and thoughtful criticisms. These gifts of time, skill, and knowledge have been of immense benefit. I would like to thank Edward L. Bowles, Paul Brooks, Alfred D. Chandler, Jr., John Cumbler, Lorna Marshall, Elizabeth M. Thomas, Cecelia Tichi, William M. Tuttle, Jr., Anne F. Scott, Barbara M. Solomon, Evelyn Stone, and my wife, Lyle L. Warner.

A grant from Boston University supported a careful final typing by John H. Orenberg. The suggestions and editing of Aida Donald and Margaret Anderson of Harvard University Press put the book in its final form, and I am much in their debt for their thoughtfulness and pains.

Finally, two people have aided and encouraged me from the very first years of this project. Robert Wiebe of Northwestern University has been my correspondent and historical companion for many years, and his letters, comments, and readings have carried me over many a hard place. Diana J. Kleiner, a research librarian at the Boston Public Library, has worked with me on this and many other research projects over the past seven years, and her skill, curiosity, and faith that there must be a source somewhere has given me access to knowledge I would never have discovered otherwise.

Boston, Massachusetts
January 1984

CONTENTS

PROVINCE OF REASON

INTRODUCTION

This book is about some of the largest events of the twentieth century, about international wars, economic collapse, new science and technologies, and about cities whose population and area are as big as whole states. But this study sees those events through the eyes of particular people in one particular region of the United States in order to understand the vastness, the barbarism, and the unimaginable that are the central experiences of recent history.

In our lifetime humankind has come to be understood as more than all Europeans and Americans, more than all Christians and Jews, more than all whites and blacks; it now means what the word says, all the human beings living on the planet. We now realize that the schoolchild's far-away Esquimaux or the novelist's Patagonians are bound to us and we to them. The century's repeated national and religious exterminations, its wars that have consumed millions, and its staggering parade of military tyrants who torture and massacre those in whose name they govern—such events tell the ordinary citizen he is but an ant, moving freely until he is crushed by barbarism. What has been unimaginable is everywhere.

In the face of daily assaults on our personal life, we seek our bearings by scanning news reports for reassurance about a probable tomorrow. The pictures on film and television, relayed instantly by satellite, heap up mounds of facts through which we anxiously pick, hoping to find clues to identify tomorrow. We cannot avoid gathering up our facts in the colors in which they are delivered to us: red and deterrent, trade and default, liberation and guerrilla, progress and high technology, know-how and bankruptcy, robots and genetic engineering, unemployment and underdeveloped. The very words and phrases by which we organize our search for understanding the world beyond ourselves partake of the vastness, the barbarism, and the unimaginable from which we seek relief.

For people harassed by the modern flood of messages, the commonplace and common sense take on fresh value. Individual experience, how a person lived as a child in a family, and in a particular place, how people did their work—such details seem a useful antidote to the floods of public messages. Perhaps we can form a reliable base for consciousness by a thoughtful review of the material of individual lives. Indeed, such reasoning has, in recent years, fostered a small vogue in autobiography and biography.[1] Readers and authors are seeking the solidity offered by the experiences of single lives.

This is such a book. It is a review of the lives of fourteen people who moved in and out of and within the modern metropolitan region of Boston. The lives and the place are bound together; the fourteen were chosen because they exemplified and contributed to important events in the region, and the region was chosen because it nourished and attracted such people.

Today the Boston metropolis, with more than six million people, stretches outward approximately eighty-odd miles from the old parent city.[2] Its boundaries include many cities, suburbs, waste lands, and resorts tied together in a social network of automobile commuting, telephone calls, and the innumerable exchanges of work, school, and play. It is a unique place with its own particular natural and human history, but it is also a very ordinary American place, typical of the nation's many metropolises.

The region has four special meanings for this book. First, when Boston was the nation's publishing center, its authors, particularly Ralph Waldo Emerson and Henry David Thoreau, wrote widely popular interpretations of the nineteenth-century romantic movement. Their views have endured as a tradition in Boston, and they continue to influence today's ways of living and understanding.

Second, as one of the world's earliest industrialized regions, Boston has known during the past hundred years the cycle of industrial prosperity, decay, and reindustrialization. The cycle has had powerful effects upon the residents of this metropolis; the suffering and success they have experienced are now being repeated in other regions of the United States and Europe.

Third, because of its early wealth and close connections to the intellectual and cultural trends of the Atlantic world, Boston long stood at the forefront of changing fashions in urban family life. It pioneered in the design of suburbs and public parks, even in vacation styles. Its women fostered a wide array of social, political, educational, and cultural institutions that totally altered the terms of modern urban family life.

Finally, Boston was an early home of learning, of invention, and of universities, and in the past century it has become a world center of modern science. Science, both learned and military, now dominates the local culture and has drawn many of the region's leaders into national and international prominence.

This book examines the interplay of these four local circumstances with the lives of fourteen Bostonians and the course of twentieth-century history. The span of the lives of these men and women reaches from 1850, when the eldest was born, to 1980, when the last of the group died. Those years form the boundaries of the period when today's existence was fashioned. In a rough way two generations appear in this book, the first born between 1850 and 1870, the second born after 1880. I do not present the lives in chronological order, however, because that would imply that what the elders did determined the course of the younger generation. Ours is a wealthy, liberal, and open society, and although the past sets limits upon the present, within these boundaries choices abound. Even in Boston's most depressed decades, and even in its meanest out-of-luck mill towns, individuals faced many choices of goals, interpretations of what they were learning, and ways to live and to work. At all times there existed more choices than any one person could take advantage of. The decisions made and the patterns formed by the multiplication of those decisions constituted the links between personal life and the large events of the century.

We must begin by recasting our familiar history in terms of the vastness of modern life. We all are aware of our ties to distant places, giant institutions, and foreign events; the very foods we purchase, the phone calls we make, the news we hear tells us that much. But to assess the meanings of this vastness we must match its presence to the trends of decades. Accordingly this book begins with the familiar history that Bostonians tell each other today, which is retold in Part I in terms of three individual lives and their discoveries of the vastness of the modern world.[3] Part II takes up the experience of four people who vigorously pursued the possibilities of their times. Part III examines the experiences of economic collapse, and Part IV takes up the lives of three persons who portray the isolation and the deep separations of modern American life. The two lives in Part V tell something of the contradictory nature of modern possibilities.

The book ends without the usual formal conclusion of a history because I feel there should be no final summary to these stories of past lives. Each reader may repeat in some way my experiences in researching and writing this book. As you read, you can lay your own life next to any of the fourteen and thereby estimate who you are and where you have been. As Alfred Kazin has so often put it, we are a nation of men and women who have endeavored to escape traditions, and therefore self-discovery is our preoccupation and delight.[4]

I ❧ THE PROVINCE IN AN EMPIRE

IN A WORLD so jammed with invented news, insistent advertisements, and special pleading of all kinds, it is useful to begin a history at a place where the reader and the historian share a common authority. Our memories make us all experts on the events of childhood, the progressions from home to school and the first steps carrying us to jobs and to marriage. There is enough that is universal in this part of life to provide us all with reliable measures of the experiences of others, and the intensity of our memories protects us against fashionable bunkum. Autobiographies and biographies vary a great deal in the amount of their detail, but the early years are always attended to.

This book begins with the recollections of two men and one woman who set down a lot of information about their youth. Robert Grant, a judge, author, and clubman, lived his entire life within Boston's center of wealth and fashion; Mary Antin, a poor Jewish immigrant from Russia, made her way through the slums of Boston to national prominence; Fred Allen, the son of an alcoholic bookbinder, was raised by an aunt in the working-class sections of the city before he began a triumphant career as an entertainer. The memories of these Bostonians about what it was like to grow up in the city seventy-five and a hundred years ago enable the reader and the historian to start together with a comparison of the universal experiences of childhood and the particulars of urban life in a time earlier than that of our own memories. Such a beginning, it is hoped, will allow us to build a framework for understanding the unexpected, the modern, and the difficult in these and the other lives that follow.

In addition to having given us rich memories of childhood and youth, these three people represent central figures in today's popular view of Boston history. They are what we have chosen to remember of our past. Like most Americans, Bostonians prefer to recall their history as a succession of triumphs of wealth and power. The pioneers came, suffered hard times, and ultimately settled themselves comfortably. After them came wave after wave of fresh migrants, and after several centuries the ranks of the comfortable and of the triumphant came to be composed of descendants of these migrations. In private gatherings Bostonians tell each other family stories of country boys and girls who made good in the city, of greenhorns from overseas who mastered local ways, of poor city boys and girls who found paths to comfort and riches. In a rough way, both private and public histories are constructed from mobility tales.

Because of the struggles of previous generations with their ethnic and religious animosities, Boston's public history has taken a special twist not commonly found in United States civic memories. The history of the region is told today in terms of ethnic stereotypes that were given written form by local novelists. In *The Late George Apley* (1937) John P. Marquand fixed the early-settler Bostonian in the form of a silly aristocrat, a wealthy Yankee who had retreated into manners and mannerisms. Edwin O'Connor cast the descendants of the Irish immigrants in the mold of a hearty popular politician, the city boss of *The Last Hurrah* (1956). Recently these stereotypes have been reworked successfully, and an attractive, hard-working, intelligent Italian gangster has been added to the local tradition in James Carroll's *Mortal Friends* (1978).

Now that these white ethnic and religious animosities have quieted, new problems have forced themselves upon us—racial fears and hatreds, prosperity and depression, the ominous powers of modern weapons. We need to retell the old stories, not just to savor the pleasures of personal success, but to discover the connections among the lives of those who came before us and the city and the world we now inhabit.

As Robert Grant, Mary Antin, and Fred Allen made their way, they discovered important things about the place of their Boston in the world beyond. Like any large modern city, their Boston proved to be a subordinate city in a highly ramified network of cities, a province in an empire.

The empire discovered by these three Bostonians took several forms, and its character and dimensions were various, as they remain today. In all its forms, however, the empire caught up the individual and the local in far-reaching and dominating webs of power. Robert Grant, traveling the short distance from his downtown clubs to his neighbors' drawing rooms, discovered Boston businesses to be national and international. He imagined the most successful of these institutions to be all-seeing and all-powerful, firms that could buy and sell politicians, scientists, and whole mill towns.

Mary Antin discovered an empire of the mind, where imagination stretched out from personal and local experience to the whole world, destroying ancient traditions and mocking personal adjustments and local adaptations. The order, stability, and comfort of the commonplace routine of family life could find no back-up, no resonance in the boundless possibilities of a modern imagination.

Fred Allen was not an anxious, seeking individual like Mary Antin, nor a settled aristocrat like Robert Grant. Through his national success in the modern role of radio star and entertainer of millions he discovered the institutions of the empire in yet another of their manifestations. He found the giant new corporations to be timid, fearful, seeking ever to disguise themselves in conventional attitudes and commonly traded platitudes. The modern imagination was the last thing they wished to deal with. His giant businesses imitated the strategy of tomato worms— large, heavy-feeding, but so matched to the body they devoured that it was difficult to tell the worm from the plant itself.

Whatever the forms, whether resembling the all-powerful, all-seeing businesses of Robert Grant or the boundless imaginings of Mary Antin, the power of modern institutions and ideas has transformed a metropolis of six million people from a city in a nation to a province in an empire.

1 ❧ ROBERT GRANT

Robert Grant (1852–1942) spent his entire lifetime within walking distance of his Beacon Hill birthplace. Like many authors in his day, he was fascinated by the manners and tensions of *haute bourgeois* family life, and it was through this concern that he discovered both modern Boston and the world beyond.

His residential life was a slow parade through a succession of houses, following the fashion in neighborhoods from Beacon Hill to the outer Back Bay.[1] Grant's father, Patrick, was a moderately successful commission merchant who dealt in flour, industrial chemicals, and merchandise. By descent and marriage, the father was linked to a number of well-to-do Boston merchant families.[2] A thoroughly conservative man, Patrick never discussed money or personal finances with his family, and unlike many of Boston's wealthy, he did not invest in the new western railroad and mining stocks and bonds. His son, however, did claim that Patrick introduced the waltz to Boston after learning the dance on a trip to Italy in 1829. An active clubman from his college days, Patrick Grant went out almost every night after dinner, which was served at 5 P.M., to play whist and socialize at one or another of his downtown clubs.[3]

Patrick Grant's first wife died after three years of marriage, leaving one daughter, who later died in childbirth while still a young woman.[4] In 1850, some years after the death of his first wife, Patrick married another Boston merchant's daughter, and in six years she bore him four children, the eldest being Robert, born in 1852, then two more boys, Harold and Patrick, Jr., and a daughter, Flora, born in 1858. In his autobiography Robert Grant says little of his mother, Charlotte, but he remembered her as the very model of the giving Victorian woman.[5]

Grant's report of his growing up some hundred and thirty years ago seems most notable for the differences between his childhood boundaries and those of today. As a child on Beacon Hill during the 1860s, Robert lived near the countinghouses, wharves, railroad stations, theaters and hotels—indeed, within walking distance of the entire city. His immediate neighborhood was not a large territory, like a 1980s suburb, nor was it set apart from either the work or the social classes of his day.

By the time they were twelve, when they went off to public and private Latin schools to prepare for college, Beacon Hill boys ran free. There were no school or city recreation departments—games were pick-up affairs arranged by the players. Hill boys like Grant and his contemporary Henry Cabot Lodge engaged in a lot of mischief, which ranged from tormenting shopkeepers and sliding down the roofs of old ladies' houses to outright delinquent destruction and harassment. Grant recalled the glories of snowball fights through his neighbors' yards and on the Common, as well as snowball wars with black children. The year Robert was a senior in the Boston Latin School his younger brother Harold was stabbed by a hoodlum on Boston Common while trying to prevent some toughs from taking twelve-year-old Patrick's sled.[6]

Yet even though they ran free once out of the house and out of school, the boys were more surrounded by families than today's suburban child. Parents, relatives, servants were everywhere. At the age of five, along with other neighborhood children, Robert was sent to a little school run by Miss Sarah M. Brown in a stables next door. Each day a children's dinner was served at 2 P.M. at home in the basement pantry between the kitchen and dining room. The hour coincided with Father's return from the countinghouse, and he would visit with the children and have a glass of sherry before going out for his afternoon horseback ride.[7] By his own account a "fairly timid and unassertive child," Robert was a bookworm who in time became a good scholar. His next school, fourth and fifth grades, only took him across the Common to Boylston Place.[8]

From age seven through age twenty, Robert Grant spent every summer with his family at Grandmother Rice's cottage at Nahant. The cottage held the six members of Patrick Grant's family, a widowed aunt and her two children, Grandmother Rice herself, a visiting uncle and other distant relatives, a butler, a cook, a handyman, and maids in numbers unremembered. Father commuted by boat across the harbor to his office in downtown Boston, leaving the family to entertain itself. The summer routine consisted of eating enormous meals, reading and chatting on the broad piazza that wrapped around the house, taking walks and carriage rides, climbing on the Nahant rocks, swimming, playing croquet and, for the boys, sailing. The summering families recognized that the vacation was too long and that the boys had too little to do, so they hired one of Robert's schoolmasters to run a summer school.[9] For girls the encasement within the boundaries of the family and its servants was even more complete. As Robert put it, recalling the possibilities even for the most grown-up, "Feminine summer recreation was still at a low ebb and except for croquet and an occasional moonlight party on the water, the chief excitement of the season lay in the yearly outing of the Cadets, the crack corps which attended the Governor. Their visit for a week with its semblance of roughing it in tents on the verge of the ocean served as a stimulus to midnight flirtation under the trees or on the improvised parade ground."[10]

Robert was frightened by the size of the sixth grade—three hundred students—when he entered the Boston Latin School (then located on Bedford Street near Tremont, across the Common from Grant's house), but his reading habits soon made him a good student. He graduated as a prize scholar in 1869 and passed his Harvard entrance examinations.

At college he again began timidly as a newcomer, but by his sophomore year he was well launched in several clubs, was playing on Harvard's pioneer football teams, and had introduced tennis to the college.[11] He lived at home and also regularly went to the theater and parties in Boston. A good but not ambitious scholar, Grant in time found himself most comfortable with the college literary set. He wrote small pieces for the *Advocate*, then became its editor. After graduation in 1873 he attempted a grand tour of Europe, but fell ill in Paris. He returned to Harvard to read modern literature. Using the university more in the style of our times than his, Grant spent ten years at Harvard, receiving his Ph.D. in 1876 and his LL.D. in 1879.[12] Through this extended education he found the place and the time to assemble his adult roles of author, lawyer, and clubman.

These years of reading literature were also years of growing up with his young sister Flora, who was just then a "bud." In 1874 the Grant family had purchased a large house in the Back Bay at 14 Commonwealth Avenue, so when Flora came out in 1877 there was a second-floor ballroom for her dancing parties.[13] Robert followed the debutante life with his sister until she married five years later. Grant fictionalized Flora's experiences in his widely read book, *The Confessions of a Frivolous Girl, A Story of Fashionable Life* (Boston, 1880).[14]

As he followed the life of a young literary gentleman of leisure, Grant, realizing that the family fortune would not support such a style, was forced to find a career. In 1876 the death of Grandmother Rice sparked a family discussion of its fortune and its inheritances. "It had dawned on me that far from being rich, my parents were only comfortably off according to the waxing standards of the day." The theme of limited means and rising expenses of ever more demanding fashion later appeared in many of Grant's novels. At the time the problem of money was matched by "the determination not to be supported by anyone else [which] was part of the social creed of self-respecting men of my day," and this spurred Grant on in his studies at the Harvard Law School.[15] By happy accident, at this time the founders of the Harvard *Lampoon*, the undergraduate humor magazine, were about to graduate, and Grant joined a fresh team of editors to keep the magazine going. His associates included Frederick Stimson, later a lawyer and author, and Barrett Wendell, who became a professor of English. Three of Grant's *Lampoon* pieces, verse tragedies in the Greek form on chaperones and wallflowers, and a little story on male timidity and advanced female courtship manners, called "Oxygen, a Mt. Desert Pastoral," he brought out as an anonymous pamphlet entitled *The Little-Tin-Gods-on-Wheels or, Society in Our Modern Athens,* in 1879. It caught on and went through nine editions.[16]

That same year Grant was admitted to the Suffolk County bar, and with another Harvard graduate, "an intelligent and witty fellow of congenial tastes," he set up practice at 19 Congress Street. Business came slowly, and Robert soon realized he had not the personality for a successful lawyer: He tended to get "rattled" and "lose my head in conflict with others." Others must have realized that the young man was not a promising champion, for there proved to be a lot of time between cases, time to write the successful *Frivolous Girl* (1880). While his law practice languished, his literary reputation flourished, and he was soon elected to the Papyrus Club, a monthly dining group whose leader was the journalist and poet John Boyle O'Reilly.[17] It was O'Reilly who helped Grant find his lifetime formula for success—a political appointment with time for literature on the side. O'Reilly secured him a post as secretary to the newly elected mayor, Samuel A. Green, and for a year Grant drew a regular salary.

Then in February 1882, Grant's mother died, and a year later his father's firm failed because of an unexpected drop in the price of soda ash.[18] Suddenly Robert was the head of his family. He had been going to cotillions, fishing for salmon in Canada, and even summering in London, trips taken in pursuit of Miss Amy Galt of Montreal, the eldest of eight daughters of a Canadian statesman. In July 1883 Robert and Amy married.[19] His sister Flora had married the previous year, so the big Commonwealth Avenue house could be sold. Robert and Amy thereupon began their family life at a new house farther out in the Back Bay at Marlborough and Clarendon streets. The young couple took in Robert's father as a permanent boarder.[20]

Grant continued his practice of law until 1888, when O'Reilly again came to his aid, this time with an appointment to fill a vacancy on the Boston Water Commission. During these years Grant established his literary audience. After writing two boys' adventure books, he began a highly successful series of tongue-in-cheek magazine pieces for *Scribner's Magazine* in New York on commonplace incidents in the married life of a well-to-do couple, Fred and Josephine. The *Scribner's* series was soon published in book form, and the volumes remained popular for years as good-natured domestic comment.[21] In 1893, once more through his club contacts, Grant secured a permanent appointment as second judge of probate and insolvency for Suffolk County, a position he held until his retirement thirty years later.[22]

As a political appointee and as a city judge, Grant was necessarily aware of immigrants because they appeared frequently in his courtroom with family and financial problems. But they seem not to have engaged his curiosity. The waves of migrants from eastern and southern Europe did not appear in his novels; his immigrants were Irish, mostly politicians whose behavior he linked to the pervasive laxity of modern Boston morals.[23] In his last novel he predicted that the Democratic Boston Irish would soon overwhelm Yankee Republicanism by their sheer numbers.[24]

Although there is little overt prejudice in any of Grant's books, and none of the commonplace ethnic and religious nastiness that pervaded the Boston province in his day, he lacked curiosity about immigrant lives and had no concern for the problems of non-Yankees. In his old age this blindness cost Grant some pain and notoriety, and it cost Nicola Sacco and Bartolomeo Vanzetti their lives. Grant served with presidents A. Lawrence Lowell of Harvard and Samuel W. Stratton of MIT on Governor Fuller's pardon review panel, and he joined with them to recommend no reprives.[25]

Domestic issues better suited Grant's interests in the courtroom. The special duties of a probate judge, to hear cases of wills, trusts, and divorce, gave direction to the themes of his domestic fiction and set him on a path of law reform. In respect to both family life and women, Grant's code of manners was that of late Victorian *haute bourgeois* society. He accepted as proper the encapsulation of women within the home. Girls in his set did not go to the city's public schools; instead they were trained at private schools in the arts, in music, in painting, and in languages and literature. They had to wait until they married before they established their own households. If a woman remained a spinster, she lived with her mother and sisters, or, at the very most extreme, alone, but within the Beacon Hill and Back Bay neighborhoods. These women were not employed in business; they were not at large in society except when they were older, when they could take charge of public subscriptions and charitable committees. The tolerated exceptions to these rules were a few wealthy widows and spinsters who were allowed eccentric enthusiasms.

For all its domestic confinement, the woman's role had a very important social function in Grant's view. Women, by example and through social manipulation, sustained the refined culture of the world at large. "Daughters were presumed to be nature's contribution," Grant wrote, "not only to the continuance of human society, but its embellishment. Without their personal interest and supervision polite usage must lapse into savagery."[26]

Modern society attacked the institution of the *haute bourgeois* family from two directions. The first attack came from the *nouveaux riches*. Grant saw in the world of 1900 a new class of women who were acquiring prominence and authority without sufficient prior training as ladies. These newly powerful women lacked respect for "modesty, sweetness and self-control," which, when joined with "elegance, wit and cultivation," are the hallmarks of a "true lady."[27] One such crass and self-aggrandizing woman appeared in his novel *Unleavened Bread* (1900).[28]

The second attack came from within the established families themselves. Grant observed the new ways of the younger generation with alarm: both young men and young women were seeking personal happiness outside the circle of family obligation and were demanding the right to sexual expression. The sexuality of twentieth-century Boston society and of modern literature were for Grant snares for self-destruction. As he watched wealthy young people follow the new path, he felt the tawdriness and hypocrisy of the divorce court seep into his cherished circle of Back Bay family life.[29]

Though he feared and deplored these modern trends, as a judge he had a concern for justice and a desire that women be dealt with fairly. He came to object to the spendthrift trust, the common instrument whereby one generation of a wealthy family endeavored to control the life of the next. He also saw from the bench the poor financial performance of the city's professional trustees, and in response he urged women to go into the profession of money management for their own protection.[30] Most objectionable of all were the contemporary frauds and hypocrisy of divorce trials. In 1903 Grant wrote a novel, *Undercurrent,* about the plight of a woman who was forbidden to remarry by religious custom, and in 1925 he wrote about fraudulent divorce in *Bishop's Daughter.* After World War I he began an active campaign for the national reform of divorce laws, and especially for the passage of a uniform divorce law by the several states.[31]

Municipal politics, Back Bay family life, and the divorce court were affairs of Grant's own daily life, but he learned of larger worlds beyond Pemberton Square and Marlborough Street from his clubs. There he came in contact with big business, national politics, high culture, and international affairs. Through golf at The Country Club in Brookline and at the Myopia Hunt Club in Hamilton he met Judge Oliver Wendell Holmes and President William Howard Taft.[32] The Saturday Club, a luncheon group that had been founded by Ralph Waldo Emerson at the Parker House, had removed in 1902 to the Union Club. Here for many years Grant dined with Harvard's President Charles Eliot and scholars like Charles Eliot Norton, Bliss Perry, and the Nobel prize-winning chemist Theodore Richards, with whom he became friends.[33]

The Winter's Night Club, a men's group that dined in each other's homes one evening a month, was a nest of Boston leaders, including Alexander Agassiz, Moorfield Storey, James Jackson Storrow, Jr., a brace of college presidents, Grant's next-door neighbor, Cardinal O'Connell, and Grant's close friend, the historian James Ford Rhodes.[34] As a Harvard overseer from 1895 to 1922, he continued his college acquaintanceship with Theodore Roosevelt, and later met Franklin Roosevelt on the same board. In January 1912 Theodore stayed overnight at Grant's home at 211 Bay State Road, and from Grant's library he held a press conference to announce his campaign for the Republican nomination.[35]

From the information and suggestions picked up from these sources Robert Grant wrote his best novel, *The Chippendales* (1909), in which he expressed his widest view of the forces transforming his provincial life. In his story, set in the last two decades of the century, he imagined modern history to be carrying Boston onward in an overlapping series of events: the migration of ambitious poor boys from rural New England to Boston;

the bankruptcy of many old families through failure to keep up with the times; the intermarrying of the successful new rich with the old families; the progression of technology from water wheels and steam engines to electricity; the expansion of finance from private trading merchants to the public marketing of stocks and bonds; the explosion of business from old local firms to national corporations; the political change from aristocratic Republican rule to rivalry between college-trained reformers and Irish city politicians.

In the face of such transformations the central question for Robert Grant became the fate of traditional *haute bourgeois* morality. Could the New England conscience, as he put it, that individualistic, Protestant, often eccentric nineteenth-century conscience, survive?[36] A quarter of a century later, in 1937, John P. Marquand answered that question in the negative. The conscience of his old Bostonian, George Apley, had shriveled into manners. For Grant, however, the nineteenth-century tradition was still viable. In their basic conflicts his heroes tested their ability to adapt traditional morality to the modern requirements for money making.

The Chippendales is a charming book because the many oppositions of the characters are handled in such a good-natured way. Beneath the major plot of courtship and the rise of a new family fortune, Robert Grant revealed both the anxieties of the Boston elite and their connections to the major public events of the day. The elite Boston tradition, as Grant knew it, held the New England conscience prisoner within the family and its property. That conscience, whether it be the withering of Harrison Chippendale, the eccentric vigor of Georgiana Chippendale, or the straight-arrow replication of Henry Sumner, always found its nourishment and meanings first within the vessel of the family. Conscience grew outward from the family business to the network of relatives and the surrounding community. In 1900 in Boston, as that conscience grew it collided with large events of imperial scale—immigrants, new technology, finance capital, the business corporation. Here it confronted possibilities and dangers far beyond its family and provincial compass. Here it faltered.

The novel followed this tension through the behavior of two generations. The patriarch of the older generation of Chippendales was the fool Harrison Chippendale, an elegant, high-minded Brahmin whose old merchant wealth had shrunk through his neglect and bad management and whose moralisms prattled into irrelevancy. Harrison Chippendale had no occupation save that of gentleman of leisure, and he had lost most of his own inheritance as well as that of his widowed sister, Eleanor Chippendale Sumner.

Harrison's other sister, Georgiana Chippendale, represented both new wealth and old conscience. Georgiana had personally supervised the investment of her inheritance and had grown rich in new ventures like western mines and railroads. She also stood for the eccentric spinster-philanthropic manifestation of the New England conscience, leading Boston charities and occasionally appearing as the champion of freak causes, like the protection of the Boston Common squirrels. Harrison's brother, Baxter, was a bachelor and a miser. His wealth had grown, but his conscience had decayed in the opposite direction from his brother's self-indulgence.

In this same generation of older people a minor character, Gideon Avery, manifested still another variation on the New England conscience. Avery was an inventor, a man who spent his entire life and all of his modest inheritance trying to devise a way to transform coke into electricity. His single-minded devotion to his vision in the end produced a powerful invention that provided the key to wealth for the next generation of Chippendales.[37]

The crucial actions of the book turned around the money-making and marriages of the younger generation, and in this field the moral outcomes ultimately escaped the novelist's imagination. Harrison Chippendale's son, Chauncey, was a Harvard College football star who became a State Street broker and investment banker. From his college days onward his was always a loose-jointed morality that skated along the margins of fraud. He was a successful money-maker who fit comfortably into what Grant characterized as an "easy-going, but efficient modernity." His behavior was the college-educated companion to Irish municipal politics.[38]

Henry Sumner, Eleanor Chippendale Sumner's only son, stood alone in the younger generation as the undiluted strain of the old tradition. Henry suffered many of the disabilities of such an inheritance. As a young man he was stuffy and awkward, and his emotions were bottled up in guilt and rectitude. His girl friend, later his wife, described him as "stiff and narrow, unornamental, self-righteous, a classic objector, and frightfully proper."[39] He intended to become a Harvard classics scholar, but Uncle Harrison's mismanagement of his mother's inheritance forced Henry out into the world of business. He became a lawyer, a specialist in lost causes.

At first his was a practice of virtue without monetary reward. For a time he seemed headed toward a life of eccentric philanthropy, like Aunt Georgiana, whom he enlisted in a campaign to save the elms and the graves of the Common from destruction by the new subway tunnel from Park Street to Boylston Street. But in time he matured from prig to idealist. Some of his cases were minority stockholder suits that brought both justice and substantial profits to lawyer and client. Eccentric civic duty also led to his reputation for public rectitude, and Henry became a vigorous, if unsuccessful, reform candidate for mayor of Boston. His final moral test arrived when he refused his Aunt Georgiana's bequest of $600,000, which had been proffered on the condition that he change his name to Chippendale. He refused the legacy in order to continue to honor the memory of his Civil War hero father. Marriage ultimately rewarded Henry's virtue. After a booklong courtship, he won Priscilla, the beautiful, intelligent, and morally concerned daughter of the inventor, Gideon Avery. At the end of the novel all the Chippendale descendants were rich, and Henry and Priscilla were not only wealthy but remained devoted to an intense personal exploration of the New England conscience.[40]

In Grant's novel the imperial representative was Hugh McDowell Blaisdell, the son of an impoverished Maine widow of no social standing. Hugh came fresh from a small country college to make his fortune in Boston. A letter of recommendation to his dead father's Civil War commander, a general who was then running Boston's largest investment banking and brokerage house, gave him his opening in business. The general found Blaisdell a job in a small firm, and by dint of being very smart, very hardworking, and in time very shrewd, Blaisdell built a firm and a fortune surpassing the general's, a fortune of imperial, not merely provincial, dimensions.

Grant was most interested in the family consequences of Blaisdell's new wealth: his marriages, his purchases of a house in the Back Bay and a summer house on the North Shore, his display, and the relationships he and his wives formed with the other elite families of Boston. In the process of telling the family consequences of Blaisdell's fortune, Grant took pleasure in poking fun at the old-fashioned manners of the generation of the 1880s, as well as at the lavish and somewhat lax style of the new generation.[41] But the central moral issue of the twentieth century, the question of to what and whom a large new imperial fortune might be accountable, escaped Grant. He knew the issue was there, but he lacked a way of even imagining its dimensions.

Blaisdell made his giant fortune in two ways. First, he successfully built a small business in investment banking into a large one. In short, he rode the wave of corporate enlargement and industrial expansion of his time. In addition, he won a truly imperial fortune by organizing and managing a giant manufacturing trust built wholly upon a new industry. He organized Electric Coke, which exploited the old Yankee inventor's process for making electricity. In so doing, Blaisdell's conscience, an unusually firm one for its day, forbade him to close out the inventor, as Alexander Graham Bell had been bought off. Perhaps because the inventor was his father-in-law, Blaisdell allowed the old man to participate in the profits of the ever-growing company. Here, then, the morality of the individual and the family held the parties to a decent standard, but beyond this scale of relationship Grant was helpless.

At one point Grant invented a scene in the offices of the new financial giant. It was a scene of bells and telephones and flunkies, a command post in a world network of business intelligence such as Hollywood later imagined when it wanted to present visible images of imperial business power. "Whatever Blaisdell undertook was initiated by pressing an electric button in his inner office. Through it and the telephone he aspired to rule the world. Sooner or later there appeared his financial factotum, his political man of all work, or whichever one of his salaried agents he desired to consult. They were like so many stops in an organ; he had but to finger them in order to test and play on public sentiment. Through them he had out feelers in diverse directions. His agents

kept henchmen on the lookout for promising investments, henchmen whose duty it was to see that accommodating candidates
were elected to the legislature, henchmen charged with the discovery of impecunious noblemen desirous to part with artistic
masterpieces."[42]

The portrait is full of wonder at modern technology and the
centralized organization of big business, but it also contains over-
tones of sinister power that Grant could not follow. The best he
could manage was a retreat into the early nineteenth-century
Boston compromise with industrialization, the happy paternal
mill town. Twentieth-century Electric Coke built another
Lowell! One spring day the family party of the inventor, Avery,
rode to the site of the works in Blaisdell's private railroad car and
picnicked on a knoll overlooking the mill valley. "They sat and
ate under a rustic arbor which, as Blaisdell explained, was the
trysting place for the younger element of the working population.
Did not the rude initials cut in the wooden benches attest to its
democratic popularity? Below them at the base of a gently slop-
ing landscape lay the factory buildings—the latest two dwarfing
the rest—breasting the water power, and from their vicinity an
imposing town—the growth of yesterday—yet with its schools,
churches, and department store, spread itself in the spring sun-
shine like a metropolis on a map. Already that morning had Mr.
Avery [the inventor] been gratified by receiving flowers from the
school children and an address of welcome from the chairman of
the Selectmen, who had saved until the last his secret that the
town which had hitherto clung to a name fastened on it when a
straggling village—Porterville—had voted to call itself henceforth
Avery."[43]

Surely an old dream, but hardly an adequate vision of the
meaning of "Electric Coke . . . one of the great industrial corporations of the world."[44] Robert Grant, the provincial novelist, clubman, and judge, had discovered the modern world, and it
frightened him. He hoped that somehow the old manners and
morals of the city's established families would survive to guide
the imperial tides of events that were then coursing through Boston. It was his best hope and his best comprehension.

2 ❧ MARY ANTIN

Robert Grant discovered the nature of his province and the existence of an empire by watching the changes taking place in his immediate circle of established Boston families. The world beyond refashioned Beacon Hill, the Back Bay, and Harvard College.

For Mary Antin (1881–1949), the process of discovery moved in quite the opposite direction. Like millions of others before and after her, she was forcibly uprooted by violent storms of religious and political attack. Her family was lured from its home in the Russian Pale by the hope of new economic opportunities and at the same time was driven out by economic failure. As an immigrant girl she had the American preoccupation with self-discovery thrust upon her. Jewish by birth and Bostonian by education, she responded by continually recombining the two traditions. Over the years her life carried her into national politics and into personal religious turmoil. Then in middle age she succeeded in finding a mystical union of her two traditions; in the end the self became the province, and mankind and the universe the empire.

It all began in the fall of 1894, when Mary's father, a religious scholar and failed merchant, took Mary and her younger brother and sister to the Chelsea public school, to Miss Nixon's first grade. Mary squeezed herself into the tiny chair, and with a class of a dozen other "green" Jewish immigrant children aged six to fifteen, she began to learn "how the common world looked, smelled, and tasted in the strange speech."[1] By midyear she had mastered English and was in Mary S. Dillingham's fifth grade.

Although Chelsea was the poorest of the Boston harborside

immigrant and industrial cities, its schoolteachers still thought that poor children could master the basic provincial culture. For Mary Antin, Miss Dillingham was the model teacher and guide. A strict Yankee schoolmarm, a woman of significant glances and few words, she trained and encouraged her able pupil in every way an elementary teacher could. She gave Mary extra time after class to help her master the sound of the English *w;* there followed half hours of poetry reading and the gift of a book of selections from Longfellow, Mary's first book of her own. Miss Dillingham published Mary's remarkable school exercises in the teachers' journal and later applauded the poems and bits Mary wrote for the Boston newspapers.[2] She became a family friend and confidante, attending Mary's sister's graduation and responding to her adolescent letters, which sometimes came daily. Miss Dillingham and her friends took Mary to the country to see autumn leaves, and it was at Miss Dillingham's home that Mary suffered the anguish and embarrassment of eating ham for the first time.[3]

In Russia Mary Antin had been excluded from public education because she was Jewish, and she had been forbidden Jewish education because she was a girl. Now, like someone slaking a lifelong thirst, she drew in everything the Chelsea schools had to teach. Within a year she overtook the native English-speaking thirteen-year-olds. Then, moved by her adopted country's image of a kindly father, George Washington, the very opposite of the demon czar, she composed a long patriotic poem that secured her position as a schoolgirl celebrity. Her father boasted of her on every occasion, and the Chelsea teachers showed her off to visiting school committeemen and teachers from out of town.[4]

While Mary triumphed and her brothers and sisters made good progress, her father failed in business again. The eldest sister, Frieda, had to give up school and travel across the harbor by ferry each day to a garment factory in downtown Boston. Slowly the little basement grocery store on Arlington Street died under the burden of the unpaid bills of its poor customers. Nothing remained but to move on, to borrow some more money from the Hebrew Immigrant Aid Society, and to try again. This time the Antins moved to the heart of the immigrant Jewish ghetto in

Boston's South End, to 11 Wheeler Street. In 1895 this was "a crooked lane connecting a corner saloon on Shawmut Avenue with a block of houses of ill repute on Corning Street."[5]

Caught in the midst of the economic depression of 1896, Mary's mother and father were buried in the anxieties of their little basement grocery. A new baby came, and while Frieda nursed the mother, Mary and her younger sister Dora took over the care of the infant girl. Frieda continued at the factory, but most important, Mary's brother Joseph developed a successful newspaper business that sustained the family and kept Mary at school.[6]

The apartment was cramped with seven Antins, including the new baby, and the occasional addition of "a greener or two from Polotzk [Russia] whom we had lodged as a matter of course till they found a permanent home." There was little there for the children except "meals in the kitchen and beds in the dark."[7] "Chaos took the place of system; uncertainty, inconsistency undermined discipline. My parents knew only that they desired us to be like American children; and seeing how their neighbors gave their children boundless liberty, they turned us also loose, never doubting but that the American way was the best way ... In their bewilderment they must needs trust us children to learn such models as the tenement afforded. This sad process of disintegration of home life ... is part of the process of Americanization ... it is the cross that the first and second generations must bear, an involuntary sacrifice for the sake of future generations."[8]

In two years' time the family history revolved through one more cycle: Mary triumphed once more, her father failed once more. But this time Mary was growing more aware of her family. She was the "smartest" girl in her class at the Winthrop School, and her graduation from eighth grade in 1897 proved a decisive triumph. It permanently set her apart within her family. At the age of sixteen she became the Antins' scholar, the one the rest would sacrifice for so that she could rush on ahead.[9]

On graduation day Mary Antin and all the other neighborhood girls, most of whom would not continue their schooling, were dressed in "fine muslin frocks, lace-trimmed petticoats, patent leather shoes, perishable hats, gloves, parasols, fans, even a sash with silk fringes." Her school success was the subject of the graduation lecture given by the visiting school committeeman. The next day the newspaper carried a half-column on her achievements since coming to Boston. Such a triumph settled the family's conviction that Mary should continue at school, "to learn everything there was to know, to write poetry, become famous, and make the family rich."[10]

And so she did. She spent that summer and many more at the Boston Public Library, and in the fall began her career as the prize-winning slum girl at Boston Girls' Latin School, class of 1901. In high school Mary became an isolate, one who did not "go with" any of her classmates. Admired for her wit and diligence, she reciprocated by admiring the manners and good looks of the Back Bay girls. Neither rebuffed nor welcomed, she stayed by herself. Her closest school relationship was to another grind, Florence Connolly. Florence, whose father "presided over a cheap lunch room," matched Mary in both diligence and poverty. Florence was "quiet as a mouse" and Mary "as reserved as an oyster." So the two girls sat side by side through high school, often staying at their desks at recess. They lived in books, gathered up honors, but found no place among their classmates.[11]

Meanwhile the Antins' last grocery store failed, again crushed beneath the weight of unpaid bills. The family moved to yet another tenement flat, this time on Dover Street (now East Berkeley Street). It was five small rooms, up two flights of stairs, past the angry, hissing Mrs. Rasnosky, a whining baby, and the drunken Mr. and Mrs. Casey. "In the 'parlor' the dingy paper hung in rags and the plaster fell in chunks. One of the bedrooms was absolutely dark and air-tight. The kitchen windows looked out on a dirty court," and across the courtyard stretched a length of line for the family wash. Here the tensions of family, school, and street pulled relentlessly at Mary.[12]

Her father, Israel Antin, a middle-aged immigrant with no craft, no experience with manual labor, with little English and no supporters, offered himself at "boy's wages." "Here too weak; here too old; here without English"; there his appearance too Jewish; the best he could manage was odd jobs. Repeatedly rebuffed and defeated, he shrank into bitterness. Mary's brother, the newsboy, was the steady support of the family. Mother, Esther

Antin, bore another baby. "I knew there was not enough to eat before the baby's advent, and she did not bring any supplies with her that I could see. The baby was one too many. There was no need of her. I resented her existence. I recorded my resentment in my journal."[13] Mary's oldest sister, Frieda, escaped into marriage at seventeen. This left Mary at home to play the lonely scholar, burning her kerosene lamp late into the night while her younger sister slept in the bed next to the desk.

Beyond the tiny bedroom and the school routine, other worlds instructed her. Often angry and depressed, she walked the streets, running away for a moment, yet always alert, inquiring. Dover Street offered supplementary education.[14] "Mr. Casey, of the second floor, who was drunk whenever his wife was sober, gave me an insight into the psychology of the beer mug that would have added to the mental furniture of my most scholarly teacher. The bold-faced girls who passed the evening on the corner, in promiscuous flirtation with the cock-eyed youths of the neighborhood, unconsciously revealed to me the eternal secrets of adolescence. My neighbor of the third floor, who sat on the curbstone with the scabby baby in her bedraggled lap, had things to say about the fine ladies who came in carriages to inspect the public bathhouse across the street that ought to be repeated in the lecture halls of every school of philanthropy. Instruction poured into my brain at such a rate that I could not digest it all at the time."[15]

There was another side to Mary's life at the time that she only hinted at in her autobiography—her experiences as a prodigy. Miss Dillingham remained attentive; Mr. Hurd, the children's editor of the *Boston Transcript*, became a friend. When she attended patriotic and inspiring public lectures she spoke up or wrote notes of appreciation, and as a result she made the acquaintance of a state senator and of Rev. Edward Everett Hale. She seems also to have been passed around the settlement house network, so she drank a fair amount of afternoon tea in Back Bay parlors. Although such introductions and acquaintanceships counted as more triumphs, there must have been some pain in these occasions, for Mary never recounted these scenes.[16]

The class strain of being a slum girl performing with her best manners in the homes of the well-to-do rested on top of a heavier burden. As a high school girl, Mary began to confront her lifelong need to reconcile two antithetical cultures: her own Russian Jewish Orthodoxy and the dominant culture of New England liberal Christianity.[17] In these days Mary played to two groups. To Boston's old residents, fearful of the new waves of immigrants, she served as an emblem of good news; for the city's small established Jewish community she was a peasant girl of wit and manners who clearly would become a fine, patriotic American citizen and an honor to Boston's Jews. She met the charitable Hecht family, who introduced her to their counterparts in New York City. She visited Philip Cowen, the publisher of the weekly *American Hebrew*, and through the Cowens met Josephine Lazarus, sister of the poet Emma Lazarus. Encouraged by these families, Mary Antin began to tell her life story to the public.[18]

Her first book was published as a serial in the *American Hebrew* in 1898, when Mary was sixteen and still a high school sophomore. Printed with an incorrect title, *From Plotzk to Boston*, it was a translation and reworking of a series of letters in Yiddish that Mary had written to her relatives in Russia just after emigrating. The Hechts introduced Mary, "the gifted Russian girl," to the English novelist and playwright Israel Zangwill, who wrote a laudatory introduction to the book. *From Plotzk to Boston* remains, even today, a charming account of the five-week journey of a Russian Jewish mother and children making their way from a small city in Belorussia to America.[19]

Ultimately it was the sociability of the settlement, not scholarly preparation for college, that determined Antin's path. Her brother and sister had joined clubs at the nearby settlement, Hale House, and the head worker there suggested that Mary join the Natural History Club, a special group of settlement house workers and their friends that attended lectures and went on outings. The club proved to be very much her métier—new things to learn, adults to please and to guide her. Though she was not a systematic observer, Antin's enthusiasm and merry spirits on the field trips soon made her the pet of the group.[20] For her, the outings and lectures on natural history and evolution began a lifelong endeavor to unite her Judaic inheritance with the modern romantic tradition of Emerson and Thoreau.[21]

It was through the club that Antin met Amadeus William Grabau (1870–1946), a handsome thirty-year-old graduate student who was just then finishing his Ph.D. in geology at Harvard. Amadeus had been raised in Buffalo, New York, the son and grandson of Lutheran ministers who taught in a seminary there. When he met Mary, he was working part-time at the Boston Museum of Natural History, giving public lectures on evolutionary topics; he was scheduled to take an appointment in palaeontology at Columbia University the very next year.

Mary Antin did not go on from Girls' Latin to Radcliffe College. She did not reach the goal that she, her family, and her sponsors had been working toward for the past four years.[22] Instead she took her sister Frieda's path, hoping that marriage and her pleasure in books would bring her a full life. As soon as Amadeus settled at Columbia in the fall of 1901, Mary married him and moved to New York City.[23] Of the five Antin sisters, the eldest three married; those who had been born in America, the South End babies, however, remained single.[24]

As a professor's bride in New York, Antin attended classes at Columbia Teachers College and at Barnard College, but she did not systematically pursue a degree. Instead she drew close to the liberal Jewish families she had met, especially adopting Josephine Lazarus (1846–1910) as her mentor. Although of very different ages, backgrounds, and experience, Lazarus and Antin were struggling with the same issues: how to orient themselves in an environment that included modern secular Judaism, anti-Semitism, and uprooted Eastern European orthodox Jewish settlements.

Josephine Lazarus and her younger sister Emma (1849–1887) had given up orthodox practices; they sought in the general romantic climate of the times some expression of spiritual order. Emma Lazarus enjoyed some success as a poet and as a translator of Heinrich Heine. She had attracted the attention of Ralph Waldo Emerson, whom she admired, and had visited at his Concord home. From Heine and Emerson she had developed a neo-Platonic sense of the unity of man, nature, and God.

The passage of the Russian anti-Semitic laws of 1879, the terror of Mary Antin's childhood, turned Emma's energies toward refugee work and writing against the rising anti-Semitism then sweeping Europe and America. She began writing on Jewish themes and speculated on Zionism. Her famous sonnet, "The New Colossus," written in 1883 for a fund-raising campaign for Bartholdi's Statue of Liberty, was part of this new activism.[25]

After Emma's death in 1887, Josephine continued her spiritual explorations. For Josephine, as for many of her contemporaries, Jewish and Christian, the answer to the problem of reconciling the many worlds of the modern Jew lay in a blending of religious tradition with secular romanticism.[26] Her book *The Spirit of Judaism* offered a solution that many Americans were seeking. Imbued with the general pantheism of romantic sentiment, along with the individual focus of Emerson, this belief held that both man and nature embodied God and that the individual could seek and find God's spirit. Josephine called upon Jews to once again take the role of world religious leadership in creating new spiritual fellowships for the like-minded.[27]

For Mary Antin, now a Scarsdale suburbanite and mother of a daughter whom she named Josephine Esther, Lazarus's ideas must have helped reconcile past and present, the traditions of the Pale with the teachings of Longfellow, Emerson, and Edward Everett Hale.[28] Perhaps, too, it was Lazarus who encouraged her to return to Russia to visit her old town of Polotzk in 1909 or 1910.

Ever since her arrival in the United States, Antin had been telling stories of Polotzk to her friends, and in her early married years she wrote a few stories of Jewish life in the Pale. The death of Josephine Lazarus in 1910 provided the final impetus for Mary Antin to make her first mature attempt to write a narrative of her own life.[29] Since the publication of her high school story of her trans-Atlantic journey, Antin's view of herself had broadened and matured. She now saw her experience as typical of the experience of many, her autobiography as "illustrative of a score of unwritten lives," and her journey in time and space as a trail many were seeking or being driven down.[30] In speaking of herself and her fellow immigrants, especially Jewish immigrants, the new book, *The Promised Land*, was an appeal for sympathy and a testament of immigrant pride and patriotic American pride. Every page of this autobiography of her childhood said that the impoverished and victimized peasants of Europe were people worthy of America, that when they came here seeking refuge they were nourished by America's freedoms even in the poverty of city slums, and that in the end, after suffering and confusion, they could become fine citizens.

Parts of the autobiography first appeared in serial form in the *Atlantic Monthly* (October 1911–March 1912), and then, having attracted favorable comment, the book was published in 1912 by Houghton Mifflin in its entirety with photographic illustrations of Polotzk and Boston.

The Promised Land struck immediate success and remained a minor best-seller on immigrant Americanization for years. The editor of the *Atlantic*, Ellery Sedgwick, wisely compared it to another recent popular autobiography, Booker T. Washington's *Up from Slavery* (1901).[31] Both books touched on the same deep tradition, a tradition threatened by contemporary racism, anti-Semitism, and xenophobia, that an ignorant ex-slave or a poor, Yiddish-speaking immigrant girl could become outstanding citizens.

An instant celebrity, Mary now took on an exaggerated form of her previous role as school prodigy. She became a lecturer in behalf of toleration. Everywhere nativism and hostility greeted the new waves of immigrants. In Washington, Senator William P. Dillingham of Vermont had just completed his extensive misapplication of contemporary social science, proving, to the satisfaction of those who wished to limit immigration and of those who were fascinated by the new eugenics, that the new eastern and southern European migrants were inferior to the earlier migrants from northern and western Europe.[32] To counter this movement, the liberal and charitable network called upon Antin to give personal testimony. Theodore Roosevelt asked her to speak in his Progressive party campaign for the presidency in 1912, which she did gladly. She entered the national lecture circuit with set pieces on "The Responsibility of American Citizenship," "The Civic Education of the Immigrant," "Jewish Life in the Pale: A Lesson for Americans," and "The Zionist Movement."[33]

In 1913 she prepared a small book as a counterattack on the contemporary anti-immigrant, anti-Semitic campaigns. It was a clever book, built upon the premise that just as the Jews were the people of the Old Testament who had kept "the word," so Americans were people dedicated to the service of all humanity, who must remain faithful to their text, the Declaration of Independence.[34] Her argument countered the immigrants-aren't-what-they-used-to-be propaganda by comparing the latest migrants to the Pilgrims. Both were characterized by youth, energy, and idealism, Antin wrote. Both suffered religious persecution and harassment, but, she added, "it takes a hundred times as much steadfastness and endurance for a Russian Jew of today to remain a Jew as it took for an English Protestant in the seventeenth century to defy the Established Church." Turning the well-known prejudices of the American eugenics movement upon itself, she noted the paradox of calling for Americanization in the New York immigrant slum just when the ministers on the Berkshire periphery were crying out for the "regeneration of the Yankee farmer." "If rural New England to-day shows signs of degeneracy, it is because much of her sinew and bone departed from her long ago." For Mary the westward-moving farmer was the equivalent of the westward-moving peasant. She concluded her argument with an attack on the hypocrisy of the labor movement, which spoke in the name of all the poor but sought the advantage of only its organized workers.[35]

Encouraged by her sudden popularity and the attentions of the powerful, and driven by a personal sense of obligation to defend the immigrant and keep America open to refugees, Mary continued on the lecture circuit for five years. In July 1916 she was reported to be lunching with Grace (Mrs. Cornelius) Vanderbilt, Cornelia (Mrs. Gifford) Pinchot, and Frances A. Kellor, the unemployment investigator, at the Hotel Astor. Mary took on the cochairmanship of a women's committee of the National Hughes Alliance. A supporter of Theodore Roosevelt, she, like others, carried her progressive Republicanism to the Hughes campaign train. The trip had its unpleasant features because in 1916 women campaigners were often the targets of derision, and the vice-presidential candidate, Charles Fairbanks, had no respect for "these good ladies." Nevertheless, Antin kept on touring and speaking to groups across the country until 1918.[36]

Although it is not clear exactly what happened next, Antin floundered in a personal crisis from which she never completely recovered. She lost confidence in herself; she suffered a nervous breakdown. Her own public explanation gives a sense that Mary Antin felt that after so many years of repetition her long-sustained public role had begun to threaten some other, more important self that lay hidden beneath the performances. "For a period of years (1913–1918) I crisscrossed the United States as an itinerant preacher, playing homely but passionate variations on one master theme, the spiritual meaning of America, before audiences ranging from university forum to state prison. In spite of major handicaps, such as an inexpert use of the voice, I was a success. But applause and fat fees and return engagements were unconvincing in the absence of a sense of vocation. I got out of the business as soon as I could, by the back door of a nervous breakdown, but glad of any kind of exit from what I considered a false position. I felt I had not *earned* the authority the public allowed me."[37]

Although she had been performing continuously since she was twelve in Miss Dillingham's class in Chelsea, clearly Mary did not regard these twenty-four years as sufficient credentials. By 1918 she was no longer willing to accept Mary Antin the performer as her authentic self. And there was trouble at home. Amadeus Grabau's brief biography presented him as a man entirely devoted to his scholarship, but in 1918 even a professional husband may have resented a traveling wife. And he too was involved in political issues. Like a number of Columbia professors, he opposed America's entry into World War I. In the turmoil of antiwar politics and family conflict, the marriage broke up. In 1920 Amadeus Grabau accepted the position of director of research for the China Geological Survey. He moved to Peking and remained in China in that and similar positions until his death in 1946. Antin returned to Boston, living in suburban Winchester and presumably resuming active contacts with her family.

In 1923, through the famous psychiatrist Austen Fox Riggs, she learned of Gould Farm, a religious and convalescent community in western Massachusetts. She lived there for several years, becoming in time an active supporter and informal historian of the community.[38] Gould Farm had been established in 1913 in the town of Monterey by William Gould and his wife, Agnes Goodyear. The Goulds took in troubled boys referred by settlement house workers and ministers from New York City. To the discipline of farm work and the security of a small community, "Brother Will," as he styled himself, added a good-natured, pantheistic, nonsectarian Christianity. With adults also in the community, it became a giant family or miniature utopian community. For Mary Antin such a setting must have seemed to combine the teachings of Emerson, Thoreau, Tolstoy, and Josephine Lazarus.[39] Mary's youngest sister, Rosemary, a social worker in Albany, also became attached to Gould Farm and its people.

From the late 1920s onward Mary Antin traveled back and forth from a farm at Spring Valley in New York to Gould Farm and New York City. What she had learned in the years since 1918, and the peace she had found, she discussed in an essay published in 1937 in the *Atlantic Monthly*, on the mystical experience. Drawing upon Boston's romantic union of God, man, and nature, Antin carried that tradition out toward its mystical possibilities. "Nothing is more characteristic of the state of subtler perception, no matter how brief its duration in any given case, than the feeling, already alluded to, that there are no inanimate things anywhere in nature. And not only is everything alive, but everything is in that state of tension of which I can only say that all things yearn toward me in a desire to penetrate my intelligence. Everything is trying to speak to me. I cannot touch this point too often, it lies so close to the heart of this whole matter: nothing is so trivial, so debased by everyday use, so buried under habitual sense reactions, but may put on life, in an hour like this, and speak direct to my intuitive perception."[40]

Mary Antin's public life ended as it began, with an appeal to Americans to honor their universal humanity. A fresh wave of anti-Semitism was sweeping over the world from Nazi Germany, killing millions in Europe and poisoning civil life in the United States. Xenophobia and racism surged across the land, despite official disapproval. The old liberal and settlement house network regrouped once more, this time as the Council of American

Unity, to foster "common citizenship" and to "uphold the freedom to be different." For the council's journal Antin wrote a little story of her experience in Scarsdale as a Jew who gave money to the local Catholic charity. It was a prelude to her appeal for the unity of all people in a common recognition of their humanity and their relationship to God. "I will pray for the world's restoration to sanity sometimes in a bare New England meeting house, sometimes in a serene Jewish temple, sometimes in a glowing cathedral interior where worshippers kneel intent on rosary and crucifix, as these many years I have prayed for things worthy to mention in prayer. In all those places where race lines are drawn, I shall claim the Jewish badge, but in my Father's house of many mansions I shall continue a free spirit."[41] What she had explored as a young woman with Josephine Lazarus and later at Gould Farm had at last become a firm unity of personal experience and belief.

3 ❧ FRED ALLEN

Fred Allen (1894–1956) was a Bostonian whose life carried him from the most local and particular of Boston settings to the center of the imperial stage. The insularity of Grant's Back Bay circles was matched, if not exceeded, by that of Boston's Irish working-class and lower-middle-class parishes where Fred Allen began.[1] A poor boy from a broken home, cursed with an alcoholic father, he made his way up the rungs from public school to odd jobs to small-time theater, to national star in the brand-new industry, radio. Throughout the years following Calvin Coolidge's presidency and prior to that of John F. Kennedy, Fred Allen was the nation's most popular Bostonian. A phenomenal radio success, with an audience estimated at as much as one-third of America's families, he captured the attention of the nation by an old-fashioned narrative approach to the world.[2]

The ultimate resource for all this imaginative work, surely, was his experience of growing up in turn-of-the-century Boston. Fred Allen was born in the working-class suburb of North Cambridge in 1894 as John Florence Sullivan, the elder of two sons of a bookbinder. At the time all of his father's brothers were bookbinders, employed by the large printing houses that then flourished in Cambridge. When Fred was three years old, soon after his younger brother Bobby was born, his mother died of pneumonia, and the father with his children moved in with Fred's maternal aunt Lizzie in nearby Allston.

Aunt Elizabeth Lovely was a common type in this world before insurance for workingmen.[3] She was a poor woman who washed, cooked, cleaned, and kept house to support herself and her invalid husband, a plumber who was becoming progressively paralyzed from lead poisoning. She rented the top floor of a two-family house on the flats of Allston, a pocket of then recently built workers' houses located on a tract bounded by the playing fields of Harvard College, the railroad tracks, and the Brighton stockyards.[4] In the five rooms and attic she boarded her two un-married sisters and her brother, as well as James Henry Sullivan and his two sons. For five dollars a week Aunt Lizzie offered a room, two hot meals a day plus a bag lunch, and laundry service. She mothered her two young nephews, and Fred became deeply attached to her. As he grew older, he assumed full responsibility for her support.[5]

The neighborhood offered little urban sidewalk entertainment; Fred remembered it as a "monotony broken by certain regular community high lights," like the nightly drill of the fire company, the passing of the police patrol wagon, and the cattle drive down Western Avenue.[6] Sundays followed a strict ritual. After Mass and the Sunday roast with Aunt Lizzie, John Sullivan and his two small sons walked over the Charles River bridge, through Harvard Square, to Grandfather and Grandmother Sullivan's house in Cambridge.[7] Here each Sunday Fred's father and uncles came for an afternoon of cards, chatter, and an early dinner. The young men each contributed a pint of whiskey to the occasion, so "after the good-bys had been said, my brother and I would flank my father, and we'd start off. It was a three-mile walk home, and if you had met the three of us along the road you would have seen a peculiar sight: we looked like two sardines guiding an unsteady Moby Dick into port."[8]

It was a poor boy's childhood, but Fred Allen recalled it as a parade of characters, each one associated with a little story. They included Miss Bancroft, who coached him in his first act, a har-monica performance in the grammar school minstrel show; "Sally Fat," the elementary teacher who had grown so cumbersome that the boys had to lead her horse and carriage up to the school en-trance; Billy Hempstead, the austere night policeman at the Bos-ton Public Library who secured fourteen-year-old Fred his first job; dapper Pierce Buckley, who bossed the library runners and stack boys; Mayor John J. Fitzgerald (grandfather of President John F. Kennedy), who sang "Sweet Adeline" all over town and who was the force behind the founding of the High School of Commerce in Roxbury, from which Fred was an early graduate in 1911.[9]

As a teenager, Fred was hungry. His first year in high school he took the streetcar from his home in Allston to school in Roxbury; after school he walked the six miles home by stages. First he walked to the public library in Copley Square, where he did his homework, ate the cold supper Aunt Lizzie had packed for him, and then ran back and forth carrying books for the library patrons. At 9 P.M., his stint done, he faced the temptation of the white-tile restaurant across the street. Here the specialty was the Trilby, a ten-cent grilled cheese and onion sandwich that could be soused with ketchup. Often Fred succumbed to the temptation, and to preserve his earnings, or perhaps quiet his guilt, he walked home to Allston to save the five-cent carfare.[10]

The next year, 1909, when Fred was fifteen, the household collapsed. His father remarried and took young brother Bobby with him for a time. One of Aunt Lizzie's sisters and her brother also left, leaving Lizzie with Fred, her invalid husband, and one paying sister. They had to give up the Allston half-house and retreat into a tiny attic apartment in the Savin Hill section of Dorchester, a cramped rookery Fred cheerfully recalled as an "indoor penthouse." Later, as Fred's earnings grew, he helped Lizzie move to a comfortable apartment in a three-decker nearby.[11]

Performing had always caught Fred's eye, and now it came to his rescue. In addition to taking roles in the ordinary school plays and church pageants, he had spent a summer helping a boy take traveling Punch and Judy shows about to picnics and parties. Now, lonely and not yet settled in the new neighborhood, he took up juggling in his spare time.[12]

He was not a good student, but he was a reliable worker, so he made steady progress at the public library, becoming in time an assistant in the Children's Room. Every Saturday during his high school years, he would go to the city paymaster's office at the old City Hall on School Street to collect his wages of five and six dollars a week. A mere two blocks away was Boston's vaudeville center, and every Saturday after he was paid, Fred would go into one or another theater to watch the jugglers and memorize their tricks. Soon he realized he should add some patter to his perform- ance, so he began what became a lifetime collection of jokes. After the show he took out his week's carfare and turned the rest of his earnings over to Aunt Lizzie.[13]

Fred Allen's stage career began in the summer of 1911, when he was sixteen years old. He entertained at the library employees' party. Following an hour of inexpert singing and dancing, his juggling captured the audience. As he recalled it, "a girl in the crowd said, 'You're crazy to keep working here at the library. You ought to go on the stage.' I often wonder who that girl was. If she had only kept her mouth shut that night, today I might be the librarian of the Boston Public Library."[14]

He was, however, not the sort of boy who ran off with the cir- cus or tagged after a troupe of itinerant vaudevillians. Instead he made his way cautiously, letting the city give him his theatrical apprenticeship. That fall an uncle who had forsaken bookbinding for piano selling found Fred a job at the Colonial Piano Company on Boylston Street, Boston's downtown "Piano Row." The block bordering the Common was typical of that era, when many of the streets downtown were hives of specialists—the engravers on Bromfield Street, the carpenters on Hawley Street, and so forth. On Piano Row the salesman stood at the door, scanning the crowd, waiting for someone to pause at the window display. A curious window shopper soon found a salesman at his side, chat- ting lightly about music and pianos and directing the shopper in- side the store, where a demonstration and sales routine awaited. Summers the door stood open, and one of the salesmen played popular tunes to attract a crowd and to slow passers-by.

Fred worked as an all-purpose office boy. He came in an hour early to dust the pianos and clean the windows and the store, he ran all manner of errands, even delivering the surburban store owner's eggs to customers in buildings nearby. When the sales manager ran out of tasks for Fred, he was sent to the basement to help out the Swedish piano finishers and repairmen. There he learned how to disassemble a piano and to chew tobacco.[15]

These were the days when every American family wanted a

piano for the parlor, and Colonial's business was the installment credit trade. Fred's employers assigned him to chasing deadbeats, and soon he became the lead player in a bit of suburban theater, the collection play. "The company . . . wanted to frighten the defaulter and cause him to bring his account up to date. Mr. Avery told me that the company was going to present a dramatic high light the following morning, and that I was to be the star. The subordinate cast of characters, Mr. Avery explained, consisted of two husky piano movers. The property list called for one horse, one wagon large enough to hold a piano, a large coil of rope, and one block and tackle. The next morning, armed with the name and address of the delinquent, I went forth to make my debut. The two husky piano movers had driven out to the scene before me.

"I approached the front door followed by the two movers, one carrying the coil of rope, the other dragging the block and tackle. When the housewife opened the door, I stepped brusquely inside, my supporting cast behind me. I informed the lady exactly how many payments she was behind and how much she owed; I told her that if she wasn't prepared to bring her account up to date, we were going to have to take away the piano. At this cue the husky mover with the rope started to uncoil. The man with the block and tackle stepped to the window and threw it open wide. This produced results. The woman couldn't make a payment on the spot, but she took an oath on the graves of a number of her dear departed relatives that she would pay up the balance immediately. Assuring the lady of the dire consequences sure to follow if her word were not kept, the block and tackle man closed the window, the rope man started coiling, and the entire cast made an impressive exit . . . On rare occasions, when the victim told us what we could do with the piano, we didn't do it. We gave the person one more chance, and withdrew with the coil of rope, the block and tackle, and as much dignity as we could muster under the circumstances. We then came back to the Colonial Piano Company empty handed. This was not good, but it was, we knew, better than the alternative: to come back to the Colonial Piano Company with a Colonial Piano."[16]

For all the excitement of these collection scenes, the job soon grew boring, and Fred's imagination was drawn more and more toward vaudeville theater. His youth, the years from 1912 to the mid 1920s, coincided with a time of transition in American popular entertainment. The era of the city "museums," those emporiums of freaks, curiosities, circus acts, and massive chorus girls, popularized by the moralizing Phineas T. Barnum, was coming to an end. The rising new forms were vaudeville, silent moving pictures, and the musical revue.

Another moralizing provincial, Benjamin Franklin Keith (1846–1914) of Hillsborough, New Hampshire, is credited with inventing vaudeville. In 1883 he closed out the freaks and curiosity rooms of his small museum on Washington Street in downtown Boston in favor of a show that amalgamated elements from the old English variety show of tricks, comic routines, songs and dances, and bits taken from American minstrel shows, to make a continuous offering of short performances. Keith's goal was to attract a family crowd, so he policed his acts and comics carefully to remove any materials he thought untasteful, like the words "hell" and "damn." He also adopted the tony French word *vaudeville* (meaning "comic song") to give his performances a suggestion of expensive taste.

Lower than the Keith theaters in price and elegance, the older forms of variety continued to flourish. Burlesque in those years still meant parodies, and a burlesque show consisted of parodies of popular theater, events, and celebrities, joined with dance, juggling, and singing, much like today's television variety show. A chorus of pretty girls offered slimmer figures than those in the old museum, and in keeping with popular trends, each year's new chorus girl stood a bit lighter than her predecessor. Nakedness and striptease, however, were not a part of the burlesque stage until the 1930s.[17]

When silent films arrived early in the twentieth century, live performances were presented along with the films. Expensive theaters provided an orchestra to support the acts and films; in the cheap neighborhood theater a piano player and a drummer furnished all the music. At the apex of the American theater was the musical revue, an elaborately staged show combining the short bits of vaudeville and burlesque with freshly composed music, star singers, actors and actresses, and elaborate costumes and scenery. This was the fame and glamour a beginner of 1912 might dream of.

A sample of all this grew up within a few blocks of the Colonial Piano Company. The new Colonial Theater was on Piano Row itself, and B. F. Keith's booking office was on Tremont Street, around the corner of the Boston Common. A few blocks farther down Tremont was the hub of the province's network of cheap entertainment, Scollay Square. Here, at the intersection of the city's subways and streetcars, the junction of the State Street of- fices and the manufacturing lofts of Cornhill and Haymarket, within easy steps from the Faneuil Hall farmer's market and a short walk from the northern railroad lines and the Atlantic docks, stood the old hotels, hearty restaurants, and cheap theaters of the crossroads of Boston, the tenderloin. "If the Boston of those days," Fred Allen later wrote, "was as proper and conservative as the high-button shoe, the average man's answer to conservatism was Scollay Square. Scollay Square was the hot foot applied to the high-button shoe."[18]

The very essence of the place was Howard Street, a short street that ran partway up the back side (now torn down and built over with state office buildings) of Beacon Hill. Austin and Stone's Dime Museum, a relic of former times, still functioned at the base of Howard Street. The museum offered the usual freaks, curiosi- ties, and a "Big Girl Show" for ten cents. The key institutions of the cheap entertainment world lined Howard Street: Walker's Nickelodeon, a shooting gallery and penny arcade that featured a man who swallowed ground glass and poison and could hold down two buckets of water before exploding like a geyser; Hig- gins's Famous Oyster House and Hotel, famous for its intimate dining rooms and its assignations; the Bucket of Blood poolroom in Higgins's basement, where gamblers made book; the Daisy Lunch, always full of actors seeking its twenty-five-cent supper of frankfurters and beans, bread and butter, apple pie with ice cream, and coffee; Hamm's Periodical Store, where the per- formers hung out because Hamm extended credit for cigarettes; the cellar ale house, where retired actors from nearby rooming houses gathered to swap memories; the William Tell Hotel and the Rexford Hotel around the corner on Bulfinch Place, whose cheap rooms made them theater hotels, where performers could rehearse, swap jokes and stories, and party all night. Still recalled by some even today, the climax of the street was the Old Howard Theater, then in 1912 the province's leading burlesque house.[19]

Around the corner from Howard Street, at 80 Court Street, in a dirty one-room upstairs back office, Fred Allen found his future—Sam Cohen, impresario of Amateur Nights.[20] Cohen, a former circus strong man, had developed a specialty in providing a package of amateur acts to neighborhood silent movie theaters. The amateurs drew in a local crowd, and Sam Cohen himself, as master of ceremonies, won the crowd's enthusiasm with his antics and jokes. Most amateurs, then as now, were singers and dancers, so Fred Allen's juggling was a welcome ingredient. When Mr. Cohen asked, "Will your parents let you go on Amateur Nights?" Allen lied. In fact Aunt Lizzie never approved of his career. She thought all actors were unreliable men who declined into drunkenness, and she urged Fred, even after he had become a vaudeville star, to come home to Dorchester and settle down.[21]

One night in 1912 at the tiny, narrow Hub Theater on Washington and Dover streets, just around the corner from Mary Antin's old tenement, Allen began his career. "And now, from Dorchester, a juggler, Johnny Sullivan." Despite his fright, the act went off presentably, and soon he became one of Cohen's regulars. Allen quit the piano company and led troupes of Sam Cohen's amateurs through the neighborhood theaters of metropolitan Boston. That summer Cohen promoted him to master of ceremonies, and he took a troupe through the amusement parks and resorts of northern New England. Next he met a professional juggler, Harry LaToy, who taught him the secrets of the trade and absconded with a lot of Allen's spare cash. Allen began collecting fresh jokes to improve his routine, and soon it became a comedy act with some burlesque juggling, not a juggling act with some patter. He adopted the stage name of Freddy James, juggler extraordinary from the West.[22]

In the winter of 1914 he supported himself by playing in local theaters and clubs: Winthrop Hall at Upham's Corner, Hamilton Hall on Meeting House Hill in Dorchester, the Imperial in South

Boston, the Ward 18 Democratic Club, the Catholic Club of Canton, the Boston YMCA, the Winthrop Lodge of Elks, and the Boot and Shoe Workers Union. That summer the booking agents who supplied acts for amusement parks then operating at the end of city streetcar lines, places like Norumbega Park in Newton, Penacook Park in Concord, New Hampshire, and Saccarappa Park near Portland, Maine, sent him to jobs throughout the province. The players he met on this circuit told him he was good enough for New York agents, so in September 1914, telling Aunt Lizzie he was off for a short trip and leaving several hundred dollars in a Boston savings bank, Freddy James, the "World's Worst Juggler," set out for New York City and the big time.[23]

There followed eight years of traveling across the nation from one small vaudeville theater to another, even an eleven-month tour of Australia, until he became a first-run performer. Along this route he adopted his permanent name, Fred Allen, given him by the Fox Theaters' booking agent, Edgar Allen.[24] As a touring professional, he established a regular seasonal routine. For ten months he traveled with teams of young vaudevillians, crisscrossing the nation as the contracts with theater chains required. Every summer he returned to Dorchester and Aunt Lizzie, to rest up by going to the nearby beach at South Boston, playing baseball with the neighborhood gang, and hanging around the cafeteria on Tremont Street and the Hotel Clarendon in the South End, which after World War I became the headquarters for the theatrical community.[25]

Called up in 1918, he escaped the army because his Dorchester draft board exempted him as Aunt Lizzie's only means of support. That year, however, he "did many camp shows ... and in the early days, shortly after the country's entrance in the war, it all reminded me of Australia: the enthusiasm, the boys eager to enlist, the girls seeing them off, the gaiety, the thought that it was all happening so far away from us and would soon be over. I hoped that I would not live to see the disillusionment and the casualties I had seen in Australia. I did, unfortunately, live to see them both."[26]

Each year, as he experimented with his routines and became more effective with his comedy, bookings came more easily, but

Fred held to the conservatism of the once-poor. He welcomed the sureness of small-time bookings against the risks of weeks of unemployment and an outside chance for billing in the grandest theaters. He turned down an opportunity to go to Hollywood for such reasons. Year by year his skill improved, and his notices as well.[27]

By 1922, after eight years as a journeyman, he had arrived in the big time, playing the Shubert theater circuit as a comedian in their musical revue, *The Passing Show of 1922.* When the revue was held over in Chicago for an extra-long run, Allen began going around with one of the girls in the chorus, Portland Hoffa. They saw a lot of each other off and on over the next five years as Fred appeared in Broadway musicals and toured the nation's big vaudeville circuits. Portland's father was a Jew and her mother a Presbyterian, but with the aid of a New York priest who ministered to actors, she converted to Catholicism, and in 1927 Fred and Portland married. In the vaudeville tradition of stage couples, Fred immediately incorporated her into his act, and they traveled together for the next four years. When Allen's scripts for Corn Products Corporation took them into the new medium, they continued as a radio couple.[28]

Fred and Portland's eighteen years in radio were an extraordinary triumph of sustained wit and energy. They lived, worked, and raised a family in their New York City apartment and spent their summer vacations in Maine.[29] Allen's success during these two decades rested upon his artful interpretation to the nation of the old city of diverse individuals.

Fred Allen wrote a great deal of his own material and supervised carefully what others prepared for him. His scripts were not one-liners or startling juxtapositions of incongruities, as in today's style. Rather, his outlook and his humor emerged from carefully composed story sequences. His regular weekly work schedule called for combing through the metropolitan magazines and newspapers to find incidents from which he could fashion tales.[30] For him the city was populated with stories: each person you passed on the street or read about in the newspaper carried a distinct story, such as Mary Antin's migration, which was the person's central being. If you came to know a person well, you would know not only the central life story, but also many of the characteristic stories he created as he traveled along his unique way.

From such assumptions Fred Allen created his famous radio formula: the weekly parade of set characters whom he interviewed in the setting known as Allen's Alley. Each character was presented simultaneously in two dimensions. First, the core story formed the recognizable image, like Titus Moody's poverty-stricken Maine farm or Mrs. Nussbaum's marriage and family. Next the character reacted to some event of the week's metropolitan news, thereby telling a fresh story that showed how he or she moved consistently through the world.

Fred Allen's world changed, in part because of far-off dictators and presidents, distant wars, and global depressions, but mostly because the city, which he perceived as a place of millions of distinct people and their stories, changed.

The old metropolitan daily newspaper, with its hundreds of small reports of police, fires, politics, oddities, and personalities, perfectly epitomized Fred Allen's city. How different this view is from our own. Boston today is a metropolis of distinct places and distinct roles, places like Billerica, the North End, and Roxbury, each place with its matching roles—senior software engineer, tile setter, food and beverage technician. In this world the residents seem to be busy inventing and reinventing themselves, just as they keep altering their job resumes. It is not a metropolis composed of an infinite variety of formed people whose interactions create change, but rather a space in which the places have stereotypes and themes, the institutions have lives and imperatives, and the roles are accountable and set. In today's understanding it is the interaction of the stereotypical places, the institutional imperatives, and the role sets that makes people change and thereby makes the city's history.

To help his audience understand the heterogeneity of his urban world, Fred Allen used two devices: he established his characters in a particular place, and he presented them within the popular ethnic codes of his day. He early realized that in radio the listener has to form a picture in his imagination of the actors and their setting in order to comprehend the plot and dialogue coming from the loudspeaker,[31] and he also realized that at that time, during the thirties and forties, radio was a device for bringing metropolitan entertainment to rural Americans who could not be reached by regular professional entertainers. Accordingly he gave careful attention to fabricating his places. First he experimented with small towns and town meetings, later he settled on his urban Allen's Alley.

In these constructions he offered his listeners the talk of people walking together to town meeting, the banter of the men and boys outside the country store, and the wit of village shopkeepers. The Allen recipe was a subtle blend of rural and urban ethnic stereotypes with a very large quantity of Fred Allen's interpretations of his own urban experiences. One of his very popular early sequences dealt with the country storekeeper Hodge White, a man who in real life kept a small variety store near Fred Allen's aunt's home in Dorchester. Such was Allen's gift that he could transform a neighborhood Boston "spa" in St. Margaret's parish into a fictional country store that listeners all over the United States could respond to.[32]

It was inevitable that he should clash with the representatives of the new society, the society of fixed institutions and roles. National corporations selling through national advertising agencies and national radio networks purchased and produced Fred Allen's show. The executives of these national institutions had their special demands and special fears, and each insisted on having control over what Fred would say. Fred's first autobiography fairly bristles with the conflict. Everywhere there appeared the "echo men," the "little men who follow in the wake of the big executive." The big executive himself was an ignoramus, a "whirling tycoon" too busy to learn anything, but an authority on "advertising, comedy, and things in general."[33]

These corporate roles, of course, had transformed the men who filled them, and Allen was quick to sense the new style. He identified several types. The "molehill man" was a "pseudo-busy executive who comes to work at 9 A.M. and finds a molehill on his desk. He has until 5 P.M. to make the molehill into a mountain. An accomplished molehill man will often have his mountain finished even before lunch." The junior executives appeared as the timid "negative men," the "fledgling executives [who] walked around their offices backwards so they wouldn't have to face an issue."[34]

These roles and these men insisted on deleting any jokes that might offend someone in the audience of millions. The advertisers insisted that competitive products never be mentioned, and the radio networks banished all political references lest they "stir up somebody in Washington."[35] Fred Allen, the poor boy from Allston and Dorchester, had studied and mastered the old city of Boston. Out of that knowledge he built the imaginary places and characters that told Americans about a rich and varied world that their class and ethnic prejudices obscured from them. Now, in New York, at the pinnacle of success, he met the new masks of the faceless empire.

II 🌸 NEW PATHWAYS

AT THE TURN of the century, Boston led the national campaign to restrict immigration into the United States. Many Bostonians forcibly argued that strangers and newcomers, Catholic and Jewish immigrants and their children, were destroying their communities, traditions, their social and political arrangements. In these years many believed that the genius of New England town meetings and progressive municipal administrations sprang from the special virtues stored within the descendants of Protestant British immigrants.[1]

Although the fear of strangers, especially people of color, still runs strong, the turn-of-the-century arguments have long since lost their credibility. To a historian looking back over the past eighty years the continuities of local government in the Boston province stand out more sharply than the changes. A locally oriented middle class of small businessmen, lawyers, and professional officeholders governs now, as it always has. Judge Robert Grant has been replaced by Judge Fitzpatrick and Judge Yasi. As English, Irish, French, Italian, Polish, Russian, Greek, and Portuguese have succeeded one another, the most noticeable political change has been a preference for conservative practice, replacing the previous century's more optimistic and innovative use of local and state governments.

Nevertheless, alongside the ethnic name-calling and the contests for political office, other events have revolutionized community life. The multiplication of imperial connections through changes in science, technology, finance, and business has transformed the nature and meaning of work. The large national and international institutions, whether based in Boston or only operating a branch in the province, now dominate the cultural and economic life. Robert Grant's business fiction and Fred Allen's career better describe the pathways to this new situation than does Edwin O'Connor's famous characterization of a Boston Irish political boss.[2] The new institutional connections have linked the region's politics and its economy to national and international events, and at the same time the institutions have reassigned people from shops and factories to offices. Bostonians are no longer help, hands, and workers, they have become personnel; they are not laborers, shopkeepers, and machine tenders, but operators, technicians, scientists, engineers, designers, writers, accountants, salesmen, and promoters.

Other streams of events have refashioned residential life. The Victorian family, which had sought order and security within the narrow boundaries of formal manners and close family obligations, has relaxed its internal bonds to become today's loose confederacy. Now the typical suburban Boston family spills out over its lawn and driveway to press its members' demands upon whole neighborhoods, even the entire town, and from all this space, which it calls home, it rushes outward to country places and seaside resorts. The artifacts of this explosion in expectations—the ranch-colonial houses, the boats, the skis, the backyard pools, and the ubiquitous automobiles—are but the visible manifestations of a revolution in family goals for education, play, and self-expression. An ordinary, comfortable family today demands more land, more public services, and a more tended environment than even the privileged circle of Henry Adams or the heroines of Henry James.

Both these revolutions, the institutional and the residential, have gone forward without much public awareness of their origins or course. Their progress has been largely invisible, hidden from our memories and attention by popular attitudes and conventions. Work and home, the office and the plant, the neighborhood and the suburb are such mundane, repetitive daily events that they ridicule analysis. The changes have occurred incrementally. Wars and depressions, to be sure, have played their parts, but most of the force for change has come from thousands of individual choices discovered and taken, pathways that people have taken without realizing that they were being carried far from the familiar. Then, too, people do not usually cavil with success. A man who makes a town or a business grow, a school or a hospital expand, or a family prosper, is a hero; and if he is not a solitary genius, but one of many who rode a winning trend, so much the better for everyone.

Our understanding of family life is obscured because it is hidden behind an emotional screen. Not only are most people's homes separated from work by commuting distances, but life within the home is not regarded as either significantly resembling, or closely connected to, the world of jobs, politics, and culture. The home, the neighborhood, the suburb, and the summer place are retreats from the larger outside world. No matter that these are all places where men, women, and children experience the most intense demands, and where they bear the most relentless responsibilities, they are not, we say, the real world. Indeed, they are not the world at all by present day terms, they are special places devoted to families. Because of this outlook, it has been very hard to imagine that wives, mothers, and families could be a powerful force that has refashioned communities.

Yet changes in the institutions of work and in the demands of families have revolutionized the province. In the world of work businessmen have continually sought new ideas, perfected new technologies, and tried out new procedures, and from their successes have come ever more circles of interaction, connection, and dependency. There are today hundreds of new networks of specialists in research and the professions; there are elaborate institutional and electronic orbits of provincial, national, and international banking and finance; and the sales, production, and marketing connections of modern business form such surprising links as those that join a Mexican peasant, a regional supermarket chain, and a teen-age baby sitter at the local shopping mall.

The international transit of ideas and skills, the buying of imports and selling of exports, are not new to Boston, but the sheer multiplication of such exchanges and their management through all sorts of formal institutions are new to the twentieth century.

This revolution in the scale and volume of business affects the daily life, the food, the commonplace goods, the politics, and the ideas of even the most inward-turning and locally oriented Bostonian; almost everyone and almost everything is dependent on networks that far transcend the visible public orders of local, state, and federal government.

It is useful to imagine the daily exchanges within these networks—the Marges and the Daves on the other end of the telephone lines, the intercity displays from the Atlanta warehouse, the daily bank balances from New York City—as inadvertent communities. Communities because they are repeated exchanges between people who depend upon each other for success at their tasks and for the continuation of their institutions; inadvertent because many of the exchanges and interdependencies are the unintended outcome of someone's having pursued what he imagined to be simple incremental steps in building up a business or offering a new product or service.

A fine example of this new world of rippling linkages and interdependencies can be found in the history of Boston's largest electrical engineering firm, Stone & Webster, begun in the late 1880s by two young graduates of Massachusetts Institute of Technology. Within twenty years their business had grown into a wide and tangled network of inadvertent communities drawn together by the imperial scale of electric power construction and utility finance.

The revolution in the family grew from another side of nineteenth-century cultural invention—the broad romantic movement. There were some parallels, however, between the cultural processes of the institutional and the family revolutions. Both began with great innovators; the institutional roles of Faraday and Gibbs, were matched by the cultural roles of Coleridge and Emerson. The Lawrence Scientific School at Harvard and the new Massachusetts Institute of Technology were matched by the women's colleges of Smith, Wellesley, Vassar, and Bryn Mawr, where the insights of the great romantic masters were taught to the first generations of college women. And parallel to the popular science lectures and magazines of the nineteenth century stood the popularizers of the romantic outlook, authors like Lydia Maria Child and Julia Ward Howe.

During the first decades of the nineteenth century, scientific and romantic thought had been joined together, and the two revolutions might possibly have gone forward in tandem—science and romanticism, business and home mutually informing one another—had it not been for the curious sexual division within the culture.[3] By the end of the nineteenth century the sons of middle-class and wealthy families were going off to college to study the new science and social science as applied to law, medicine, business, and engineering, while the daughters of the same families, excluded from these fields, were taught what had by then become an old-fashioned literary and artistic culture. Educated, restless, active, furnished with the classic ideas of romanticism and the informal wisdom of magazine articles and novels, these women continued to explore the possibilities of the romantic outlook upon the world. What the men had abandoned for realism and modernism in art and literature, and for science in business and the professions, the women continued to develop in the residential nonworld of families, neighborhoods, suburbs, and summer places.

At the core of the romantic outlook lay the proposition that all things and all persons take their value and meaning from their relationships to the observer.[4] For some women the popular sentimental interpretations of this attitude furnished a source of wisdom and a positive direction to their reforms. Laura Richards, children's author, mill owner's wife, pioneer clubwoman, and model town reformer, exemplified this most common kind of family and community leader. For a few, however, the insights of romanticism were able to transcend sentimentality and the confines of the family. Taking the view that relationship is the key to understanding, these few could encompass the latest scientific knowledge, and from this union came a rich source of insights and social inventions at all levels of modern life, from the provincial to the imperial. Emily Greene Balch, young lady scholar, settlement house volunteer, economics professor, and peace worker, was one of these few.

4 ❧ CHARLES A. STONE and EDWIN S. WEBSTER

The provincial environment that fostered Boston's twentieth-century institutional revolution was the same as that of the theater circuits that later offered Fred Allen his start. Around the corner from the Old Howard Theater and Austin and Stone's Dime Museum, on the upper floors of a building at 109 Court Street, Charles Williams ran a machine shop. During the 1860s and 1870s he specialized in the manufacture of electrical equipment and the building of inventors' models. His shop served as the hangout for many of the city's inventors and tinkerers. Here Thomas A. Edison had brought his first ideas for improved telegraph equipment, and here the young machinist Thomas A. Watson built Alexander Graham Bell's telephone equipment.[1]

A few blocks to the east was the heart of the city's financial district. There at 113 Devonshire Street the partners of Kidder, Peabody & Company, an important bank, had located their Boston office. The names and home addresses of the men at Kidder, Peabody told of Boston's position in the Atlantic banking network. In 1889, four of the eight listed partners lived in the Back Bay. Three of these Bostonians were Peabodys, their names suggesting the great fortune that the family had amassed through marketing United States government bonds in London during the Civil War. Indeed, New York's famous banker, J. P. Morgan, a Boston shopkeeper's son, had received some of his earliest training in the Peabodys' London office. Of the four New York partners, one bore the name of a London banking family, Baring, thereby completing the outlines of the Boston–New York–London capital network.[2]

Along Boylston Street in the heart of the Back Bay stood the classrooms and laboratories of the Massachusetts Institute of Technology, founded in 1865. Here Bell learned of new developments in electricity, and here the city's first electrical engineers were trained.[3] Outside Boston the suburbs and provincial mill cities were still important sources of new technology and venture capital. Suburban Cambridge offered Harvard University's scientists and a number of wealthy investors, like Bell's Gardner Hubbard, and in Salem, Haverhill, Lowell, Lawrence, Worcester, Providence, Fall River, and New Bedford the owners of textile, shoe, paper, and machinery mills both fostered new devices and put up money for new companies.

With such resources the province of Boston entered the electrical age. The technology of electric power—the generators, transmission lines, motors, lights, and appliances—developed on both sides of the Atlantic. In 1879, while Thomas Edison in New Jersey worked on improving the light bulb, Antonio Pacinotti in Italy, Werner von Siemens in Germany, and Zenobé Gramme in France were perfecting the dynamo to generate electricity. In 1882 the New York Edison Company started up its first central power station with a steam-driven dynamo capable of making enough direct current to light four hundred lamps.

Boston did not lag in all this activity. Bell's telephone inventions led in 1885 to the formation of the immensely important American Telephone and Telegraph Company, and that same year the city started up its own Edison Electric Illuminating Company. The nearby shoe city of Lynn was the home of the Thompson-Houston Electric Company, which soon joined with Frank Sprague in developing electric street railways; subsequently the firm became the heart of J. P. Morgan's General Electric Company.[4]

This climate of electrical invention and progress attracted two brand-new MIT graduates, Charles A. Stone (1867–1941) and Edwin S. Webster (1867–1950). The two had met and become friends while taking the examinations for admission to Tech. Stone had been born in suburban Newton, the son of a wholesale butter merchant, and he had graduated from Newton High School. Webster had been born in Roxbury, the son of a partner in Kidder, Peabody, and he had been educated in private schools.

At MIT both young men decided to major in the new field of electrical engineering, and as classmates they grew to be such fast friends that they were known to their fellow students as Stone & Webster. (Today they hold the distinction of being the only joint entry in the *Dictionary of American Biography.*) For their senior paper they collaborated on an analysis of the efficiency of a Westinghouse alternating current generator.

Upon graduation in 1888 the two planned to set up as partners, but their senior professor, Charles R. Cross, discouraged them. He doubted there would be sufficient business to support one consulting electrical engineer, and surely not two. So Stone spent the next year at the Thompson Electric Welding Company in Lynn and then worked for an electric motor company in Boston. Webster toured Europe, then went to work at Kidder, Peabody.[5]

However, in 1889, the year Henry M. Whitney undertook to electrify the street railways of Boston, the two young men decided to test the field. In November they rented two small rooms on the top floor of 4 Post Office Square and staffed the office with MIT students. Uncertain of the outcome, neither partner quit his other job for a few months. In the brochure announcing the firm, Stone and Webster called attention to the rapid pace of electrical invention and offered their services to help inventors perfect their work, to evaluate inventions for investors, and to test electrical systems and equipment for manufacturers and users. The two men also would lay out wiring and design small power plants. In short, they stood prepared to bring all they had just learned in physics and electrical engineering to the world of practical application. As references they listed the president of MIT, Francis A. Walker; their physics professor; and Webster's father, combining the seals of knowledge and of finance.

Some of the new firm's first work consisted of testing the wiring, insulation, and appliances listed in the fire insurance underwriters' book of safety rules. They soon discovered that much of the fuse wire of the day did not melt under the loads it was rated for, so Stone & Webster began to test and label wire according to their own standards. Six years later, in 1895, the Insurance Underwriters Union established its own testing laboratories, so Stone & Webster redirected the work of the laboratory to electrochemical explorations.[6]

Their first big job came in 1890 as a referral from the president of MIT. The Warren Paper Company, which had surplus capacity at its Saccrappa dam on the Presumpscot River, near Portland, Maine, wished to generate electric power there and transmit it to their Cumberland Mills plant a mile away. At that time the transmission of electric power had not yet been mastered, but the young men succeeded in devising a workable 500-volt direct current system, which they later experimented with and improved. This initial job soon led to the firm's getting commissions to design and build more power stations, including two for the Lowell, Lawrence, and Haverhill Street Railway.

Once under way, the firm of Stone & Webster quickly took on its enduring roles as a gathering point for new science and new industrial techniques and as a broker for the separate and unpredictable worlds of science and investment capital. During the 1880s and 1890s the new fields of chemistry and electricity surged forward with a rush of answerable research questions. American investment capital swung between taking cautious risks in areas that were known to be profitable and going off on wild chases for bonanza opportunities. In arbitrating among the scientific academy, the investor, and the operating corporation Charles Stone and Edwin Webster not only made their personal fortunes, but they also played leading roles as makers of our modern provincial culture. Their cultural force expressed itself directly through their electrical and industrial constructions and indirectly through their contribution to the forming of new American institutions—the huge engineering firm, the privately owned public utility, and the private industrial corporation.

All the essential elements for this institutional revolution came together during the firm's first ten to fifteen years. Because electric power was a new venture, in many cities investors had been slow to come forward with sufficient capital, but this shortage had been made up by the manufacturers of electrical equipment. Companies like Westinghouse and General Electric accepted shares of stock from their customers as part payment for their supplies. Then, when the panic of 1893 struck and the banks called in their notes, many new utilities failed. The electrical manufacturers were left short of cash but with lots of shares of stock. J. P. Morgan, father of the General Electric combination, immediately organized a syndicate of trustees to finance General Electric's receivables and to take over, manage, or dispose of the properties that had given shares of stock in part payment. Morgan hired Stone & Webster to examine each utility, and soon this work became an important and enduring side of the firm's business. As Russell Robb, an early partner, put it: "Depression spurred this business . . . Hundreds of examinations were made in these years by Stone & Webster and invaluable experience was accumulated . . . All this work led, naturally, to the business side of the operation of properties, the preparing of plans for the reorganization of old companies, the organization of new companies, the building of properties, and the employment of Stone & Webster managers."[7]

Examination and reorganization of companies immediately led the firm into management. Small and middle-sized utilities could not support a staff of specialists, but through Stone & Webster, they could hire the services of a manager and a team of experts. The first contract was written in 1895 for the Brockton, Massachusetts, Edison Illuminating Company, and management services soon became a hallmark of the firm.[8] It was a comfortable union of engineering and financial services, and it carried the partners by easy stages into the utility investment banking business. J. P. Morgan offered the young men the Cumberland Electric Light & Power Company of Nashville, Tennessee, for $60,000, and on his advice they borrowed enough money to purchase it. After operating the company for a few years, they sold it for $500,000. Soon thereafter, beginning with the Puget Sound Light & Power Company of Washington, they took on the task of forming power companies, as well as operating, constructing, and assessing them.[9]

The New England paper business brought the men further opportunities and useful connections. In 1884 the new sulfite process for the manufacture of paper from wood pulp had been introduced into the United States at a mill in Providence, Rhode Island, whose superintendent was a young chemist, Arthur

Dehon Little. Two years later Little established his own chemical consulting firm in Boston, and he worked frequently with Stone & Webster. When Stone & Webster set up their own Fort Hill Chemical Company, Arthur D. Little served on its board of directors. It was the beginning of a lifetime of collaboration among the three former MIT students.[10]

From this rather typical turn-of-the century beginning there emerged a common modern pattern: a business life of revolutionary impact but a private life that followed the conventions of its day. In 1893 Edwin Webster married Jane dePeyster Hovey of Brookline, whose father was an editor of the *Boston Transcript*. The couple had three daughters and one son.[11] Edwin S. Webster, Jr. (1899–1957) worked at Stone & Webster's office from 1926 to 1930, but then followed his grandfather into Kidder, Peabody. Webster, Sr., raised his family in a large suburban house at 307 Hammond Street in Chestnut Hill, Brookline, and later purchased a grand town house in Boston at 306 Dartmouth Street on the corner of Commonwealth Avenue. The Websters had a country place at Beverly Cove on Boston's North Shore, and another on Squam Lake in Holderness, New Hampshire, near the White Mountains. Webster became a permanent member of the MIT Corporation in 1910 and continued to be an active alumnus. He served for many years as a trustee of the Boston Museum of Fine Arts and as president of the Massachusetts Horticultural Society, and he sat on the boards of such local corporations as United Fruit, Pacific Mills, and Ames Shovel & Tool.[12]

His partner followed a similar path. Charles Stone married Mary Adams Leonard of Hingham in 1902, and the couple had two daughters and two sons. The younger boy, Whitney Stone (1908–1979) later took an active part in the business, ultimately leading Stone & Webster into the fields of oil, gas, and atomic power. For a time Charles Stone and his wife lived in a proper Back Bay town house (234 Beacon Street), and he belonged to the usual Boston clubs and boards. With his partner he became a leader in MIT's move across the Charles River to its present site in Cambridge.

To direct the securities business of Stone & Webster and to serve as head of a private corporation formed to promote American exports, Charles Stone moved to New York City in 1915. There he quickly became a major figure on Wall Street, serving as a director of the Federal Reserve Bank of New York from 1919 to 1923 and as a director of the International Acceptance Bank, the Bank of Manhattan, the International Mercantile Marine Company, and the Union Pacific Railroad. He also secured for Stone & Webster a great many construction contracts in the mid-Atlantic region.

Stone belonged to twenty-three clubs. He also followed the then-popular English country-gentleman model of family life. The family spent winters at their town house at 907 Fifth Avenue and summers at a number of vacation homes. The principal estate was "Solana," at Locust Valley, Long Island, but Stone also owned Thomas Jefferson's farm in Virginia, where he raised thoroughbred horses. At his farm at Holderness, New Hampshire, he raised prize-winning Morgan horses and Welsh ponies.[13] Charles Stone and Edwin Webster used their new wealth to reenact the roles of the nineteenth-century Boston rich; they played the parts of Robert Grant's heroes and heroines, Mr. and Mrs. Chauncey Chippendale and Mr. and Mrs. Hugh Blaisdell.

It was in their business that the two men helped to form the twentieth century. Riding the wave of the first development of a major new industry, their firm expanded rapidly, carrying Stone & Webster into the new forms of the large American corporation, the new styles of office work, and a new culture where goals were set and values determined by a union of advanced accounting and engineering. Evaluation and management of utilities continued to be a specialty of the firm, and evaluation remains an active side of the business today. Consulting carried the company along the pathways of American finance to the assessment of properties all over the continental United States, and then, after World War I, to studies of utilities in Japan and Europe.[14]

The securities business and investment banking also grew in an easy, logical fashion from the earliest business services. At first the partners invested in a few companies they had studied or managed. Then in 1902 they began to offer the companies they managed a regular securities service as transfer agents, brokers, and underwriters. In 1907 they opened a branch securities office in Chicago, and in 1910 another in New York. Soon they extended these operations to underwriting the bonds and stocks of their engineering clients. In 1911 they successfully floated $15,-000,000 in bonds and $6,000,000 in preferred stock for the Mississippi River Power Company, the client for the giant dam at Keokuk, Iowa.[15]

In 1906 Stone & Webster managed twenty-eight utilities from Nova Scotia to Puerto Rico, from Georgia to Texas and Washington; by 1929 the list had grown to sixty-seven. Then, on the eve of the Great Depression, the firm absorbed its managed properties, transforming itself into the nation's thirteenth largest utility holding company. During these same years, as an investment banker, the firm participated in underwriting syndicates of one quarter of all the new issues offered publicly. Many of Stone & Webster's customers were savings banks and insurance companies, and the value of these 1929–1930 securities came to $1,-200,000,000.[16]

The engineering side of the business similarly followed the demands of new industrial corporations. What had begun with small dams, street railways, and city gas works rapidly grew to the largest electrical and industrial contracts. By 1903 Stone & Webster offered a full range of design and construction services for everything from simple trolley car barns to complex steam power stations and steel mills.[17] The core of the engineering work, however, remained electrical, and a succession of large power projects established the firm's national reputation. In 1909 the Pacific Light & Power Company ordered a series of three dams in the Sierra National Forest near Fresno, California, and a 275-mile transmission line to Los Angeles.[18] In Georgia the Columbus Power Company had the firm build a dam and power plant on the Chattahoochee River (Goat Island). Major consumers of this power were the new cotton mills that were competing with the Boston province's established mills.[19] The largest project of the years before World War I, and the one that confirmed Stone & Webster's reputation was the dam, lock, and power station at the Des Moines Rapids of the Mississippi River, near Keokuk, Iowa. At the time of its completion in 1913, it was the world's largest power dam.[20]

Their successes with huge installations brought the firm a continuing flow of commissions for hydroelectric and steam power stations. There were more giant dams, like the one at Conowingo, Maryland (1926–1928), and new high-pressure steam plants like the Charles Levitt Edgar Station for the Boston Edison Company at Weymouth in Boston Harbor (1924). Industrial firms, like the Ford Motor Company and American Sugar & Refining, also ordered power plants, and the company even tried building some utilities overseas—water works in Uruguay and a reservoir for the city of Athens, Greece, which brought its water from Marathon on an aqueduct built by the Emperor Hadrian.[21]

The firm's other industrial engineering jobs of the teens and twenties read like a gazetteer for the twentieth-century industrial revolution. Close to home there were factories for Simplex Wire & Cable and Boston Woven Hose & Rubber in Cambridge, a foundry for the United States Army's Watertown Arsenal, the downtown office headquarters for the First National Bank of Boston and another for its branch in Buenos Aires, Argentina, the MIT Cambridge campus (1913–15) and later its Daniel Guggenheim Aeronautics Laboratory, and the Boston Lying-In Hospital. Beyond the province the contracts spread outward with the expansion of American corporate enterprise: a ball bearing factory for SKF in Hartford, a large factory for Standard Oil Cloth in Peekskill, New York, and roundhouses for locomotives for the New York Central and the New Haven railroads, two factories for General Electric in Schenectady, New York, several office buildings in New York City, the most notable being the fifty-story Radio Building in Rockefeller Center, the Pratt School of Naval Architecture in Brooklyn, three factories for the Celluloid Company in Newark, New Jersey; a lamp factory for Westinghouse in Trenton; in Philadelphia the vast wartime Hog Island Shipyards, the Jefferson Medical College, the Insurance Company of North America, and the Bryn Mawr Hospital; to the west the University of Pittsburgh stadium and Tower of Learning; a plant for B.F. Goodrich in Akron and another for National Carbon in Fostoria, Ohio; a steel mill in Peoria, Illinois, and twelve buildings for the Moline Plow Company, a giant warehouse in Chicago; two small factories for Carnation

Milk in Wisconsin; and so it went across the nation from Minneapolis to Galveston, to Long Beach and Seattle. For the first thirty years of the twentieth century Stone & Webster's Boston office at 147 Milk Street served as engineers to the new institutional America.[22]

The range and scope of their business forced the firm to abandon its early form as a provincial private partnership; after successive adjustments it finally became, on the eve of the founders' retirement, a large, publicly held imperial corporation. In the beginning the two partners' desks had been placed side by side in the small office in Post Office Square, and from there they had dispatched young MIT and Harvard graduates to manage utilities or oversee construction jobs. As the firm grew, it moved from one downtown office building to another, settling in 1907 at the corner of Milk and Batterymarch streets. By then partners had been added, each one representing some aspect of the firm's specialties.[23]

Over the years partners came and went as related corporations offered them opportunities. The number of partners fluctuated, from three in 1905, to seven in 1912, to four in 1918, and ten during the 1920s.[24] Then, with all the postwar activity and expansion of utilities, Stone & Webster in 1925 formed the Engineers Public Service Company, a holding company to control a string of southern utilities. A few years later this subsidiary purchased control of the utilities Stone & Webster had previously managed. In 1929 the parent corporation transformed itself into a series of distinct subsidiary corporations, each one held to its own accounting, but answerable to the parent officers and board. Stone & Webster Incorporated, with headquarters at 90 Broad Street, New York City, topped the hierarchy. Beneath were Stone & Webster Service Corporation, the utility appraisal office; Stone & Webster and Blodget, Incorporated, the underwriting and brokerage firm; Stone & Webster Engineering Corporation, whose offices remained in Boston; the Engineers Public Service Corporation, the utilities holding company; and A. L. Hartridge Company, a New York office and industrial building contractor.[25]

By the 1930s, when the founding partners were retiring into their chairmanships, Stone & Webster had taken on all the characteristics of the twentieth-century institutional revolution: its business was national; its financial interdependencies were international; it managed a large office of almost a thousand engineers and draftsmen.[26] Its expertness and problem-solving skills rested upon a very particular fraction of modern culture, a technique that combined engineering with cost accounting; its corporate form of ownership promised that Stone & Webster would in the future be directed by small groups of leaders drawn from the national network of high finance. To a historian looking backward from 1983, the situation of Stone & Webster in 1930 reads like an announcement of today's social and political agenda. The scale of its construction jobs and its clients' operations foretold the metropolitan social and environmental concerns that now occupy our attention, while the organization of Stone & Webster's office and its engineering and accounting techniques lie at the heart of today's question about the adequacy of our modes of employment and the relevance of our measures of quality of production.

During Charles Stone's and Edwin Webster's active years, Americans had been so preoccupied with conflicts over the regulation of rates and the policing of private utility financing that they lost all track of equally significant social consequences that flowed from the mass use of electricity. When, at the turn of the century, the electric power industry had grown large enough to be of political significance, it had inherited all the habits and conflicts of private water and gas works and of railroad and streetcar companies: municipal conflict and corruption, lobbying and purchase of state legislatures, monopolistic favoritism in pricing, irresponsible and fraudulent stock and bond issues. There followed thirty more years of hot utility politics until the discipline of the Great Depression brought a lasting public-private compromise.[27] Since the thirties the federal government has shouldered the responsibility for supervising the marketing of private utility securities, the states have taken on the task of setting rates for utility customers, and the private corporations have been largely freed from local municipal controls to operate within the federal and state guidelines.[27]

The exceptions to this compromise have mostly proved of little consequence. In the east a few of the early municipal power companies carry on; in the far west the federal government's giant hydroelectric projects sell their power to private distributors. Only in the Southeast did a promising alternative to the compromise appear, the Tennessee Valley Authority. In this case the provision of electric power was joined to the goals of social and economic revitalization of an impoverished region. The TVA proved unable either to help the poor farmers to the degree that many had hoped or to bring prosperity as quickly as desired. Yet it was a promising attempt to combine power, land, and economic planning to achieve important human improvements. The objections of private power companies, and the conflicts among competing bureaucracies within the federal government itself, prevented the experiment from ever being repeated in the United States.[28]

In the grueling course of these utility debates the parties generally lost sight of the social and cultural consequences of the institutional revolution attendant upon the rise of large electric utility corporations. Stone & Webster, like other large firms, exerted on Boston the confusing and contradictory forces that increasingly dominate the province. As a large employer of college-trained help they provided all the current amenities of white collar work: it was neat, clean, orderly, and generally polite in the firm's offices. Yet its professionals were not much safer against layoffs in hard times than their factory neighbors, and they labored under that peculiar mix of external command and internal self-control that is the special quality of modern corporate endeavor.

Stone & Webster distributed its hundreds of engineers and draftsmen into project teams. As in the past, executives and supervisors directed the speed, skills, and costs of the work of these teams, but now the men themselves also participated in designing their tasks and in setting the cost accounting measurements as well. The result of such management has been the curious culture of large-scale office work—comfortable, neat, clean surroundings in giant office building spaces, employees enmeshed in small and large social networks; informal work styles and strict hierarchies of salaries and promotions; some degree of individual and group responsibility; and the workers' willingness to judge themselves and the organization according to the conventions of modern ac-

counting. Within the new downtown office towers and beyond
the city, scattered about the metropolis, these swirling social, economic, and cultural cross currents now support more and more of
our fellow citizens and define their consciousness. They are now
the heart of the work culture.

Such a work setting was made possible through the development of measures of accounting, a field in which Stone & Webster was one of the leaders. From the firm's earliest years
accounting required the two partners' closest attention. Their engineering consulting work was done on a cost-plus basis, so careful accounts had to be kept for the clients. Moreover, to compete
successfully, Stone & Webster had to complete its jobs on time
and bring them in close to their initial cost estimates.[29] Similarly,
the management of gas works and street railways and electric
companies for stock- and bondholders required reliable accounting practices.[30]

But Stone & Webster was more than an electrical engineering
firm with a business office employing a lot of accountants; its approach was to unite the two arts. First as engineers exploring applications of the science of electricity, and then later as engineers
helping to plan large capital investments, they were concerned
with output per dollar, kilowatts per ton of coal, horsepower per
foot of dam, losses per mile of transmission. Whether in the optimistic early years (1887–1912) when the cost of electricity fell
from twenty-five cents to ten cents a kilowatt hour, or in the discouraged Great Depression years, the firm concentrated upon reducing unit costs through building ever-larger installations.[31]
Stone & Webster engineering designs for clients, its own management bookkeeping, the special statistical services it created to
monitor systems performance, and its elaborate examinations for
bondholders, bankruptcy trustees, and investment banking syndicates, all were directed toward this narrow goal of balancing
capital investment with kilowatt output costs.

With the political debate on utilities focused on rates and capital structures, and the internal business of the firm directed toward measuring output and costs, it is no wonder that both the
culture of the office and the social consequences of electricity
escaped public notice. Yet these cultural and social issues were

part and parcel of the new technology and the new institutional arrangements, and every year they have grown more urgent. Just as employees know that job cost tickets do not closely resemble either the output or the quality of a work group, so the regulation of rates and capital returns offers few clues to the range of social effects of electric power. The social dimensions—dispersal of the metropolitan population, segregation of the classes, air pollution, traffic flows, community structure—all the current issues of the electrified and automobilized Boston province lay outside the engineers' and the regulators' accounts.

A few contemporaries of Charles Stone and Edwin Webster immediately grasped the significance of cheap electric power distribution and tried to add their concerns to the discussion. It was no accident that these pioneer social visionaries were enthusiasts for wild nature, advocates of public parks and forests, people whom we would now call environmentalists, but who were then called conservationists. For them the analysis of any problem began with an examination of human relationships, and the values that directed their policy proposals stemmed from their understanding of those relationships.[32]

Benton MacKaye of Shirley, a small town that in the twenties was far removed from the reach of Boston suburbanization, quickly grasped the possibilities of cheap long-distance transmission of electricity, the sort of metropolitan scale that Stone & Webster had demonstrated in 1913 with their lines from Big Creek to Los Angeles. MacKaye and a group of architects and planners concerned with New York city and state proposed an organized string of settlements placed along regionally planned transport routes. Their social analysis called for preserving wild land and farm land and for building networks of comfortable low-density small towns and cities. The means to this end was to be a coordinated setting of the location of limited access highways and electric power services.[33] Some of these conservation ideas were incorporated into the land policies of the TVA, and others cropped up in state plans for parks and parkways,[34] but generally the institutional revolution in electric power left the process of metropolitan settlement to find its own way according to the constraints of the private pricing of land.

The corporation of Stone & Webster continues, although it suffered a major shock during the Great Depression. Under the new federal Public Utility Holding Act of 1935 it was forced to distribute its utility stock to its stockholders[35] and to turn back to its original specialties of engineering and consulting. Under the leadership of Whitney Stone, son of the founder, the company soon recovered. Its deserved reputation for skill in designing and executing big jobs carried it to the center of World War II construction. It built ammonia and TNT plants, synthetic rubber and alcohol plants, the giant uranium refineries at Hanford, Washington, and the whole of Oak Ridge, Tennessee.[36]

World War II, with its emphasis on petrochemicals and atomic bombs, gave the firm its present configuration. What had begun with two provincial college engineers testing fuse wires and managing bankrupt streetcar lines now became a high-technology, worldwide business. Today Stone & Webster drills for oil in the Arabian Gulf, lays gas pipelines in Malaysia, outfits coal mines in Utah, builds oil refineries in Ohio and an atomic power plant in Illinois, and is building the breeder reactor at Clinch River, Tennessee, as well as carrying on its familiar utility consulting.[37]

The pace of change in the firm's history exemplifies the unpredictability of both modern technology and modern economies. Its range and scope of activities exemplify the new imperial scale of many modern Boston institutions. To whom is Stone & Webster now responsible? Its directors are directors of other imperial corporations, as well as officers of Stone & Webster.[38] The firm reports to a man from the First National Bank of Boston, a man from American Express, a man from W. R. Grace & Co., a man from the Chase Manhattan Bank of New York, and itself.

5 ✿ LAURA ELIZABETH RICHARDS

In truth we and our parents are still closely tied to the idea of the sentimental family of the nineteenth century. In many ways we live the kinds of metropolitan lives they intended for us, and we persistently use sentiment to express our longing for harmony and to reassure ourselves that we have found it. No less than our nineteenth-century predecessors, we try to maintain our emotional balance by pretending that the world is governed by stable laws.

Our grandparents live in our memories hidden by a peculiar nostalgia of gaslight and ragtime. In our memories their sentimentality means only songs, valentines, and bouquets. We no longer remember what they were straining toward. Today's sentimentality, of course, is not sweet. We no longer pretend that love governs the world, or that home and mother are the embodiments of love and benevolence. Our sentimental fashion is an obsession with the lurid and the horrible. Whether in apocalyptic science fiction or in films of explicit personal brutality, destruction fascinates us, and the scent of pain and death perks us up and makes us feel alive again. These pleasures of negation are no less partial and sentimental in their popular enactment than the former visions of sweetness. Ours is the negative pole of the sentimental axis, but the current is no less powerful for being negatively charged. In the old religious language of seventeenth-century Boston, today's sentimentality would have been called an ignorant fascination with the devil's work, and the popular nineteenth-century style would have been called an equally ignorant assumption of knowledge of God's ways. Today these outlooks are labeled cynicism and perfectionism, but behind both dwells the common relief of sentimentality.

Because of its partialness, its willful screening out of information, sentimentality is always an obstacle to comprehension, no matter what form it takes. Instead of giving knowledge, a sentimental view joins heart and mind and thereby works as a surefine remedy for the pains of alienation. This union is its compelling force, and the reason why sentimentality remains so popular. Despite the secularization of the various sects Bostonians remain a deeply religious people, so they cry out ceaselessly for order somehow, somewhere. Sentimentality answers the cry by spreading half-truths thickly over commonplace experiences.

The hopeful, perfectionist sentimentality of the nineteenth century provided islands of familial comfort in the midst of a sea of wrenching change. As families were driven from their farms and villages by economic force or political violence, alternately buoyed up and cast down by the possibilities for new wealth, given giants' powers over distance, men, and nature, the idea of the sentimental family, however contradicted in fact, stood as a worthy goal to cling to for relief from the aches of heart and mind. And if such an idealized home accorded with the benign laws of nature itself, as one branch of romanticism taught, why should it not serve as a standard for the larger society, a force for goodness that might press outward from home to neighborhood, to entire suburbs and cities, indeed, to direct the worlds of man and nature?

Such a vision of perfection lent both comfort and direction to the well-to-do families of Boston at the end of the nineteenth century. It gave relief and meaning to the inevitable conflicts and suffering within their homes, and it provided a goal for the men and the women of these families. The women, especially, held the standard of the sentimental family up to measure the world, and made the demands that effected the residential revolution. As a movement dependent upon the half-truths of sentimentality, in time this revolution played us false. Its hopes for security proved to rest upon the social mechanisms of segregation, and its ignorance of business, politics, science, and war denied it leverage against the destructive forces of the twentieth century.

Laura Elizabeth Howe Richards (1850–1943), as daughter, wife, and mother, lived this sentimental family life, and after many years of triumphs, her ideal led her down dangerous, narrowing, and destructive pathways, as it did everyone. Compared to the global reach and corporate power of Charles Stone and Edwin Webster, her power for good and evil always remained extremely modest. Her compass was that of a married woman: a large house and a large family, a summer camp, a town with its many committees, charities, and clubs, provincial friends and acquaintances, and a national career as the author of popular children's stories and poems. By any standard hers was a happy and thoroughly successful life, one she enjoyed immensely, and which gave pleasure and example to many. Surely, Laura Richards was one of the most successful women of her province and her era. As such she stands as complicit as anyone else for making Boston what it is today.

Her life began in a sheltered *haute bourgeois* home in South Boston. Her father was Samuel Gridley Howe (1801–1876), and her mother Julia Ward Howe (1819–1910). Laura was the third daughter, fourth child, in a family of four girls and a boy. Many things conspired to make the Howe family into a little world of its own, and that was how Laura always recalled it.[1] Because only ten years separated the youngest (Maud) from the eldest (Julia), and because the family was well-to-do, the Howes could and did make their home into a school for their children. The family was rather isolated in what was then suburban South Boston. They lived in an old colonial house with a large new addition, situated on four and a half acres of land at the end of Story Street (a dead-end lane off G Street), overlooking Dorchester Bay.[2] The household also included a gardener, a cook, a governess, a nurse, and servant girls. And the father's daily rounds as director of the nearby Massachusetts School for the Blind (Perkins Institute) surrounded the home with still more children and servants. Indeed, Laura was named for one of Samuel's famous blind and deaf pupils, Laura Bridgeman.

Samuel and Julia seem to have intended for their home to be a child's garden, a perfected miniature world. Their arrangements, if more elaborate and complete than most, followed the established lines of the era. Father settled the family in its house, ceaselessly rebuilt and remodeled it, and guarded the fence about his household. As an internationally famous pioneer in the education of the handicapped, Samuel stood at his gate to welcome a stream of interesting and important visitors who came to observe his work (Charles Dickens visited and wrote of his work in *American Notes*).[3]

Not content to be merely the protector of his home and his family, father did battle against the dragons of his day. He began as a Byronic hero, a young physician who joined the poet in the Greek revolution against the Turks. Byron's helmet rested on the hatrack in the hall. Later he turned to the cause of Polish independence. He made his career an attack on blindness, deafness, feeblemindness, prisons, slavery, and a host of lesser issues. Samuel's wife always called him "Chev" (for Chevalier, his Greek revolutionary title), and his daughter Laura thought of him quite literally as a knight, as did the poet John Greenleaf Whittier.[4]

Father supervised the gardens and managed the fruit trees and roses himself. "He liked to make companions of his children . . . We followed him about the garden like so many little dogs, watching the pruning and grafting which were his special tasks. We followed him into the wonderful pear-room, where there were many chests of drawers, every drawer full of pears lying on cotton-wool . . . He had many delightful stories—one of Jack Nory which had no end and went on and on, through many a walk and garden prowl."[5] Samuel taught all his children to ride by taking them on pony rides before breakfast through the quiet streets of South Boston. He read to them from the Bible, Sir Walter Scott, and his favorite poets, Pope and Byron. He had no ear for music, but music and singing were Julia's forte. For Laura, "I suppose there never was a tenderer or kinder father";[6] after his death in 1876 she edited and published two volumes of his letters and journals (1906 and 1909).

Within the fence Julia Howe tended the children's world. A New York City banker's daughter, she had mastered the encapsulated life of the women and children of the families of the rich. As an heiress she had been taught all the womanly skills of music, foreign languages, and polite crafts. Her own mother had died when she was six, and although her two brothers and two sisters provided companionship, their New York home suffered under the father's austerity. Julia Howe, like her fellow New York heiress, Emma Lazarus, had escaped into books, and from childhood on she remained an active scholar, especially a student of German and ancient authors. She was not shy and retiring, however, but a quick, lively woman with a sharp wit that could bite and a love for parties and fun.[7]

In her South Boston home, which she named "Green Peace," she invented a daily schedule that concluded with a long children's hour. At the end of the day, to entertain her children, she played the piano while they danced, she sang to them and taught them all manner of English, German, French, and Italian songs, and she helped and encouraged them to write stories and poems and to present little family recitals and plays. Occasionally Chev joined this end-of-the-day fun, playing bear in his old fur coat and taking part in the readings and dramatics. "The time for singing was at twilight, when the dancing was over, and we gathered breathless and exhausted about the piano for the last and greatest treat. Then the beautiful voice would break out, and flood the room with melody, and fill our childish hearts with almost painful rapture. Our mother knew all the songs in the world—that was our firm belief. Certainly we never found an end to her repertory."[8] In summer the music and dramatics moved to the outdoors at Lawton Valley in Newport, Rhode Island. As Laura Richards later wrote about her childhood, Julia Howe made the home into a kind of energetic, upper-class version of Louisa May Alcott's *Little Women.*[9]

Many things divided Julia and Samuel Howe besides his inability to carry a tune. Samuel hated to sit still, he always had to be doing something, but he wanted Julia to remain within the miniature world of the home. Most particularly he resented her public life. First the publication of her poetry and the presentation of her plays offended him. Later he exploded when she followed him out of the home to the lecture platform, speaking on subjects from abolitionism and prison reform to world peace and woman suffrage. After one of their recurring arguments, this one on the occasion of their twentieth wedding anniversary, Julia wrote angrily in her journal: "I have been married twenty years

today. In the course of that time I have never known my husband
to approve of any act of mine which I myself valued. Books—
poems—essays—everything has been contemptible in his eyes
because not his way of doing things . . . I fear to do wrong in dis-
obeying one who has a husband's authority. God help me for I
am much grieved and disconcerted."[10]

The conflict between them died down only when Julia learned
to quietly slip off to her public activities; perhaps, too, Samuel got
tired of objecting as he grew old. And Julia was not always able to
play the role of perfect housewife and mother.[11] Her son-in-law
recalled that as the children grew beyond the dining room songs
and dancing, Julia "could not always wholly cope with her maternal responsibilities."[12] It was Laura who was the peacemaker
in the Howe family, and later she served this role in the Richards
family.

This is the background we must understand to appreciate what
Laura Richards herself created. Officially she resolved her memories of parental conflict by saying she learned from her mother
that the husband was "the skipper" and the wife "the first
mate."[13] Pretending that such labels tell anything about how a
man and a woman can live together, she went forward to make
her own family and home and to convince thousands of Bostonians and Americans of the soundness of family and community,
her goals.

In Laura's autobiography she described herself as the least outstanding of all the Howe children. Julia, the eldest, was shy,
beautiful, and literary; Flossie, the next, was imaginative and active, the inventor of family games and sport; brother Henry,
whom Laura was closest to, was full of mischief and pranks (later
he became a famous metallurgist); Maud, the youngest, was a
beauty. Laura, herself, was "dreamy, indolent, thoughtless,"
awkward at the piano, a "donkey fingers" at sewing.[14] During the
Civil War the only task she could do was to pick lint for the Sanitary Commission, not sew for the soldiers.

When Laura was eleven the family moved to the first of a series
of rented houses in Boston, one on Boylston Place (an alley off
what was later Fred Allen's Piano Row), others on Beacon Hill.
Laura attended a small private girls' school nearby on Boylston
Street, and her life remained confined to the family and its circle.

Mr. John Sullivan Dwight, an old Brook Farm resident and the founder of the Harvard Music Society on Beacon Hill, took Laura and her sisters to symphony concerts. She attended the Handel and Haydn Society concerts in which her mother, brother, and sister Flossie sang. Her father's best friend, Senator Charles Sumner, whom Laura called the "harmless giant," and a lawyer, John Albion Andrew, governor of Massachusetts during the Civil War, talked of the larger political world. The summer when she was seventeen, she traveled abroad with her parents and eldest sister on a relief mission for Crete.[15]

Laura was sent to Lorenzo Papanti's dancing school to learn the waltz, polka, quadrille, gavotte, and schottische.[16] There, in the winter of 1869, at an assembly dance she appeared "as a vision on the steps of the ladies' dressing room" to Henry Richards (1848–1949), a shy Harvard senior. The following summer Henry invited Laura and her brother, who had been his classmate, to visit at the family place in Gardiner, Maine, and in September they became engaged. Laura was nineteen, Henry twenty-one. Although a suitable young man, Henry had yet to establish himself, and Laura was sickly. Accordingly, the Howes insisted on a lengthy Victorian courtship.

Henry, while making rapid progress as an architecture student and draftsman, wrote fondly of their courtship. "During these two years, I passed up and down Mt. Vernon Street, four times a day, looking up at my vision in the window at number 32 to receive a smile, and allowed to call, while Aunt Flossie hovered, once a week."[17] On June 17, 1871, Bunker Hill Day, Henry Richards and Laura Elizabeth Howe married. With a handsome subvention from the Howes, the couple took a year's honeymoon tour of the architectural sights of Europe and Greece.[18] Later her husband remembered her as suffering the delicate health of a Victorian lady. She was sickly during the years before their marriage and delicate throughout their honeymoon, so he bought her a cane with a seat so she could rest as they went about to see the sights; he always carried her up flights of stairs, indeed he carried her all the way up the campanile in St. Mark's, Venice! Apparently her lifelong style, like her mother's, was to balance energetic activity with periodic retreat, thereby sustaining her "delicately poised" constitution for ninety-three years.[19]

On their return from Europe, Laura was pregnant. They settled into the "old part" of the Howe homestead in South Boston; Samuel, Julia, and Maud retreated into the more commodious "new part." Here Laura made her first home, a sheltered corner fenced and tended by her father and her husband. The matron of her father's nearby School for the Feeble Minded, Mrs. Macdonald, long a devoted servant of the Howe family, helped her hire a cook and a nurse. Henry, a young man with little fortune and a lifelong concern for economizing, furnished the house with his old college furniture and purchases from the second-hand stores of downtown Boston. The old house lacked central heat, so Henry rebuilt the fireplace, bought a small stove for the nursery, and sawed, split, and daily carried in the firewood. Mrs. Macdonald advised Laura on the purchase of kitchen utensils and taught her to order groceries. Henry completed the preparations for being a family by purchasing a Saint Bernard dog, "Brownie." When her time came to give birth, however, in July 1872, Henry was off at the architectural office in downtown Boston, and Laura's father superintended the birth of her first child, Alice Maud.[20]

Laura Richards flourished as a mother. These years were all "bearing, nursing, and rearing; my first housekeeping; my first loaf of bread; my first quince marmalade; my first Baby."[21] Indeed, three babies in four years; after Alice came Rosalind (1874) and Henry Howe (1876). To the "surprise of all the family"[22] and to the delight of her husband and children, Laura broke into song, rhymes, jingles, and bits of fantasy to express her imagination. She held baby Alice face down on her lap, placed a pad on her back, and began writing.

> Little John Bottlejohn lived on the hill,
>   And a blithe little man was he.
> And he won the heart of a pretty mermaid
>   Who lived in the deep blue sea.
> And every evening she used to sit
>   And sing on the rocks by the sea,
> "Oh! little John Bottlejohn, pretty John Bottlejohn,
>   Won't you come out to me?"[23]

She never stopped thereafter: ninety volumes in all, filled with numberless rhymes, fables, children's stories, occasional poetry by the yard, bits of history, genre novels, her own autobiography, her father's papers, and, with her sister Maud Elliott, a prize-winning biography of her mother.[24] Motherhood was a liberation, making her an immensely successful children's author and an important advocate for the moral ambitions of comfortable Boston families.

In 1876 the stays of Laura Richards's world gave way. Her father, to whom she had been extremely close, died. At the same time the building boom collapsed, and with it her husband's promising Boston practice. When Henry's eldest brother offered him a position in the family paper mill, the young couple moved to Gardiner, Maine, a mill town 150 miles northeast of Boston to find security for their growing family.

Gardiner, situated where the steep falls of Cobbossee Stream meet the tidal Kennebec River, typified the industrial village life of the Boston province of those days. The houses of the 4,400 residents were perched along the slopes of the town. A water power company controlled the dams and reservoirs for the factories: four large lumber mills, three paper mills, of which the Richardses was the largest with seventy-five workers, a foundry, a woolen mill, a tannery, a leather belting factory, a flour mill, three machine shops, a spring and axle factory owned by Henry's brother, several carriage factories, many sash and blind shops, and many blacksmiths. A special feature was the winter harvest of ice from the millponds, a crop whose value the census taker estimated to equal the year's output of all the factories.[25]

All of these businesses were managed and operated by local people, and much of the capital was local too. The trade was provincial and coastwise, and the Richardses' paper mill was no exception. Most of their output was bought by a big publisher in nearby Augusta and by the Sunday edition of the *New York Herald*. Because the firm required a lot of money for buying paper-making machinery, Boston banks and funds supplied a growing, and in time, a controlling share of the corporate capital.[26]

In coming to this fringe mill town, Laura joined a large family.

The five Richards brothers, of whom Henry was the youngest, were descended from the Gardiners, after whom the town was named, the first Gardiner having been a Bostonian who had been agent for the Plymouth Colony's vast Maine purchase. The family had English relatives and connections as well as ties to Boston. All the Richards boys received some of their education in England. Frank, fifteen years older than Henry, was a graduate of Cambridge University and was married to an Englishwoman. He owned the largest share of the mill, and after the father's early death, he ran the family. Next there was George, a successful Maine lawyer, and John, an active investor in local manufacturing schemes, a veteran of the Civil War and the Spanish-American War, and director of the Disabled Veterans Home in nearby Togus. His three daughters were the same ages as some of Laura's girls, and the cousins grew up together. The next brother, Robert, was a metallurgist, a professor at MIT, and husband of Ellen Swallow Richards, the pioneer home economist. Robert and Ellen lived in the Jamaica Plain section of Boston and so were not part of the frequent visiting among the Maine Richardses, but they later helped finance the higher education of Laura and Henry's daughters.[27]

This family, her home in the mill village, and the village itself became Laura Richards's new world. At the center, as in South Boston, stood house and home, in this case "the yellow house," a large rambling 1814 structure at 3 Dennis Street in Gardiner village, a mile from the paper mill. Over the years Laura and Henry enlarged and remodeled the house, ultimately installing running water and bathrooms, "Statlerizing it," as Henry scornfully characterized these last improvements.[28]

At first Laura Richards kept within her home and circle of relatives. She had come to Gardiner with three young children, and now she gave birth to four more: Julia Ward (1878), Maud (1881), John (1884), and Laura Elizabeth (1886). With the Richards brothers and their wives, there were outings, picnics, dancing, and evening parties with home dramatics. Her husband and John Richards rented a room in the house across the road, where the two families kept a little school for their daughters, classes emphasizing literature and the mastery of French and

German.[29] Laura and Henry created a wonderfully lively and pleasant family life, and everyone who knew them commented upon its ebullience. A fellow townsman, the poet Edwin Arlington Robinson, became a frequent visitor. He wrote a letter to a friend saying, "The only trouble with that family is they are too abnormally happy and unconscious of the damnation that makes up nine tenths of life."[30]

All the while Richards continued her nursery writing.

> Once there was an elephant,
> Who tried to use the telephant—
> No! no! I mean an elephone
> Who tried to use the telephone—
> (Dear me! I am not certain quite
> That even now I've got it right.)
>
> Howe'er it was, he got his trunk
> Entangled in the telephunk;
> The more he tried to get it free,
> The louder buzzed the telephee—
> (I fear I'd better drop the song
> Of elephop and telephong!)[31]

As her children grew older, her stories advanced; soon Richards was telling stories for ten- and twelve-year-olds, then tales with teen-age girl heroines. From 1885 through 1897, as her children reached high school age, she perfected her talent and wrote a series of extremely popular stories: the Toto books of animal stories (1885, 1887), *Captain January* (1890), and the teen-aged Hildegarde books (1889–1897). *Captain January,* the story of a shipwrecked baby girl raised by a lighthouse keeper sold 300,000 copies and was twice made into a movie.

The death of her fifth child, the infant Maud, in 1882 prompted Richards to venture beyond her home and immediate family. One remedy for her grief was writing the Toto stories, in which animals played like children.[32] Next, in imitation of her doctor father, she began regular visits to the shut-ins and the disabled of the village and to John Richards's soldier's home in Togus. An easy, cheerful, sociable woman, Richards wrote of her education as a visitor. "I read to the old men—at first—a merry short story, recited a brief stirring poem; they listened kindly, responded civilly; but I soon found out that what really interested them was to talk themselves. They were full of 'tells,' what they wanted was an audience. So they began to teach, and I to learn many things."[33] Finally, joining forces with the local Episcopal minister, a former assistant to Phillips Brooks at Boston's Trinity Church, she conducted an energetic and successful campaign to build a public library and public meeting hall. The new library became a center for Laura's life, the scene of books read aloud, clubs, meetings, and theatricals—public versions of the private family activities of the yellow house.[34]

In the village people called her "Mrs. Harry," after her husband, the mill manager.[35] What she accomplished in her move outward into the town was to transform a woman's role of long standing. She accepted the position of local squire's wife and then remade that role into its modern suburban form of the well-to-do housewife, clubwoman, and volunteer. What formerly had been restricted to church-related activities and private family charitable errands now became a public role of volunteer committees and community politics.

In Laura Richards's version of the modern volunteer and clubwoman, she attempted to bring all the fashionable big-city ideas of liberal Boston to her small town. Indeed, her life in these years repeated the history of American social reform. Visiting the sick led to a Public Health Association, the District Nurses Association, and the Gardiner General Hospital. Beginning in 1895, for twenty-six years she served as founding president of the Gardiner Women's Philanthropic Union. From here she launched her successful campaign of 1917–1919 to raise private subscriptions to build a new high school. This group carried her to the larger issues of prison reform and the protection of women and children.

Like her mother before her, and like all the settlement house workers of her own day, Laura Richards believed in the efficacy of clubs as a device for teaching and for self-education. She ran the Howe Club herself, in the yellow house, for high school boys. From 1886 through 1930, every Saturday evening she read to the boys, then served them ice cream and good humor, in order to acquaint them with great literature and to encourage the ambitious among them. She established a whole series of clubs, ranging from a "sociable club for wage earning girls" to a current events club for herself and her friends.[36]

This round of activities can best be understood as an expansion of her family ideals into the surrounding community. The work was useful and efficient enough to make the lives of her children, relatives, and neighbors safer, easier, and more joyful. With good will and practicality Laura Richards nourished the Boston soul. Emerson had grasped this necessity. "Thought, virtue, beauty, were the ends; but it was known that men of thought and virtue sometimes had a headache, or wet feet, or could lose good time whilst the room was getting warm on winter days."[37]

Richards directed her reforms in such a way that her antagonists seemed to be the unimaginative, the backward-looking, the fearful. She presented herself as the agent of progress, and her many letters to the local newspaper, the *Gardiner Reporter Journal,* were written from this popular position. A long poem written for the high school campaign showed her good-natured style of attack.

> "I wonder what is the matter with me!"
>   Said good old Gardiner town.
> "I seem to feel so queer this year,
>   I cannot settle down.
> I used to sit in my good old chair,
> And knit, and nod, and doze,
> Until my good old spectacles
> Dropped off my good old nose.
> But now I feel such pains, my dear,
> Shooting and darting there and here;
> I cannot sleep, and I cannot knit,
> And sometimes I cannot even sit,
> But have to get up and stir about;
> And what it all means I can't find out.
> And when they see me awake, you know,
> My children come and *annoy* me so!

Begging and teasing to have things new—
You know the way all children do;
Good gracious! the things they want, my dear!
Why such demands I never did hear.
More room to work, and more to play,
A new High School and a Y.M.C.A.,
Playgrounds, gymnasiums, basket ball,
Nurses and helpers, too, for all;
You cannot even be sick today,
Unless you do it in the proper way."[38]

Behind Richards's reforming clubwoman's role lay an outlook on life that was then sweeping the Boston province. She set forth her version in a pamphlet, "The Social Possibilities of a Country Town," written for an Episcopal laymen's organization. A better and more ample future can be anticipated, she wrote, from the dissolution of the narrow denominational boundaries that formerly isolated small town residents from one another. "At the Methodist Fair no Congregationalist ladies bought the aprons and dolls. Calling was in great measure confined to the church circle, and at an evening party one was apt to meet the same people one saw in the pews on Sunday, without their bonnets . . . All this is mercifully changing today."[39] Urged on by the example of the local ministers and carried forward by the women's clubs and social and charitable organizations, a fresh spirit of common human fellowship was coming to be the dominant outlook and practice of the Boston province's small towns.[40]

Richards lamented the petticoat rule and objected to the separation of the sexes that prevailed during her lifetime, and she anticipated the mixing that later came to be the hallmark of middle-class suburban schools, country clubs, recreation, and family life. "In the ideal town," she wrote, "the clubs shall be of men and women, studying, working, playing together, as the Lord meant them to do."[41]

The new spirit of fellowship, however, was not directed merely toward forming a more cohesive community. Such a goal would hardly be in the tradition of Boston province. Instead, the minister, the women's clubs, and the new public libraries, schools, and clubs were all servants to the task of "nourishing distinctive individual lives." The special advantage of the country town, the feature of the small place, as opposed to the city, lay in its encouragement to individualism. "The dweller in the country town may, if he so will, possess his soul, instead of having it snatched from him every hour of the day, and can live for the most part his own life. He can be himself, and not a well-executed model of his next-door neighbor."[42]

To this end the agents of progress should identify the particular in each person and help that person cultivate his special bent. The librarian "knows his books and his people; he studies the taste and disposition of each reader so far as possible, and helps him to his choice." "If a boy goes to sleep over his Latin, the teacher tries him with mathematics; if that fails, there are the natural sciences." The modern school was to be "the rallying ground for all kinds of pleasant things."[43] Indeed, the entire community was to be formed into one large school for the nurture of families and their children.

In reading over these old specifications for the good life, it is hard not to ask, as generations of American boys have asked, why must our world be turned into a school? Why, with the universe stretching out before our eyes, must we be confined to narrow rooms by ministers, teachers, and mothers? If we "should grow up hand in hand with Nature,"[44] as Laura Richards herself wanted, why force the parlor, the schoolroom and the backyard garden on people in the name of individuality? It was Thoreau's conceit to side with the boys against the schoolteachers and the adults. "Children, who play at life, discern its true law and relations more closely than men, who fail to live it worthily, but who think they are wiser by experience, this is, by failure."[45]

To such questioning, Richards had a ready answer, the answer of generations of Boston divines and schoolmasters. The world must become a school because "eight boys out of ten require to have their eyes opened for them: they cannot find their sight unaided."[46] Once they have been taught to see, "their walks and plays are in the fields and the friendly woods; from every hill-top they see the world fresh and green and lovely; their eyes learn to look far abroad, yet miss no smallest flower at their feet. The birds teach them to love music; what they study at school, they can prove by going a few rods from their own door."[47] In short, the community was to be a garden for the nurture of wise and godly human beings. When failure occurred, the fault lay with the parents. Fathers who did not know or did not play with their children, mothers who kept drab homes and didn't talk with their daughters were the source of ignorance and evil in Gardiner. It was they who fostered the lounging boys at the railroad station and the "loitering girls" in "showy attire" on the back streets.[48]

Like all gardens, Richards's garden nourished noxious weeds as well as the fellowship of families. The most dangerous weeds were the tactics and politics of exclusion, which her community as school required. Hers was a woman's vision, and as such it extended the nurturing goals and employed the boundary-maintaining tactics of the family she and her husband managed. Her community was not Gardiner, but particular Gardiner families and a network of established families that extended through the major institutions of the Boston province and to the imperial capital at New York City. Her sons went to Gardiner's grammar school, then to Groton School and Harvard College. The Richards's kept their own small school for their daughters, then sent them to fashionable finishing schools and on to Smith College or the Boston Museum School of Fine Arts, or had them come out into Boston "society."[49]

The idea of the Gardiner community as a school was philanthropy; it was an idea and a set of instructions intended to benefit others. A province dominated by schoolmasters and ministers, as Boston once was, easily falls into such a trap and has often been admonished for this blindness. "Rescue the drowning and tie your shoe-strings. Take your time, and set about some form of free labor . . . Do not stay to be an overseer of the poor, but endeavor to be one of the worthies of the world," Thoreau had warned years earlier.[50]

Laura Richards's idea caught the imagination of many. Why should the family and its children exist as an island surrounded by a hostile and dangerous world? Might the family not settle in a community where it hopes and its children would be encouraged and supported? Many women and men in Richards's generation took up this vision, discarded its philanthropy, and transformed whole towns into school communities. By the time she was writing her autobiography in 1930, her kind of community of families, clubs, and schools had become the common ambition and the frequent achievement of the suburbs and summer vacation towns of the Boston province.

Yet by chance the experiences of lives other than the Richardses' found a voice in Gardiner. Thanks to this accident, a memory of the breadth of the forest and the thickness of the mill town survive for us today. Cobbossee Stream, whose falls drove Gardiner's mills, were also the cascades of the poet Edwin Arlington Robinson.

> I found a torrent falling in a glen
> Where the sun's light shone silvered and leaf-split;
> The boom, the foam, and the mad flash of it
> All made a magic symphony; but when
> I thought upon the coming of hard men
> To cut those patriarchal trees away,
> And turn to gold the silver of their spray,
> I shuddered. Yet a gladness now and then
> Did wake me to myself till I was glad
> In earnest, and was welcoming the time
> For screaming saws to sound above the chime
> Of idle waters, and for me to know
> The jealous visionings that I had had
> Were steps to the great place where trees and torrents go.[51]

Robinson (1869–1935) accepted Gardiner, as he later accepted Boston and New York, on the realist's grounds that what was somehow had to be, but he doubted the direction of his times. He found no substance in the contemporary language of progress, no escape in the puffing up of nature. Robinson would not let go of the crucial question of whether "the great place where trees and torrents go" was heaven or hell.[52]

Laura Richards had extended to the young Robinson the same sort of maternal philanthropy she gave to the rest of the town. The Robinsons, once a prosperous family of shopkeepers, collapsed into poverty and personal disaster soon after the death of the father. Despite their former prosperity, the Robinsons were nobodies and were never included in the Richardses' social circle. But neighborhood proximity brought the children together. One of the Richards boys met Edwin and later, when Laura Richards learned that a serious young poet lived a block away, she invited him to tea. Thereafter the active Richards family welcomed Edwin, the girls went on long walks through the woods with him, and Henry Richards introduced him to a cousin, John Hays Gardiner, a young Harvard professor who became Edwin's steady literary and financial supporter.[53]

In 1904 Richards's eldest son, Henry, a teacher at the Groton School, was the intermediary in an exchange that bought Robinson his first national attention. Kermit Roosevelt, Theodore's son, went to Henry Richards, his teacher, to ask what he should be reading. Henry gave Kermit a copy of Robinson's *Children of the Night* (1897), and Kermit was so taken by its poems that he sent a copy to his father in the White House. The president caught his son's enthusiasm and wrote a favorable evaluation for the magazine *Outlook*, thereby drawing some testy comment from professional literary critics, but helping Robinson into public notice. When the president learned of Robinson's ill-paid job as a timekeeper in the New York subway tunnels, he found him a sinecure in the U. S. Customs House in New York.[54]

Substantial differences separated Robinson's imagined countryside and village from Laura Richards's. Robinson's Gardiner, which he called Tilbury Town, was carefully located in the author's experiences of the present. His gift was the ability to present honestly the alterations of triumph and suffering of ordinary lives. His characters were people of force whose lives interacted with the obdurate facts of small-town life in the Boston province of 1900: the "skirt-crazed" John Evereldown, the dying Luke Havergal, the grieving butcher Reuben Bright, the drunken Mr. Flood, the New York *litterateur* transformed into Tilbury's dying Captain Craig. Neither nostalgia nor imagined natural landscape obscured their circumstances. Robinson refused to admit "that nature, not man, was the proper study of mankind."[55]

By contrast, Richards's Maine genre novels floated in place and time.[56] Because the action had no concrete social surroundings, the characters moved in clouds, despite the verisimilitude of local language, the plots of commonplace family events, and the carefully specified clothing and rooms. Laura Richards's literary places were in fact Boston and New York places, and her characters ran on big-city nostalgia time. Their background was the sentimental repainting of the scenery of Emerson and Thoreau.[57]

"At the gates of the forest, the surprised man of the world is forced to leave his city estimates of great and small, wise and foolish. The knapsack of custom falls from his back with the first steps he takes into these precincts. Here is sanctity which shames our religions, and reality which discredits our heroes."[58]

There were, inevitably, more forces at work in Gardiner than those of the family and the local community. The mill town, like the suburbs of Boston, was part of the modern empire. The Richardses' paper mill burned in 1893, and the Boston bankers who financed its rebuilding refused to put up enough capital to allow the business to expand and compete successfully in the evergrowing world of newsprint manufacture. After floundering for several years, the rebuilt Richards mill sold out to the new J. P. Morgan trust, International Paper Company.[59]

In 1900, with all but two of their six children grown, Laura and Henry began still another sort of home and community, a summer camp. As pioneer camp founders they were part of still another branch of the residential revolution—the transformation of the rural fringe of the metropolis. Thanks to the Richardses and many others, the dying farm and fishing settlements surrounding Boston were being repainted for the imaginative life of modern city dwellers. Bankrupt villages and broken-down farms were reinterpreted as a special heritage of charming New England small towns nestled within a friendly forest or ocean wilderness.

Although the new metropolitan fringe was compounded of the most ordinary elements—old houses and antique furnishings, the village characters on the post office porch, the running and splashing boys at the summer camp lake—its scope was anything but modest. It purported to be an entire world. The new garden embraced the entire province, from Boston and its satellite cities to the lonesome spruce forests of Maine. The residents of the cities were urged to visit, to enjoy, and to learn from the newly refurbished outer places. Instead of seeing impoverished farms, pastures grown to pines, rotting barns, slashed forests, pinched mill villages, and soapy rivers, the city dwellers and their children should seek renewal in the religion of nature.

During Richards's lifetime Maine, along with the scenic metropolitan fringes of the entire province, became a popular retreat for city dwellers. Its transformation by writers and artists into a semtimental landscape gave it an important dimension in our twentieth-century provincial life. As a collection of falsely imagined places, Maine deceived Richards and the thousands who shared in her wishfulness. By choosing not to look closely at the vacation surroundings, the city dweller lost his bearings and gave up any chance of discovering the consequences of his own presence. This same sentimentality blotted out history and blocked from view the presence of significant contemporary events.

Such self-deceptions immediately overtook the Richardses as they set about building their summer camp to teach young boys the skills and sports of the "country." The family had lost its mill to the advance of imperial business, yet neither Laura Richards's writing nor the couple's boys' camp had any place for such events. Within their new garden International Paper Company could not be seen. For a time the Richardses had considered setting up a school. When they consulted Endicott Peabody, rector of Groton School, he encouraged them instead to open a summer camp, and he promised to refer many prospective campers.[60] At that time the summer camp movement was in first flood.

The impetus to establish boys' summer camps arose from a novel social problem that followed upon the elaboration of vacation styles of rich Americans. Deprived of chores and work, the teen-aged boys of such families idled about and got into mischief, as Henry Cabot Lodge and his gang had done during their long summer vacations at Nahant. The founder of the first summer camp (1881) spoke of "the miserable condition of boys belonging to well-to-do families in summer hotels."[61] Another pioneer camp founder, a private school headmaster, observed a repeated summer decline in his students and assigned the cause to families who owned "large and somewhat isolated estates [where] . . . the boys had been reduced to the company of stablemen and servants."[62]

The notion of summer camps caught on with well-to-do city families, and numerous boys', and later girls', camps were founded between 1886 and 1900 in Maine and New Hampshire and all over the rest of New England and upstate New York. Many of the camp founders were masters in private schools who saw their camps as useful additions to the winter classroom. The boy's summer would be a blend of individual and team sports, tutoring in academic subjects if necessary, hiking, swimming and canoeing, absorbing the benign effects of living close to nature, and following the powerful example of energetic college student counselors.[63]

The Richardses, with their schoolmaster sons and teacher daughter Alice, fitted easily into this trend. Characteristically, at the outset they expected that "camp would be little more than an enlargement of the family."[64] Henry purchased a beautiful piece of land on the shore of Belgrade Great Pond and, aided by former mechanics from Gardiner, built a lodge, tent platforms, and a dock. In June 1900 the first boy's camp in the Belgrade region of Maine was ready to open. They named it Merryweather after a family in Laura Richards's teen-age novels.[65] The camp remained a comparatively small, family affair for forty boys, many of them from Groton and St. Paul's schools, until Laura and Henry retired from it in 1932.

Laura supervised the reading, singing, and dramatics and with her daughters managed the camp's domestic arrangements. Henry and his two sons, instructors at Groton and St. Paul's, ran the water sports, canoe trips, and hikes. The camp seems to have trained another generation of Boston schoolmasters, and three of its boys later became famous as writers: Conrad Aiken, Ogden Nash, and Joseph S. Alsop.[66]

The sentimental blanket of stories and nature descriptions deceived the Richardses as to the meaning of their role as camp directors and misled them about their place in the modern metropolitan world. Unwittingly, perhaps, and surely without a sense of the grave consequences, they became active participants in a costly social retreat. Their camp, in its small way, joined the general American and European movement of the early twentieth century toward heightened ethnic and racial prejudice. Closer to home, the Richardses joined with many other established Protes-

tant Boston families in erecting barricades of privilege and advantage—the Groton School, St. Paul's School, and Camp Merryweather.

In 1924 the Richardses listed their camp in the official directory
in the new language of exclusion. "Merryweather, the first camp
on the Belgrade Lakes, was established in 1900 by Mr. and Mrs.
Henry Richards, who now have as co-directors their sons . . . Mr.
Richards and his sons are Harvard graduates, and with Mrs.
Richards, daughter of Julia Ward Howe, and author of well-
known children's books, strive to give their campers wholesome
influence and strong sympathetic understanding. Merryweather
aims to combine home and family influences with camp life, and
the program is filled with out of door activities that appeal to the
wide awake boy. Tutoring is given if necessary. A discriminating
standard of admission has always been maintained."[67]

Only an occasional camp mentioned its "discriminating standard" in the directory. In 1924, for both camps and private
schools, such language meant no Jews, no Catholics, and no
blacks, except under circumstances of very special sponsorship
and patronage. In their falsely imagined countryside the Richards
were joining, or being swept along by, deep forces of prejudice
and violence that they could not comprehend. To measure the
distance they had drifted from the moorings of their parents, we
can recall that a century earlier Samuel Gridley Howe's romantic
universalism had led him to join the Greek war for independence.

Unexamined memories of their families also misled the Richardses in respect to the meaning of the great wars of their lifetime. Laura remembered her father's heroism, her mother's patriotism, and the triumph of Boston during the Civil War. Henry's
brother had served in both the Civil War and the Spanish-
American War. Consequently, when World War I came, the family was intensely patriotic.[68] In the blindness of their summer
community they detected no links between war and the ever-
narrowing exclusiveness of their own definition of the human
community.

Boys have always loved to play at games of hunting and war.
The high point of the Richardses' summer camp season was a
game of war called "scouting." Laura Richards described it with

pride, and without awareness. "This game, first played in 1904, this mimic war, so long waged on Scouting Ridge, has proved of such enduring precious qualities that I must be forgiven for lingering over it. . . The gathering of two parties, Algonquins and Iroquois, at the two bounds, half a mile apart, with hill and field, wood and shore between; the khaki-clad figures, tense, alert, waiting the signal. . . The Skipper mounts the Scouting Rock, from whose height he is visible to both parties, hidden from each other; and a whisper passes through the waiting ranks like a wind through grass, 'Skipper's up!'

"They are off; the guards each to his station, beside a rock, in the branches of a tree, in a raspberry bush; the Scouts rushing like flame up the two sides of the steep hill, along its flanks, crawling like little brown snakes amid the sweet fern, reconnoitering from behind rock or tree. Dead silence for a time; then at intervals, a 'shot,' the name of a combatant shouted aloud by one of the opposite party, who has seen and recognized him.

" 'Smith!'

"Smith rises promptly; turns his khaki cap inside out, the white lining showing that he is a corpse, and makes his way sadly to the top of the hill to report, 'Killed.' Perhaps also, he can say proudly, 'Shot one,' or 'two.' "[69]

Her son and other former campers later told Laura that the training of the game had saved their lives in France; another taught it to recruits in the Philippines.[70] Today, it is hard to imagine a mixture of symbols better calculated to confuse both the camp masters and the campers. The game itself was named for the spying of American frontiersmen in wars against the Indians. The game took the form it did because Henry Richards had been reading Baden-Powell's Boer War training manual to the campers, and they invented the game from one of Baden-Powell's training exercises.[71] The boys wore khaki, a Persian word for the color of the uniforms of the British Indian troops who suppressed the Sepoy Rebellion of 1857. The two teams took their names from obliterated American Indian tribes.

Here were the unlooked-for weeds in Laura Richards's garden.

6 ❧ EMILY GREENE BALCH

Emily Balch (1867–1961) possessed no special knowledge that was not accessible to other Bostonians. Like Laura Richards, she drew upon the romantic poets and novelists in fashion in her day, and like Charles Stone and Edwin Webster she mastered the new scholarship and science. Yet throughout a long life of charity work, teaching, research, and political action she managed to escape both the unintended evil of Laura Richards's sentimentality and the moral helplessness of Stone's and Webster's engineering. Her background resembled theirs, but in the course of her lifetime she found a way to live wisely and responsibly within the modern world, while they did not.

The resources she drew upon were those readily at hand. As a child of a *haute bourgeois* Boston family, she began with her family's and her minister's Unitarianism. Then, as an endlessly reading schoolgirl she mastered the romantic outlook of a world valued according to human relationships. She completed her formal education by learning the new social science, economics. So equipped, Emily Balch progressed steadily outward from home to city to the entire world, learning and refashioning her knowledge as she went. By the 1920s she and her associates had clearly mastered the basic facts of modern life: the sheer extent and multiplicity of the world, the unpredictability of events, and the awesome human potential for both creativity and destruction. Given such an understanding of the modern condition, her wisdom lay in stressing human processes and relationships as the keys to both power and sanity.

This life of discovery began in the most settled sort of comfortable Boston home. As a child she was sheltered within the family and its circle, and her entire life was characterized by curiosity and wonderment about what might lie beyond. Her father, Francis V. Balch, exemplified the Boston Victorian. The son of a wealthy merchant, he managed a successful downtown law practice in conveyancing, the drawing of deeds and leases. He had married his first cousin, Ellen Marie Noyes, a doctor's daughter from Newburyport, and the young couple lived in a succession of houses in Jamaica Plain before finally settling in a large house at 130 Prince Street in 1879. The house, which remained in the Balch family until the youngest daughter died in 1961, had the then-fashionable mansard roof and a capacious piazza across the front, facing Jamaica Pond, with an elm-lined lawn that extended down to the pond. Here the Balches raised their five daughters and one son. Emily, born in 1867, was a middle child with two older sisters.[1]

For a well-to-do family like the Balches, the Jamaica Plain section of Boston during the seventies and the eighties was a kind of peaceable kingdom safe from the turmoil of the nearby world of poverty, factories, strikes, unemployment, immigrants, and even the fear of revolution. Emily's grandparents lived in the neighborhood, and an aunt lived with the family and helped with the children. Prosperous downtown families had settled here, men like the lawyer Richard Olney and the historian Francis Parkman. Laura Richards's brother-in-law, an MIT professor, and his wife, a pioneering chemist, lived nearby, as did Harvard president Charles Eliot's two sisters, Mary Lyman Guild and Catherine Storer. All these families visited in and out of each other's houses, dined together, met at the Unitarian Church on Sundays, planned picnics, and journeyed into the city proper for concerts and assembly dances. The children ran in and out, watched over by an army of Irish girls.

The Unitarian minister, who had removed to Jamaica Plain from Bangor, Maine, in 1876, recalled it as a suburban idyll, the kind of community Laura Richards and her fellow clubwomen were attempting to spread throughout the province. "I doubt whether anywhere around Boston," he wrote, "there was a more eligible place to enjoy a restful home and to command the best conditions for bringing up children than Jamaica Plain offered when we went there to live. You had there, as in the neighboring villages of Brookline and Newton, a community composed in an unusual proportion of the people of the energetic and enlightened New England stock, generally well-to-do, but no worshippers of money, with a fairly clear sense of the values of life, much devoted to their institutions of education and religion. Most of them had gardens with flowers and fruit, and it was still possible to eat your own peaches and pears without being forced to yield them up to hordes of marauders."[2]

The large suburban family, with its daily rounds, seasonal moves, and network of friends, neighbors, and visitors, established the first boundaries to Emily's life. There were family Bible readings and Sunday night prayers; no one in the family could carry a tune, so the Balches memorized and recited hymns. Two women in the neighborhood ran a private elementary school to which Emily was sent.[3] Winslow Homer might have painted the domestic scene Emily's mother described in a letter of June 1883, when Emily was sixteen. The mother was writing to her husband and her second daughter, Annie, who were traveling together in Europe. "It is a very warm afternoon. We are all scattered about the piazza and parlor, reading, and playing, with our fine agapanthus and the orange tree promoted to the front piazza. Alice and Madie are in white, Frank in his white waist and blue trousers. Bessie in her pink satin, Emily in her linen lawn, Auntie in her batiste with the blue ribbons, and I am in blue linen lawn. Opposite are a fanning group of Frothinghams and everything goes on in the familiar round."[4]

Emily's father, a keen botanizer, who had studied with Asa Gray at Harvard, taught her the names of the plants and a love of gardening. A plain, awkward, bookish girl, she suffered the tortures of dancing school, but aside from this failing, Emily mastered all the Victorian lady's skills of gardening, sketching, and poetry writing, and she enjoyed them throughout her lifetime.

Religion and books opened the pathway that carried Emily beyond the confinements of the family circle. In 1876, when she was ten, a new minister, Charles Fletcher Dole (1845–1927), came to the First Congregational Society (Unitarian) at Eliot and Centre streets. He served for forty years, until 1916. A prolific writer and popular speaker, he had a strong influence on his parishioners. He especially helped Emily Balch who, as an uncertain adolescent raised in a family of guilt-inducing New England consciences, agonized over her selfishness. When she was fourteen she pledged herself to "goodness."[5] For Dole, goodness meant not just family obligations and tears in the pantry, but an active life in the larger world. He himself was an opponent of immigration restriction, and he viewed labor unions, anarchists, and socialism as reasonable responses to the conditions of the industrial age. Emily was much influenced and encouraged by such preaching, and his recommendations for the management of immigration closely resembled those she later advocated.

The Spanish-American War shocked Dole, as it did many Bostonians, who regarded it as a corrupting piece of imperialism,[6] and from 1898 on he took a Christian pacifist position. "Whatever issue has separated men in other times, the issue of our time is coming to lie between the faith and the efforts of men of good will on the one hand and the harsh impatient reaction of those who still put their confidence in violence."[7] Dole, however, never figured out a promising way to cope with the conflict.

All the time that Emily was confiding in and listening to Dole, she was making her own path as an able, hard-working schoolgirl. When she was thirteen the family sent her to Miss Catherine Innes Ireland's school at 9 Louisburg Square, Beacon Hill, in central Boston. Miss Ireland's was not a college preparatory school, since college was still a rarity for women in those days, but it was an ambitious course of instruction for young ladies who presumably would have to educate themselves as adults. Modern languages and literatures furnished the core of the curriculum, and the outlook of the teachers was that of the great New England romantic figures: Emerson, Thoreau, Hawthorne, Longfellow, Lowell, and Oliver Wendell Holmes. Family botanizing here joined the science of Louis Agassiz, and views of the Adirondacks suggested Italian painting. Science, literature, and art fused in the romantic tradition in which Emily Balch was trained. In these works the crucial tensions and anxieties were not the uncertainties of human actuality, but questions about the presence of God.[8] It was this training that provided Emily with the lens through which she would later discover the nature of the modern world.

"The Supreme Critic of the errors of the past and present," Emerson had written, "and thereby the only prophet of that which must be, is that great nature in which we rest as the earth lies in the soft arms of the atmosphere; that Unity, that Over-Soul, within which every man's particular being is contained and made one with all other; that common heart of which all sincere conversation is worship, to which all right action is submission."[9]

During her five years at Miss Ireland's, Emily made a number of friendships that sustained her all her life.[10] When she graduated she and another scholarly friend canvassed the possibility of attending the new Harvard Annex (now Radcliffe College), but the friend's father, a Harvard professor, forbade it. He feared his daughter would become a bluestocking, an unfeminine intellectual. Emily's father, however, took pride in his daughter's skills and even proposed that she study law in order to practice with him. When Emily suggested the new Quaker women's college at Bryn Mawr, Pennsylvania, he visited it and approved. The two girls entered in the fall of 1886, and both finished in three years, graduating with the first college class in 1889.[11]

At Bryn Mawr, especially under the guidance of the self-taught sociologist Frank Giddings, she discovered the basic social questions of her day—the problems of industrial work and wages, the growth of great cities, international poverty, and migration. Like many of this early generation of college-educated women, Emily Balch wanted to apply her studies to the human suffering and conflicts that seethed in the world beyond home and campus. Studying was ever her way of beginning and, encouraged by Professor Giddings, she took up the study of economics. Giddings was an empiricist who believed in examining institutions and laws to discover how they actually worked, in studying conditions as people experienced them, and in talking to workers and the poor. Balch adopted this style, and to this fact gathering she later added a mastery of contemporary capitalist and Marxian economic theory.[12]

An outstanding student, Balch was awarded the Bryn Mawr

faculty's European traveling fellowship, and for the year after her graduation she studied in Paris with the distinguished French economic historian, demographer, and geographer Emile Pierre Levasseur (1828–1911). In Paris she found the life of the lonely "intellectuelle" difficult and took little satisfaction from her researches there, a descriptive review of the French system of public assistance. A reader of this beginning study today can see that Emily Balch had already acquired her lifelong strategy for dealing with the indeterminacy of the large social events of the modern world; she showed a thoughtful appreciation for the social and historical setting of the human institutions under examination. What a physicist might call inertia, and what a heedless reformer might call reactionary custom, she recognized as the thickness of human society and human experience.[13]

Returning home in 1890, Balch was "determined to see something of things for myself. I had read much of *l'ouvrier* but had so to speak never known one to talk to."[14] She began, conventionally enough, by offering herself as a volunteer to help with delinquent and neglected children in Boston. She met with a group of young Italian girls, tried unsuccessfully to be the mentor of a delinquent black girl, and served on the board of a municipal home for children. From this vantage point she followed the teachings of the director of the Children's Aid Society, who was then instructing Harvard College students in the new art of social work, and she watched Mayor Josiah Quincy encourage and reward reformers and ward politicians alternately. Characteristically, she dug out the law and relevant articles on juvenile delinquency and compiled a case manual for her fellow workers.[15] After two years of this volunteer work she attended a Summer School for Applied Ethics in Plymouth, Massachusetts, run by the Ethical Culture Society of New York. It was a place where the new group of young settlement house workers gathered to exchange ideas. Here Balch met her later-to-be colleagues at Wellesley College, Vida Scudder and Katherine Coman. Her Bryn Mawr classmate Helen Dudley and her former professor Frank Giddings also attended. The leading figure was young Jane Addams, who reported on her experiences with the first three years of Hull House in Chicago.[16]

In December 1892 Emily Balch and some of her fellow Plymouth students founded a settlement, Denison House, in an old row house in Boston's South Cove. Located on the edge of Boston's downtown industrial district and in the middle of a large immigrant slum, the settlement stood but six blocks from Mary Antin's apartment.[17]

Encouraged by the activities of the Women's Educational and Industrial Union, and following Hull House precedents, Balch made her settlement the meeting place for the neighborhood girls working in the tobacco, laundry, and sewing industries. Mary Kenney O'Sullivan from Chicago, a young organizer for the American Federation of Labor, visited and later moved to Boston to join Denison House. Balch and some of her fellow workers became regular attenders at union meetings; she joined the A.F.L. and served as a delegate for the Cigar Makers' Union.

This intense activity of 1892–1894 carried Balch to the center of Boston's reform group. At its countless meetings she came to know Robert A. Woods, head of the nearby South End House; Joseph Lee, the pioneer of the playground movement; Elizabeth Glendower Evans, then involved in prison reform; Rev. John Graham Brooks, who had just resigned from his Brockton parish to become a full-time labor investigator; and Mary Kehew (1859–1918), director of the Women's Educational and Industrial Union. Kehew, like Balch, came from a wealthy Boston Unitarian family, and her example seems to have confirmed Emily Balch's sense of herself and to have helped her fix on a career combining research and study with public activity. As director of the Union (founded in 1877), Kehew gave its program a strong educational and legislative direction. She stressed vocational training and investigation of working conditions. Out of these efforts ultimately came a whole package of useful state legislation, from milk inspection to minimum wages and old age pensions. Not a publicity seeker, but an energetic fact gatherer, a vigorous and charming committee organizer, and an energizer of others, Kehew offered a congenial example to Balch.[18]

Caught up as she was in all the activity of a new settlement house, Emily Balch recognized her scholarly curiosities and her personal need to understand the human experiences she was participating in. She spent the fall semester of 1893 at the Harvard

Annex (later Radcliffe College) studying sociology. There she met a young Latin teacher from Somerville High School, Mary Kingsley (1867–1951), later Mary Simkovitch, who was preparing herself for what was to be a long career as a New York settlement house leader and housing reformer. The two women became fast friends. In 1895 Balch spent the spring semester at the University of Chicago, where she tried to write a description of the current distribution of goods and services based on marginal analysis. That work failed to jell.[19] Finally, encouraged by Rev. John Graham Brooks, who had studied in Germany himself, she and Mary Kingsley set out for a year at the University of Berlin during 1895 and 1896. Emily studied German culture, economic and social policy, and politics—preparatory, she thought, to taking a Ph.D. at MIT. On the ship home she traveled with Katherine Coman, then Wellesley College's only professor of economics. Katherine offered Balch a halftime position as her assistant, and from 1896 until 1915 Balch made her life as a professor of economics at the new suburban woman's college.[20]

For Emily Balch and her reform and settlement house group, human suffering was not general but specific, and as they discovered its particular manifestations through their visiting and work, they proposed very specific remedies. For industrial injuries and poisons they proposed state factory inspections and insurance; for hungry and neglected children, city milk stations and public nurseries; for overcrowded and dangerous houses, fire codes, sanitary inspectors, and subsidized building construction. As an economist Balch concentrated on the study of wages, income, and employment. During her years at Wellesley she served on several state commissions, including the first minimum wage board in the United States. In 1902 she and Mary Kehew founded and shared the presidency of the Boston Women's Trade Union League, an organization of labor reformers and working girls designed to help young women join and found trade unions.

For Balch and the young women she taught in her classrooms and led into Boston, the city was a discovery, a place of previously unknown people and novel institutions like factories, saloons, ward clubs, and unions, which no one at home had talked about. They came to study and to live in the provincial capital and its mill towns in order to learn about the world beyond their own suburban and Back Bay houses. They all had experienced a sense of confinement and isolation within their *haute bourgeois* family homes, and they wished through study and social action to establish some sort of firm basis upon which to stand amid the world's actualities.

If there was a single fault common to so diverse a group of young people, it lay in the fragmentary nature of their outlook and experience, which limited their understanding and proposals for change. Although there was much common sense and practicality in all their undertakings, most of the explorers in this generation were blind to the links of social and economic conditions within the province and the empire that caused needless human injury. Emily Balch was an exception. She declared herself a socialist in 1906, and with her colleague Vida Scudder organized a socialist conference in Boston. She regularly taught a course on the history of socialism at Wellesley. Indeed, she was chided by the English utopian novelist, H. G. Wells, for her reliance on Marx. However, he found the subject matter of Professor Balch's courses a great relief from the art classes of the college and the drawing rooms of Boston, which seemed overcome by a preoccupation with the past. "One feels in Boston," he wrote, "as one feels in no other part of the States, that the intellectual movement has stopped."[21]

At dinners and teas on Commonwealth Avenue the visiting English celebrity encountered Emily Balch's opponents, men and women who did not see their own, or their ancestors', hands at work in making the province's present history. Instead they imagined a kind of human flood drowning their formerly virtuous republic. They focused all their disappointments and fears on one target—the immigrant. With their inability to speak English, their wrong-headed religion, and their inappropriate culture, the new immigrants were the source of all difficulties—unsanitary, overcrowded housing, low wages, shoddy work, vulgar entertainments, ignorance, promiscuity, unruly children, lawlessness, and political corruption. The human difficulties that Balch and her group were at such pains to delineate and to cope with in specific ways, these long-descended Bostonians carelessly threw together as the inevitable manifestations of non-English origins.[22]

It was in such a climate that Balch, now an assistant professor of economics, decided to undertake a study of immigration, and particularly to examine the migration and settlement of America's newest and least understood arrivals, the Slavs—Poles, Hungarians, Czechs, Yugoslavians, and Ukrainians—the migrants from the Austro-Hungarian Empire. She began, at the outset of her 1904 sabbatical year, by living among coal and steel workers near Pittsburgh. Then she visited settlement houses in Chicago and Cleveland and in the fall settled in New York with a Czech family Mary Simkovitch had found for her.[23] There in an Upper East Side tenement she learned some Czech and began her common-sense social research: she canvassed such literature and sought out such authorities as existed, she read the local foreign language press, talked to the neighbors, and sought the aid of the local priests. These techniques remained her method throughout the two and a half years of study. At the very outset they led her to a Czech priest in Yonkers, New York, who confirmed her choice of subject and gave her the theme for her work. "My people do not live in America. They live *underneath* America."[24]

In 1905, accompanied by a young woman from Greenwich House, Euphemia Murray Abrams, Emily Balch left for a year's tour of the Austro-Hungarian Empire from the Adriatic to the Polish provinces. As the two women journeyed by train and carriage, they collected maps and government publications, but most of all they sought out the villagers themselves, visiting their homes, markets, inns, churches, and mosques, trying to get a sense of what was causing people to move.[25]

Beneath the surface of peasant village life the new economy—the railroad, the telegraph, the factory, and factory-made products—was undermining every element of common life. The new money economy forced new divisions of land, closed old occupations, offered new opportunities in the city, and thereby started peasants on the move. It was Balch's general finding, confirmed by subsequent scholarship, that the children of the middle strata of the villages, those whose families had a trade or some land, were the ones most squeezed by the new circumstances, but they were also the ones who were most able to raise the small sums necessary to make their way to America.[26]

Balch's study was unique for its thoroughness, its wide sympathy, and its use of economic theory. Not only were the facts skillfully gathered, but they were accurate because they were placed in their proper context—the international process of economic development and migration. Here, at last, the local particulars of slum alleys and peasant landholdings assume their proper relationships. Through her observation and economic theory she joined all the human actors, from neighborhood landlords to steamship companies and national armies. The immediate import of Balch's book in 1910 was an appeal for human understanding. She intended it to be a blow against contemporary "alarmist writing."[27] Like Mary Antin, she urged Americans to have the courage of their traditions of liberty and fraternity.

In terms of both scholarly and popular following, however, the book proved a failure. Her urgent calls to substitute knowledge for prejudice, and concern with human experiences for angry political posturing, went unheeded. The red scare deepened each year, and the presence of more and more Eastern European immigrants in the Boston province and the nation intensified, instead of relaxing, public fears and antagonisms. In 1916 Emily Balch tried to warn her Wellesley College students of the "false paradise" of ignorance, prejudice, and willfulness that they were being drawn into.

"Alone of modern industrial countries we are made practically a country of caste. The 'poor,' i.e. those living by labor with no income except from hiring out their labor, are in the South Negroes, in the North 'Honkies,' 'Dagoes,' 'Wops,' 'Sheenies,' 'Polacks,' 'Guineas,' 'Micks,' 'Greeners,' all the ugly names invented by prejudice and class feeling for the newcomer."

"Equality at least nominal, at the polls and before the court stands side by side with inequality in industries, with lack of opportunity and with hierarchical authority in the workshops, for the most part unalleviated by any right of representation or any chance of appeal from arbitrary power."

"We live in a fool's paradise if we do not face these things."[28]

Although she was a prescient scholar of immigration, it is not her mastery of the subject that speaks to us most today. Balch's understanding of the links among the local, the provincial, and the imperial was her best creation and her most useful gift. Hav-

ing discovered the size and complexity of the world, she understood what the price of such a discovery was—it was, and would
ever be, ignorance and uncertainty. Not pride, but caution,
proved her sure guide to the difficulties of large affairs. At the end
of her long study she had mastered enough to conclude, "Before
such a vast world movement as the modern wage migrations it is
impossible not to feel awestruck, not to realize how little it is
possible for contemporaries to gauge the results and to compute
the advantages."[29] And from such indeterminacy it naturally followed that the fashions of the latest science must be handled with
extreme caution and subjected to thorough verification. Contemporary science in 1910 suggested that "the most important issue
involved is the racial one. But here we are paralyzed by our comprehensive ignorance."[30]

Although an appreciation of the various scales of living in the
twentieth century necessarily carried with it such admonitions,
caution and timidity were not Balch's goals or ways. Beneath the
respect for facts and the attention to the details of human experiences rested her deep commitment to the values of her Emerson-
ian religion. Though in her youth this Protestant variant was
narrowly based in her class and her region, as a species of romantic neo-Platonism it could be enlarged for childhood, family, and
garden out into the larger world. In gifted hands, like Emily
Balch's, such an outlook could nourish wonder and deeply held
values able to withstand heavy conflict. The wonder, the fusion of
heart and mind appear throughout *Our Slavic Fellow Citizens* in
her pleasure in what she discovered. The view of a "Passaic
handkerchief factory full of Polish girls in kerchiefs of pale yellow
and other soft colors, the afternoon sun slanting across the fine
stuff on which they were working";[31] the pleasure in watching a
young Lithuanian couple shopping for the bride's trousseau in a
Pennsylvania mining town;[32] "the beautiful elm-shaded street
[of] ... old colonial mansions" now occupied by Polish onion
and tobacco farmers in western Massachusetts.[33] These aesthetic
observations were ever Balch's way of registering her sense of the
presence of spirit and value everywhere.

This simplified, but deeply held, religious sense led Emily
Balch to place great stress on process. Ignorance and indetermi-

nacy in human affairs both suggested caution, but the fact that humans would suffer or prosper according to the processes in which they lived made her, and her colleagues, extremely attentive to processes. It was to process that they lent their best science and investigations, and it was for process that they would initiate and sustain heavy political conflict.

Prepared only by such wisdom, Balch was suddenly cast into the whirlwind of the First World War and forced to transform her knowledge and beliefs into radical political action. The outbreak of the war in August 1914 caught her by surprise, as it did many people on both sides of the Atlantic. She later reasoned, "My formative years were passed in the long Victorian peace, and war seemed as obsolete as chain armor."[34]

The rise of internationalism, peace organizations, and new institutions like the World Court at the Hague, which Balch had taught her students about, had misled many people. Her family had direct links with Boston's long peace tradition. Her father had been secretary to Senator Charles Sumner, who as a young man had been an impassioned speaker in behalf of the American Peace Society, founded in Boston in 1828. Some of the nation's earliest pacifists came from the city, men like Elihu Buritt, and the more radical Charles K. Whipple of the New England Non-Resistance League (1838). This early generation had been followed by a post–Civil War revival led by such notables as Edward Everett Hale, Julia Ward Howe, and Phillips Brooks. In addition, a very popular disarmament group, the Universal Peace Union, had sprung up in Providence, Rhode Island, in 1866. In 1898 old-fashioned Bostonians gathered at Faneuil Hall to establish the Anti-Imperialist League to oppose the Spanish-American War and its annexations. The local textbook publisher Edwin Ginn (1838–1948) had donated a million dollars in 1909 to endow an educational foundation called the World Peace Foundation, and department store owner Edward A. Filene was active in the International Chamber of Commerce. This provincial tradition joined those of Philadelphia and New York to create during the early twentieth century a swelling tide of internationalism and planning for alternatives to war among nations.[35]

In the hopefulness of that time, no one could appreciate the degree to which the imperialist and military enthusiasms of the Spanish-American War, the fears of socialism, and the anti-immigrant prejudices had already undermined the patience of American leaders for finding alternatives to war. Within a year of the outbreak of World War I, the major peace organizations, such as the Carnegie Endowment and the World Peace Foundation, and leaders like William Howard Taft, Theodore Roosevelt, and Nicholas Murray Butler, had rushed toward the position of doing good after slaughtering millions. Theirs was the old crusader's dodge: first defeat the Central Powers, then reform the world. At a meeting on June 17, 1915, at Independence Hall in Philadelphia, Taft's League to Enforce the Peace swept up the established peace organizations and announced a war policy that President Woodrow Wilson shortly made official United States policy.[36]

Emily Balch's group followed an entirely opposite path. As women they respected their timeless role as "the custodians of the life of the ages."[37] As women, too, they stood outside the formal political process, but this time they were organized to demand the vote from the Atlantic democracies. In the fall of 1914 Balch attended a very fruitful meeting of social workers called by Lillian Wald, Jane Addams, and Paul Kellogg of *Survey* magazine, and in January 1915, when Jane Addams and Carrie Chapman Catt formed the Women's Peace Party in Washington, D.C., Balch immediately became an active member. She began to take a succession of leaves of absence from Wellesley College so that she could concentrate on her peace activities, based in the radical branch of the movement in New York City.[38]

The next few years of activism resembled nothing that had happened previously in her life. Travel in wartime, hectic meetings and rallies, fund raising, lobbying, and political conflict were all new experiences. Because she was older (she was forty-eight in 1915), a leader, and a college professor, the younger women in her peace organizations depended upon her for judgment and guidance. Balch's test was to find a way to translate her previous knowledge and values into effective political action. In the end she came a lot closer to success than either President Wilson or his opponent, Henry Cabot Lodge.

The European leaders of the woman suffrage movement, frustrated by the cancellation because of war of their planned meeting in Berlin, issued a call in the spring of 1915 for a peace conference at the Hague. Urged on by Jane Addams, Emily Balch sailed with a delegation of forty-two American women on the *S.S. Noordam* to that April conference.[39] On the twelve-day voyage she cemented her fast friendship with Jane Addams, the group leader, and thereafter the two became captain and lieutenant in many peace activities. While at sea and while passing through the British blockade and the German submarine zone, Balch characteristically turned to her books to find the basis for her forthcoming campaign.

She reread Edwin D. Mead's edition of *Eternal Peace and Other International Essays* by Immanuel Kant, the German philosopher who had inspired Emerson and other Boston romantics. Kant's essays expressed a faith in the progressive course of history, a vision cherished by Balch's generation. For Kant, progress did not depend either on violent competition or unremitting benevolence; rather, an antagonism within human nature, between individualism and the desire for sociability, established a tension that would drive human progress forward.[40] In the past this tension had given rise to law and to local political order; therefore, in the fullness of time, just as the democratic state had succeeded the monarchy, so a world federation of nations would succeed nation states and empires. National competition within international legal and institutional bounds would thus become the final stage of human organization.[41] In these late eighteenth-century essays Kant turned the order of neo-Platonism into a progressive history. Emily Balch, rereading this Bible of the peace movement, found justification for her adventure. In her journal she contrasted her group's sense of connection to the world with the impatient drive for power of political leaders and journalists.

"I think one thing that is disarming is that although we are proposing to put forward all sorts of Utopian plans we do not ourselves greatly misconceive the situation. We do not suppose that we have power or knowledge or importance. We just mean to do what we can and hope to stir little waves of thought and feeling that may multiply and expand as every living thing can do and so add our little momentum to the great wave that is rolling up against war."[42] One person may not succeed, and indeed this mission was thwarted by President Wilson, but small actions that draw upon the union of human feelings and intelligence may succeed if they touch the common elements of "living things" and if they find accord in the nature of the species.[43]

Despite harassment from the British and attacks in the world press, the women delegates to the Hague conference successfully maintained their process of finding consensus across the lines of the belligerents. As Emily Balch wrote in her published report, the women at the Hague believed "that every belligerent power is carrying on a war deadly to itself, that bankruptcy looms ahead, that industrial conflict threatens, not at the moment, but in the none too distant future, that racial stocks are being irreparably depleted. The prestige of Europe, of the Christian Church, of the white race, is lowered inch by inch with the progress of the struggle which is continually closer to the debacle of a civilization."[44] The resolutions of the Hague Women's Congress anticipated President Wilson's Fourteen Points by calling for a future international organization, national autonomy, and the guarantee of democratic process. In addition they voted to establish a permanent women's peace organization, which later became the Women's International League for Peace and Freedom.

More immediately, encouraged by Rosika Schwimmer of Hungary, the congress adopted the so-called Wisconsin Plan. This was a proposal put forth by Grace Wales of the University of Wisconsin and later endorsed by the Wisconsin Legislature, calling for the neutral nations to set up a conference so that there could be continuous negotiations among belligerents even while the war was going on. The idea was not a new one—it had been employed by Sir Edward Grey, the British foreign minister, during the First Balkan War of 1912–13—but it was the only effective plan put forth at this time, and it later became the essence of League of Nations and United Nations practice. From that time on the methods and practice of continuous negotiations became Balch's lifetime concern.[45]

To urge the Wisconsin Plan forward, the congress set up two delegations and assigned each one a tour of belligerent and neutral capitals. The delegations were to determine whether the various governments would be willing to participate in such a process. During May and June 1915 Balch toured the northern capitals of Holland, Denmark, Sweden, Russia, and the United Kingdom as secretary to her delegation. Everywhere they met with a favorable reception and a willingness to treat with a neutral negotiating team.[46]

Meanwhile Secretary of State William Jennings Bryan, the leading figure in the administration working to keep America neutral, resigned over President Wilson's *Lusitania* note, which Bryan interpreted as leading the nation toward war with Germany. The new secretary of state, Robert Lansing, along with Wilson's personal adviser, Colonel Edward M. House, and President Wilson himself, all agreed that the defeat of the Central Powers must come first. They therefore temporized when meeting with peace delegations. Jane Addams visited the president several times during the fall of 1915, and Emily Balch spent an hour with Wilson reporting on the Hague conference, but he was unwilling to be the leader of the neutral world for mediation.[47]

In December 1915 the focus of publicity in America turned toward Henry Ford's peace ship and his attempt to discount war propaganda and to foster negotiation through dramatic public relations moves. Balch participated in an interesting series of panels on "war and militarism" at the meetings of the American Sociological Society in Washington, D.C. The other leading speakers were Theodore Roosevelt and the Boston intellectual Brooks Adams.

Roosevelt gave a firm speech, restricting himself to a statement of his conviction that personal and national morality were one and the same and that just as the soldier's virtues were good for citizens, so imperial conflict is good for nations. He regarded the militarism of Europe as the means whereby it had preserved its "social value," and he cast his appeal for American armaments in terms of national self-defense. "No nation can permanently maintain any 'social value' worth having unless it develops the war-like strength necessary for its own defense."[48] On this occasion the former president was specifically identified as a winner of the Nobel Peace Prize. Yet reading his speech today, one cannot help being shocked by his equating of all non-Western cultures with barbarism and by his complete inability to imagine any significant human organization other than the nation state.

For Balch, who spoke on the effects of militarism on the status of women, an international outlook was the one possible source of hope. She noted, with some humor, that war tended to reestablish the woman's old chivalric position—she was to nurse, cheer, make bandages, and admire the men. Indeed, she said, these ancient roles of Venus and Mars had made many a woman into an enthusiast for national adventures. Emily Balch hoped that the recent women's movement was producing more thoughtful and independent women, so that the new generation, though it might differ about the current war in Europe, would "never fall victims to the characteristic hallucinations of war."[49]

Brooks Adams (1838–1918), then an old man of seventy-seven who had completed his series of books on the unfolding of modern history, spoke in the voice of the frightened provincial Bostonian. Addressing the topic "Can War Be Done Away With?" he reviewed his geopolitical history of the world and concluded that armies and war were both inevitable and progressive institutions. He summarized all of human history in terms of the conflict for food and goods, which he said, was expressed in wars to dominate strategic trade routes. From this Malthusian geography he concluded that "man has no other destiny than to conquer or to die." In the instant case, the conflict pitted Germany against England for the control of the Atlantic trade and the resources of the Americas and Europe.[50]

Today Adams's interpretation of the evidence from science is thoroughly discredited, but two aspects of his speech carried an ominous significance for later twentieth-century affairs in the province and the empire. The first was the loss of sympathy and contact between many intellectuals and their fellow citizens in the middle and lower classes; the second was the call for national warfare as a relief from domestic turmoil. Brooks Adams considered his fellow Americans "heedless, helpless, reckless, vain spoiled children . . . careless pleasure-seekers and money-makers."[51] Ours was a "hysterical and feminized population, which had been so long petted by nature that it resembles a peevish and spoiled child impatient of restraint."[52]

Like Roosevelt, Adams believed in the military as a mode of disciplining his "feminized society." It was a canard of late nineteenth-century imperialism that a little war could serve as an antidote both to the "decay" of populations grown soft on the new bourgeois comforts and as a distraction to the restless poor and working classes. And so the Great War itself followed a string of such supposedly therapeutic little wars, and Adams, to encourage us all forward, spoke at length of the virtues of Rome as if that ancient empire's bloody habits were to be imitated instead of avoided.[53]

Such language was a call to human intolerance and violence, and it added the celebration of war to the mélange of fears already fueling Boston's immigrant red scare. The long-range purposes of this imperialist thinking were to restrict the public's comprehension of the world to the narrow terms of military power and conflict and to persuade the public to substitute an "administrative" government for its established "deliberative" democracy.[54] Adams's immediate goals were to encourage the United States to enter the war against the Central Powers and to silence all who were opposed. One of the voices to be silenced was that of Emily Balch.

During the spring of 1916 Balch traveled to Stockholm to work for the International Committee on Mediation, established through Henry Ford's support. She assumed her usual secretarial role, gathering documents that would tell the belligerents what they were saying about each other and what they were telling their publics were their peace terms. This research led to Balch's later book of documents, published during the last year of the war as *Approaches to the Great Settlement.*[55]

Since the vast economic and diplomatic resources of the United States still seemed the greatest opportunity for beginning negotiations among the belligerents, she returned to New York City to work against the war preparedness campaign. Despite the efforts of the peace organizations and the leadership of David Starr Jordan, president of Stanford University; former secretary of state William Jennings Bryan; and Wisconsin Senator Robert J. LaFollette, and despite the doubts and misgivings of many Americans, the United States declared war on April 6, 1917. Immediately the Wilson administration unleashed a full campaign of wartime propaganda, and worked to repress pacifists, socialists, and radicals of all kinds. Eight months before the Russian Revolution (November 6, 1917) the fears and angers of the immigrant red scare spread through the nation, borne forward by the voices of super-heated patriotism. The Women's Peace Party retreated to trying to work for a postwar league of nations and for civil liberties. Jane Addams found a role for herself in food relief, and Emily Balch turned her attention to the defense of pacifists.[56]

As a socialist and an informed observer of the circumstances of the conflict, Balch declared herself an opponent of the war and a pacifist. This extreme position placed her entirely outside the wartime anxieties and triumphs of her fellow citizens and cost her the deep pain of isolation and ostracism. In this position she especially feared the defense of becoming a narrow doctrinaire. She wrote to the president of Wellesley College that she wanted to be able to follow her mind and conscience as she continued to learn of the world.

"I fully realize that wiser as well as infinitely more spiritual disciples of Christ believe that they were following him in taking part in the war according to their respective functions. This does not excuse me however from doing what seems to me right as I see it. I may have a larger vision some day, then I can follow the new leading. Meanwhile one of the hardest things about holding the position I do is that it is so hard to keep it clear of Pharisaism."[57] In 1920 Balch joined the London Yearly Meeting of the Society of Friends.

Since 1915 she had taken a series of unpaid leaves and a sabbatical from Wellesley so that her political activities would not embarrass the college. When her five-year contract came up for renewal in 1918, however, the trustees voted not to renew it. "This left me at fifty-two with my professional life cut short and no particular prospect."[58]

While controversy swirled at the campus for the next eighteen months, Balch's friends came to her aid. Oswald Garrison Villard offered her a position at the *Nation*, which she took for some months. An old friend and classmate from Miss Ireland's School, Helen Cheever, sent her a check each month, and others helped with money and housing. As was commonly the case in her pioneering generation, a network of wealthy women made up for the gaps in the limited list of places society then afforded its educated women. Many also urged Balch to make a dramatic public campaign of her dismissal, as had been done in similar cases at Columbia University and the University of Pennsylvania, but she was not by nature a public fighter. Besides, she knew her personal goals in the controversy. She had been at Wellesley off and on for twenty years, and she loved the college. She wanted it, and her adversaries within it, to learn her antimilitarism and her internationalism. Her dignified defense of her position in time led the college administration to pay attention to her views, and after a long interval, on November 11, 1935, to honor her example by inviting her to speak.[59]

In May 1919 the Hague women reassembled in Zurich to revive their peace efforts. They welcomed delegates from France and Germany and dramatized their hopes for international unity by electing a German woman their vice-president. Their first business consisted of a thorough critique of the Versailles Treaty, which they regarded as sowing the seeds for future wars with its provisions for reparations. On Emily Balch's initiative the Zurich meetings also passed resolutions in favor of racial equality and in opposition to restrictions against Jews.[60]

During the next twenty years, during which Balch served the Women's International League for Peace and Freedom (WILPF), she adapted what she had learned in settlement work and as an economist to the problems of internationalism. For herself she tried to live the new role of a private citizen of the world.

> Dear to me, beyond worlds dear to me,
> Is the Earth:
> Wherever I pass I am at home.
>
> In the vast expanse of the universe
> With its moving worlds
> All that I know of sentient life
> Is borne by earth
>
> Wherever I pass upon the earth I am at home . . . .[61]

She proposed a series of partial steps that the nations of the world could take to practice and learn cooperation. She thought the League of Nations should encourage a functional internationalism in which technicians would work on specifically defined problems of common interest, like world health.[62] By thus breaking down the issues, the League could establish the beginnings of a worldwide civil service, setting up international trustees to manage aviation and neutral sea channels and to take over European colonies to speed the process of closing out colonial empires.

Emily Balch regarded the impoverishment of non-European peoples to be both a glaring injustice and an explosive problem. She visited Palestine and wrote on the Jewish question there, and in 1931, when the Japanese invaded Manchuria she proposed an American boycott and a negotiation process. At the request of Haitian members of the WILPF, she, with senator-to-be Paul Douglas and a group of other experts undertook in 1926 an investigation of conditions in Haiti, which had been occupied by the United States since 1915. She revealed the deep racial antagonism that prevented the Americans from comprehending the Haitians, and she and Professor Douglas proposed land reform for relief of the island's impoverished peasants. When fascism spread to Spain she set forth, in 1936, a scheme for a "mediated peace" as an alternative to the "progressive suicide" she saw Spain undergoing. In all these studies and initiatives Balch and the WILPF were learning and following what are today regarded as the best practices of the United Nations.[63]

In these years of international conferences, observation at the League of Nations, and WILPF research, Balch gathered a great deal of wisdom about the art of containing international conflicts by breaking down the controversies into parts the opponents could then negotiate. Also she knew that her proposals were at most the beginnings of a process, not solutions. They were a means whereby, she hoped, the world's inevitable and endless conflicts could be adjudicated without resort to war. In her religious background, her "creed" as she called it, she lacked an explanation for the origin or presence of evil, but from her experience as a settlement house worker, economist, and peace activist she knew that it abounded and that it would not disappear. Her response to the force of evil was always to mobilize the opposing forces of reason and benevolence through openness and respect for the humanity of all adversaries. If any quality in Balch's international work seems a relic of her era of progressive reform, it is her optimism about professional civil servants. She liked to refer to Kipling's futuristic story of the world mail service as an example of what an international civil service might do.[64]

It was, however, the new scale of national power that caused Emily Balch the greatest difficulty. In her time the issue surfaced in the conflicting concerns of world disarmament and the question of the appropriate responses to European fascism. The members of the Women's International League for Peace and Freedom, horrified by the suffering of World War I, established their organization's position as "disarmament, universal and complete." At the same time American pacifists, isolated from their fellow citizens by their own wartime experience and by the peacetime red scare, moved toward the extreme position of absolute pacifism: no participation in any war. Balch often worried about this position, feeling at times that the world must first consider the underlying causes of war.[65]

For a time, however, in the horror of the immediate postwar period, these positions fitted with a trend in world and United States diplomacy. Athough the United States failed to join the League of Nations, it promoted an antiwar memorandum, the Kellogg-Briand Pact of 1928. There followed the London Naval Arms Limitation Conference of 1930 and the League of Nations Conference on Reduction and Limitation of Armaments, which the United States joined, and which met off and on from 1932 through 1937. These talks, however, got nowhere. All the major European powers, and Japan as well, pressed against disarmament. Concurrently, the rise of fascism in Italy, Germany, and Spain, with its glorification of war, made the process of negotiation impossible. As Balch later wrote, "The world chose disaster."[66]

Because of the failure of the peace initiatives of the twenties and the thirties, disarmament has come to be regarded by United

States politicians, and by much of the public, as a sucker's move. And although Emily Balch, Jane Addams, and the WILPF learned a great deal about the world's conflicts and the possibilities for managing them, their experiences did not enter into the general experience of Americans, nor did they gain admission to American politics. Instead, the red scare of the twenties and the Great Depression of the thirties turned the national consciousness inward, and international issues ceased to have salience for either provincial or imperial politics. During the 1930s Balch, like Addams, became a distant figure of goodness, a wraith of an earlier era of imagined virtue; she ceased to be an important, attended-to teacher of new ideas and new experiences.[67]

Balch first confronted the issue of fascism in France in 1931. She recorded her experience as one of the significant shocks of her life. One evening she attended a meeting in Paris on world disarmament at which the American ambassador and some French dignitaries were to speak. A mob of French fascists broke into the hall, overran the speakers' platform, and with shouts and nationalist songs drowned out the proceedings. In the balconies hand-to-hand fighting broke out, and for a time the forces of evil and violence could not be controlled by good will, patience, or reason.[68]

The spread of fascism and the resumption of the Great War in Europe in 1939, added to the 1931 incident, forced Balch into the painful position of not being able to choose peace and freedom, but of having to choose the evil of war as an alternative to unchecked fascism.[69] Her solution, which cost her the support of many of her colleagues in the American peace movement, was to support America's participation in the war and to concentrate on helping Jewish refugees[70] and the Japanese Americans in concentration camps. Beyond this work, she tried to speak and write in behalf of future world organizations. Even though war had been thrust upon her one more time, she argued, she could still work for its future prevention.

During the war she opposed the Allies' policy of unconditional surrender on the grounds that to fight a war without clearly stated goals was to throw away the possibilities of lasting gains at the peace table, as the United States had done in 1918.[71] When the United Nations proposal was announced she was delighted, seeing it as evidence of a growing internationalism in the United States, which she hoped would help secure world peace. Nevertheless she chided the UN proponents for their stress on military security. Modern warfare, she observed, abolished all the old concepts of security by drawing all of society into its orbit—science, industry, the whole civilian population. Therefore, she wrote to the United Nations conference in San Francisco, "modern human cooperative efforts ought to be concerned with *establishing* security rather than *upholding* a security which does not exist.[72]

Americans and their leaders had yet to understand this sort of human process approach to international affairs. Speaking to the Philadelphia chapter of the WILPF at the darkest time of the war in May 1942, Emily Balch summarized her wisdom and her hopes. "I have a considerable distrust of government as such," she said, "and I see no reason to be sure that a world government would be run by men very different in capacity and moral quality from those who govern national states." Moreover, "international unity is not in itself a solution. Unless this international unity has a moral quality, accepts the discipline of moral standards, and possesses the quality of humanity, it will not be the unity we are interested in. If it is autocratic and not cooperative in tone, it may indeed be a Frankenstein."[73]

In 1946, when she was seventy-nine, the Nobel Prize for Peace was granted to Emily Greene Balch, the third American woman to win a Nobel Prize, along with Jane Addams and the writer Pearl Buck. Too infirm to travel to Norway for the presentation, she received the medal in her Wellesley home in the spring of 1947. By then she had the sense that she was being dissolved into a myth, and that the reality of her life was already moving out of reach of her fellow Bostonians.[74]

Today the distortions of publicity and the passage of time obscure what Balch experienced and learned. The American empire and its institutions now stand between us and our memory of her successes and failures. The thrust of post–World War II internationalism has not been toward learning and process, but toward great aggregations of power, pressing both outward from the

United States to peoples overseas and inward upon the provinces of the empire. Both the postwar red scares and the propaganda of the Cold War deny the very qualities of humanity that Emily Greene Balch knew to be America's one best, indeed its only, hope.

III ❧ FAILURE OF
COMMUNITY

IN THE MODERN WORLD both the sources of bounty and the
sources of misfortune have multiplied. In Boston's preindustrial
days the whims of nature, such alternations as fair winds or
storms, an early spring or a May frost, warm summer days or a
scorching drought, carried good fortune or suffering. The rivalry
of nations, the clash of armies and navies also brought power and
wealth to some and death or poverty to others. All these alternations of nature and politics still prevail, but to them must be
added the fortunes and misfortunes of modern business.

As the nation's earliest industrialized region, Boston experienced the economic benefits and hazards of business sooner than
other sections. After many decades of inventiveness and expansion, the machinery, the techniques, and the organizations of the
region's core industries, textiles and shoes, had grown commonplace and routine by the end of the nineteenth century. Thereafter, no special advantage accrued to such firms doing business
within the Boston province. It is clear today, as it has been clear
since at least 1930, that although work in the textile and shoe factories employed a lot of machinery, it was not work in which the
machine predominated. These industries were labor intensive,
employing armies of machine tenders and relatively few skilled
workers. Such businesses could thrive only so long as there were
long queues of low-paid workers waiting to tend the machines. In
the 1820s the sons and daughters of poor New England farmers,
and later the sons and daughters of poor Canadian and European
farmers, stood in these queues. Then, in the late nineteenth cen-

tury, textile and shoe manufacturers began to leave their early bases in New England in search of cheap labor and cheap raw materials. In America manufacturers established new textile mills in the south and new shoe factories in Missouri, Illinois, and Wisconsin. Overseas Egypt, India, and Japan resounded with the new machinery, beginning the worldwide dispersion of the first forms of modern industrial practice.

Although the older Boston specialties experienced increasing competition from other regions, newer industries and products provided fresh sources of employment, greater productivity, and higher wages. The textile and shoe workers then organized and tried to win the standard wages of the times, but in response to the new competition the mill owners organized to lower their wages and increase their work loads.

Thus there began in the Boston province the long and painful process of economic obsolescence. A cluster of businesses that had faced an expanding future now became backward-looking, narrow, and pinched. As time went on, and more and more industrialists built new plants elsewhere, the labor conflict and the haggling over wages and prices grew more intense; whole communities were torn apart by conflicts between owners and workers and by competition and rivalries among creditors and mill owners. Labor strife and management turmoil, however, did not end the suffering. After the union busting and union recognition there followed years of short time, lengthened shutdowns, reorganizations, failures, more reorganizations, and then decades of final mill closings. The years of labor strife from the 1890s through the 1920s were followed by thirty years of mill closings, until by 1960 the textile industry had all but disappeared from the Boston province, and shoe manufacturing had become a survival of a few skillful operators who had found some specialty within national and imperial markets.[1]

This is a parsimonious history, merely summarizing tens of thousands of separate business and mill town events. Economists have documented the trends and theorized about the sources of provincial advantage and about national and imperial competition. They have collected the statistics about firms, machines, wages, hours, production, and sales that make possible such a ready summary. These enumerations reveal that until World War I Boston was a region of above average wages and incomes. Then, slowly, year by year, it lost ground as other areas prospered with new industries, until by 1960 Boston had become what it is today, a province of low wages, a place where a secretary or a truck driver, an engineer or a hotel keeper, a doctor or a physicist, works for less than a counterpart in Texas or California.[2]

The statistics and the comparative analysis give useful information, as does the weather report, but abstraction turns even the most thoughtful economics into a process of communal forgetting. The interpretations of the economists do not attend to the workers' daily experiences or to the social and political relationships among workers, shopkeepers, managers, and the residents of our cities and towns; the economists' accounts contribute more to our amnesia than to our enlightenment.

The years of labor strife and the succeeding years of unemployment and plant closings were not comfortable or heroic times that people in the Boston province like to recall. These were times of anger and frustration, of false hopes and helplessness, which are much easier to forget when they are called the inevitable process of obsolescence. Yet the helplessness of the communities, of the cities and towns and states, is the central fact we need to understand. During all those long years of suffering no way was found to express or mobilize the community of interest in the failing businesses. No way was discovered for all to share in the power of or responsibility for those institutions. That failure is now forgotten, but in the high-technology prosperity of inflation, armaments, dangerous products, and periodic unemployment, the people of the Boston province are even more helpless than they were fifty years ago.

As any plow in New England soon strikes a stone, so the slightest historical curiosity soon uncovers a buried record of community suffering. The rebuilt towns on the outer fringe of the Boston metropolis are currently the province's proud examples of recent prosperity. Such a model is Marlborough, Massachusetts, an old mill city twenty-five miles west of Boston, situated at the edge of the new outer circumferential highway, interstate Route 495. You enter this small city the way you enter any place in America; the highway becomes the strip, and you pass through a receiving line of suburban subdivisions and highway retailers: Norm's Shell, Mobile Home Park, Royal Crest Estates, Bubble Laundromat, Post Road Shopping Mall, Rich's Department Store, Big Discount, McDonald's, Pizza Hut, Annie's Book Swap, and the Salon de Venus. After a few miles the strip becomes a typical old New England Main Street, and you pass white churches and a few pillared houses of the apple orchard era before the Civil War. Most of Main Street, however, reflects the little city's two eras of industrial prosperity, the brick blocks of the 1880s and 1890s, now refurbished with urban renewal, and the parking lots of prosperity of the 1970s and 1980s.

The sources of the new wealth lie scattered about the old city and in a few surviving mills, as well as in new factories near the highway. Honeywell, Digital Equipment Corporation, Data Translation, High Voltage Engineering, Space Age Electronics, Syntest Corporation represent the new electronics. There are also less glamorous newcomers, companies making products that did not exist half a century ago: molded plastics for aircraft and boats, polyethylene bags, wire racks and display shelves, custom packaging, portable lighting equipment, aluminum windows, and sliding patio doors. All of this has been added to a remainder of earlier products that are still in demand: printer's ink, rubber rollers, floor wax, tools and dies, paste and glue, planed and custom cut lumber, shoe boxes, women's sport shoes, and leather boots.[3]

The mix now yields prosperity and growth. The population of Marlborough doubled between 1950 and 1980. What then has been forgotten? Half a century of helpless stagnation. In 1900 Marlborough's population was 13,609; in 1950 it was 15,787. An economist would call those five decades a half century of obsolescence; a historian would call them a half century of experiences whose meaning has been lost.[4]

If you drive down Main Street, heading west through town, you pass the ambitious turn-of-the-century high school, now converted into offices, and then at a fork in the road you see monuments to World War I and the Spanish-American War, flanking the First Baptist Church. Turn right at that intersection, venture up Mechanic Street (that most apposite of mill town names), and on your left, surrounded by abandoned buildings and open lots, stands a large red-brick block. High above the sign for the karate school, a sign set in terracotta reads "The Frye Building, 1892." Across the street the new wire display company carries on an 1860s mill, and at the top of the hill, on Pleasant Street, in two old wooden mill buildings, the John A. Frye Shoe Company still does business. Indeed, with 600 workers it is still the city's largest employer. After a financial reorganization in the 1950s the Frye Company managed to capture the fashion in big leather boots, and it survives in this little cowboy corner of the national and international shoe market.[5]

In 1898 almost everyone in Marlborough worked in shoe factories; the city was the nation's fifth largest producer of shoes, and 3,500 men and women worked in the mills of John A. Frye, Rice & Hutchins, S. H. Howe, John O'Connell & Sons, and J. F. Desmond. A few years before that, the many shoe craftsmen and operators had banded together into a confederation, and their union representatives and the mill managers would set the payments for the workers' output through arbitration before a branch of the Massachusetts State Board of Arbitration. Then the mill owners combined to destroy the unions. The owners wanted to set the rates for piece work in their mills without any interference from unions or state arbitrators, and they wanted to lower the pay.[6]

On November 10, 1898, the S. H. Howe and Rice & Hutchins mills took the lead, posting notices of what were then called "ironclads," warnings that each employee would have to sign an individual contract setting his rate of pay for the coming year. The language of the owners' aggression was the bland language of law and economics. "Believing that the success and continuance of our business in Marlborough demand a change . . ." the notices began. And they concluded with an appeal to the discipline of in-terregional competition. "By the change of method and reorganization we believe we shall recover and be able to hold our place in the first rank of manufacturers, thereby providing steady employment for the greater numbers."[7]

William Ball Rice, of Rice & Hutchins, was a local boy who

had risen in the shoe business. His corporation's office was in downtown Boston, his home in nearby Quincy. The summer before the lockout, when all negotiations between the union and management had stalled, he had been in Europe.[8] Over three thousand workers struck against the cut in pay and the loss of union bargaining. After a month the companies began reopening their mills, importing Italian laborers to fill the strikers' places. That winter over a thousand men left Marlborough in search of work elsewhere, and another thousand were trapped in town, unemployed. Savings were used up, mortgages were defaulted, retail credit was stretched to bankruptcy. On Friday, May 5, 1899, the council of unions gave up. It voted to let its members—those who could—return to the mills without stigma. The unions had been broken, the wages cut, and 2,000 more workers would soon have to leave the city to find steady employment. A third of the city's population was driven out of town.

So it went in the province of Boston decade after decade. Many conflicts were smaller and lasted less time than this incident in Marlborough. Some lasted longer, some turned violent, some the owners won, some the unions won, but no matter what the outcome, the tide of mill closings was not stemmed. In all cases the communities stood by helpless as the using up and wearing out of the textile mills and shoe shops went relentlessly forward. In Marlborough a committee of ministers tried to get the companies to meet with their employees; the Massachusetts Board of Arbitration investigated and reported, as did a committee of the state legislature. All were refused.[9] There was public suffering, but no public power or responsibility.

Not only did company after company, mill after mill, town after town, suffer such wounds and humiliations, but no one knew what to do to ease the conflict or relieve the pain of dying businesses and dying towns. Having failed to find any mutual interest in these institutions, people turned to promises of instant relief. Businessmen talked of the wonders of new forms of management, like centralized office control, of the magic of Henry Ford's mass production, and the panacea of mergers into giant enterprises. The workers listened just as hopefully to preachers of syndicalism and class warfare. By 1930 the process of regional industrial obsolescence had become clear to all, but by then the collapse of the national and international economies was preempting everyone's attention. Provincial failure and provincial helplessness were buried under a larger catastrophe.

Two lives, when remembered, show what heavy burdens of failure await the province when economic obsolescence returns yet another time. One life, that of William Madison Wood, tells a story of unchecked business fantasy, of how a self-made millionaire, following the business fashions of his day, hastened the destruction of Boston's woolen textile industry. The second, that of Fred Erwin Beal, tells a story of ignorant millennial faith, and a tale of business and government crimes turning a man—who was following Boston's missionary tradition—into a useless eccentric.

7 ❧ WILLIAM MADISON WOOD

William Madison Wood (1858–1926) spent his early working life as a junior to Yankee factory owners and managers. In 1915, as a rising executive, he gave an interview in which he identified himself and his parents with one of Boston's favorite pasts, that of the old whaling families of Martha's Vineyard Island. The puff said: "His ancestors were prominent in the colony of whalers and seamen who had made the coast of Massachusetts famous in national story and song."[1] Later, when he and his company were rolling in World War I profits and he owned several yachts and four houses, he corrected his story to conform to the biography of a poor immigrant boy who had found riches in America.

William Wood's parents had emigrated from the Portuguese Azores to Martha's Vineyard. The father, whose name had been Jacinto, had worked his way as a cook's assistant on a whaling ship. Soon after his arrival in Edgartown he changed his name to Wood; William's mother, also an Azorean immigrant, changed her name to Madison. The young couple married, and William, their first child, was born at Edgartown, Martha's Vineyard, April 5, 1858. William's father found a job as steward on a small steamer that shuttled between Edgartown and New Bedford, then moved his family to New Bedford, the steamer's home port. There William went to public grammar school, working summers as a cash boy in a local store. When his father died in 1870 William quit school and went to work in the counting room of the city's Wamsutta Mills, manufacturers of fine cottons. The owner of the mills, Andrew G. Pierce, Sr., took an interest in the young clerk; William became his protegé and a lifelong friend of the family.[2] After the boy spent three years in the counting room, Pierce transferred him to the mechanical departments, so by the time he was eighteen, William Wood had undergone a thorough apprenticeship in cotton manufacture.

Thereupon young Wood set out to find his future. He tried six months in a broker's office in Philadelphia, but it didn't suit him. He returned to New Bedford, where he worked for three years as a clerk in a shipping and banking firm. Then he found a post as paymaster and assistant to the treasurer of the large Border City Mills in nearby Fall River. In 1885, when he was twenty-seven years old, his opportunity arrived through the good offices of one Thomas Sampson, a well-known cotton agent in Rhode Island. Sampson had been asked by the purchasers of the Washington Mills in Lawrence, Massachusetts, to reorganize their plant, which at that time processed both cotton and wool. Sampson in turn asked Wood to join him as his assistant and to take charge of the cotton department. It was a risky venture.

The Washington Mills were first constructed in 1848 for the manufacture of cotton cloth, but the original company collapsed during the 1870s depression. New operators tried to make a go of the plant by adding a woolen department, but they went under during the 1882–1885 recession.[3] In 1885 the mill was standing idle.

The next purchaser, Frederick Ayer (1822–1918), who hired Sampson and Wood, was a new investor in textile mills. He had begun his career as a shopkeeper in Syracuse, New York, made a small success there, sold out to his partner, and then joined his physician brother in Lowell in 1855. There the two established a thriving patent medicine business, bottling sarsaparilla, hair re-tainer, and some sort of cherry-flavored relief. In 1871 the brothers bought a controlling interest in the Tremont and Suffolk Mills in Lowell, and this venture prospered. In 1885 they hoped to re-peat that experience.[4] The special quality that Frederick Ayer brought to the Washington Mills purchase was his willingness to try new things. He had become by then a financier; he was in-volved with Lowell banks, was a founder of the New England Telephone and Telegraph Company and later was an organizer of

Lake Superior mines and shipping and an active member of corporate boards.

At first the reorganized Washington Mills fared poorly, running at only a quarter of their capacity. Sampson quit or was fired; a fire destroyed some of the plant in 1887. Wood, however, instead of losing confidence, proposed to reorganize the mills along the latest lines, introducing the new worsted process, which was then considered the cheapest and fastest way of making woolen suitings. The cotton machinery was to be entirely phased out. Frederick Ayer trusted Wood with the expansion, the mills were rebuilt and steadily converted to worsted manufacture. In 1888 William married Ayer's eldest daughter, Ellen.

Wood's gamble with the new process succeeded, in part because it was the new way, in part because he proved to be an excellent manager and salesman. It was said that his "dancing black eyes hypnotized people," and that he was a super salesman. By cutting back the number of patterns offered and by dumping the inventory that didn't move, he cut his losses, and he found the market often enough to pull the mills out of debt. In the decade after 1887 he expanded the Washington Mills in Lawrence from 2,500 to 5,000 employees.[5]

This youthful triumph drew William Wood toward his future of unchecked power. As a young assistant treasurer he probably hoped to own and manage a mill of his own some day. Now he and Ayer were heroes of the industry. Despite an intense depression in the woolen trade, and a national depression besides, they had succeeded. Wood's special contribution was the vision of large-scale mechanized production. "There is no money in idle machinery," he said: put in the latest process, run the mills full tilt, search for the widest market, cut the costs, lower the prices, and make standard products for those newly imagined people—the masses. Ayer contributed the necessary confidence and the necessary long line of credit, Wood contributed the formula.

Now in the late nineties, while other mills were running on short time or failing, Wood urged his father-in-law to enlarge their operations and to organize a trust.[6] To do this Ayer and Wood employed the services of an old-fashioned Yankee trader, Charles R. Flint (1850–1934). Flint, the son of a shipbuilder, had been born in Thomaston, Maine. During the Civil War the family removed to Brooklyn, New York, where the father managed a shipping business. After graduating from Brooklyn Polytechnic Institute, Charles began his career as a clerk on one of the piers in New York City. Clerking led to ship chandlery, and ship chandlery to trading to Chile and Peru and to a lifetime of Latin American commerce, intrigue, and arms deals.

In 1885 Flint joined an offshoot of his father's business, Flint & Company, commission merchants with a flourishing worldwide trade in lumber, general merchandise, and rubber. Flint's other public label was "the Rubber King of America," because of his management of the Brazilian rubber crop. The arms business also flourished. Flint sold a fleet of ships to Brazil in 1893 and sold Spanish-American War surplus to Japan for its 1905 war with Russia. His firm served as international agents for the Wright brothers' airplane and for an American manufacturer of submarines. Flint continued his traditional American free-trading ways, supplying arms to the Soviets in 1917, even though the American government opposed the revolution there.[7]

As was appropriate to his day, Flint operated out of New York City, the new imperial capital, but he did business in the manner of the old China merchants. He did not seek an industrial empire, like Andrew Carnegie or John D. Rockefeller, but continued the traditions of the dockside. So successful had his adaptation of the merchant style become that in 1900 a Chicago newspaper called him "the father of trusts." His rubber specialty had put him in contact with the rubber boot and shoe manufacturers of the Boston province. During the nineties, when they were suffering from intense competition among themselves, Flint brought them together in a successful merger as the U.S. Rubber Company. Therefore, he was playing a familiar role in 1899 when he assisted Ayer and Wood in merging three small groups of woolen and worsted mills to become the American Woolen Company.[8]

Wood rapidly expanded the corporation. First as treasurer and then as president after Ayer's retirement in 1905, Wood was the real force in the new enterprise. By 1901 he had bought up twenty-nine mills, and he kept buying more until the firm reached its peak in 1919, with fifty-six mills and a capacity of 30 million yards of cloth per year. What had begun as nine mills with a peak employment of 15,000 now put 40,000 people to work.[9] The mill owners of the Boston province sold readily to the new combine after the depression of the 1890s, trading the uncertainties and harsh problems of old plants, old machines, and short time for 50 percent cash and the balance in 7 percent preferred stock.[10] And many investors were foolish enough to believe that Wood was right, that centralization of purchasing, manufacturing, and sales would save everyone—mills, millhands, and mill towns—as it had apparently rescued Lawrence's big Washington Mills.[11]

The American Woolen Company was the Boston province's attempt to follow the fashion for giant industrial enterprise. Although scattered about in large and small units all over the province, from Old Town, Maine, to Yantic, Connecticut, and even west to Utica, New York, and Kentucky, American Woolen shared many superficial characteristics with the new giant steel and auto corporations of the midwest. Like them it had the lure of mechanized production of standard products. Its factories contained long vistas of machines and armies of employees daily streaming through the mill gates. It too offered seemingly limitless power to its captain and the sudden flash of riches to its managers and stockholders. It too alternated harsh denials of employee demands with impulses of paternalism. And like the nabobs of steel and automobiles, the free-floating leader of the enterprise precipitated his fantasies into silly reconstructions of farm and village pasts.

The resemblance to the new giants in oil, steel, electrical machinery, and automobiles, however, was only superficial. In spite of its size, American Woolen could not control the key elements in its costs and prices, which still depended upon the fluctuations of the world market in wool. United States Steel might purchase a few mines to assure itself of a steady supply of iron, limestone, and coal, but William Wood could not purchase the sheepfolds of Montana, New Zealand, and Australia. At the output end of the business, despite its dominant position in woolen cloth, it could not control fashions in clothing the way an automobile manufacturer could manipulate the fashions and the prices of his automobiles. Finally, only under the most sophisticated of decentralized management could each of the scattered plants run most efficiently. A one-man central office could not possibly manage it successfully.[12]

If it had not been for the insatiable demand for uniforms and blankets during World War I the province might have learned its lesson sooner. The original nine mills had in fact made more money as separate units than they did when combined, burdened as they were with the watered stock of merger and the inefficiency of overcentralized management. In the years when Stone & Webster's far-flung and varied branches were experimenting with independently responsible departments and subsidiaries, Wood was trying to run all of his scattered mills from his own desk. Common stock dividends stopped altogether in the panic of 1907, depreciation accounts had to rest unfilled, and for several years the preferred dividends were paid out of surplus.[13] But Wood charged forward, certain that his formula was the right one, or at least right enough. He concentrated his efforts on a narrow line of goods, standard men's and women's suiting materials. Soon, with but 10 percent of the nation's machinery, his company was producing 20 percent of the nation's woolen goods for clothing.[14] Even at the very end of his career, Wood proudly advertised that 70 percent of his company's output was dyed blue.[15]

In 1931, at the outset of the Great Depression, when American Woolen's common stock had fallen from its 1919 high of $169½ to $9, a *Fortune* magazine reporter saw the business as a familiar American confection—a blend of get-rich-quick dreaming and financial jobbery. "The war decade," he wrote, "was an era of enthusiastic and absolutely fatal expansion under the glorious American delusion that right or wrong, merger is wonderful."[16]

In 1905, the year Wood assumed the presidency, he began construction in Lawrence of the world's largest worsted mill, covering three million square feet, along the banks of the Merrimack River in one vast six-story wall of brick and glass.[17] He named it the Wood Mill, and he installed in it all the latest worsted manufacturing machinery. For the 7,000 employees he added the most modern conveniences, including an escalator, the building's most remarkable novelty. It prompted one millworker's old country grandmother to see it all as frills and pampering: " 'Twon't be long before they'll have a horse an' buggy take 'em to work."[18] Others saw the new mill as continuing the Boston province's tradition of manufacturer's paternalism.[19] Two years later Wood added a large spinning mill, the Ayer Mill. These constructions, along with the new mill jobs, created a minor industrial boom in the province, adding 16,000 jobs in Lawrence alone.[20]

When the American Woolen Company began losing money regularly year after year, as it did from 1924 onward, Wood's financial arrangements became the focus of controversy. Indeed he was forced out in his first year of disaster. Yet it is now clear that the hopes of many people were hitched to American Woolen, that it represented much more than the cupidity of one man.

After his retirement Wood was accused of having used special accounts to defraud the parent company in the construction of new mills and in the buying and selling of old ones. Professor Arthur H. Cole of the Harvard Business School, however, surveyed the company's construction practices and found them a model of sound accounting procedures.[21] Whatever the truth, Wood soon began acting the part of the new industrial millionaire, spending money like Robert Grant's fictional millionaire, Hugh Blaisdell. To his large house in North Andover Wood annexed a country gentleman's model farm, which he called the American Woolen Farm. When its cattle won prizes, they were the American Woolen cattle.[22] He bought a large house in Boston's Back Bay, a few yachts, and a spread on the North Shore at Pride's Crossing.[23] On Cuttyhunk Island, near his early home in New Bedford, he established a summer house for himself and a vacation spot for the woolen company employees. He named it Avalon for the Arthurian island of the blessed.[24]

To afford all of this, he paid himself a whopping salary of a million dollars a year. He gave his two sons, William, Jr., and Cornelius, executive jobs.[25] Like Henry Ford, Wood seems to have lost all sense of the boundaries between himself and his business. American Woolen surely was an institution, as Emerson would have said, "the lengthened shadow of one man."[26] As Wood grew rich and powerful making mass-produced products, his fantasies turned toward a nostalgic past, just as Ford's had.

When Ford built his vast, overintegrated River Rouge plant in Dearborn, Michigan, after World War I, he also restored his family's farm and built the Greenfield Village and Henry Ford Museum of Americana. In 1918 Wood purchased a large tract of land in North Andover and poured twenty million dollars of American Woolen's wartime profits into building a neo-Georgian village for his company's staff and head office.[27]

So long as he seemed successful, Wood was admired, and his riches, if not also admired, were at least expected. Yet it is perfectly clear now that his short-lived success was the last fever of Boston's dying textile years. His mass production was a fashionable error, an outpouring of intemperate images borrowed from the meat packers and farm machinery builders. And through it all there was no community or organization that could call the American Woolen Company or William Wood into question.

The clothing trends of the twentieth century went against Wood's plans. In 1905 Americans were growing richer, and as they prospered they wanted to enjoy their comfort with objects they could personalize, not in the blue uniform of standard men's suits and women's coats, long ago popularized by the Union troops in the Civil War. Smaller firms, oriented to the fashions of Paris and New York, were the ones that fitted the times—firms like Wood's neighbor, M. T. Stevens Sons of North Andover, or Furstman & Huffman in Passaic, New Jersey.[28] The steady advance of central heating killed the market for woolen underwear, then the demand for heavy wool suitings. Young women wanted to wear the new light sport clothes of the rich and the new fabrics woven of silk and rayon. By the mid 1930s the average American woman was buying only two-thirds of a yard of woolen garments a year, whereas in 1909, her mother had bought almost seven yards.[29]

The lure of bigness, however, propelled Wood forward despite poor sales since the first merger in 1899. It took World War I to match bigness, centralized management, standardized products, and mass production to a profitable market. Then so intense was the demand for blankets and uniforms that Wood was indicted for profiteering—he was acquitted.[30] American Woolen made millions and paid handsome dividends. It established a department of labor to find homes and coal for its workers, it gave the employees life and health insurance, and it set up baseball teams and picnics. Then, when the wartime boom collapsed in 1921, the whole structure came tumbling down, revived only by the intervals of World War II and the Korean War. Finally, in 1955, the company was swallowed up by a still newer fashion in imperial capitalism, a conglomerate. From the beginning American Woolen had been a mistake, a fantasy of high finance and big business talk, a misconception that, instead of improving industrial efficiency, piled the burdens of new capital upon the old and thereby hastened Boston's textile industry toward collapse.[31]

After such a long time it is no longer possible to judge who was the seducer, who the innocent. William Wood surely was a man of great enthusiasms and magnetism, and surely he acted as if drawn by the sirens of giant enterprise. Yet so common was the enthusiasm for mass production in his day that he may well have been the innocent led to his own and the province's destruction by the lure of machines and their promise of personal aggrandizement. Indeed, as late as 1933 the department store owner and reformer Edward A. Filene argued that what Boston's failing economy needed was more of Ford's mass production and more of Frederick W. Taylor's scientific management.[32] Whether Wood was victim or villain is not a question that matters much today. It is the helplessness of the thousands of workers and townspeople in the Boston province that we must recall.

"In August, 1922 [Wood's] elder son, William Wood, Jr. while racing his auto from Boston to Andover was almost instantly killed just this side of Reading. Young Wood was a vice president [for Labor Relations] of the American Woolen Company and was, according to those who knew him, a man of keen mind, and one who ordinarily would have followed in the footsteps of his father."[33]

"Daytona Beach, Fla., Feb. 2 [1926]—William Madison Wood millionaire, formerly president of the American Woolen Company of Andover, Mass. committed suicide at a lonely spot above Flagler Beach this morning by placing the barrel of a revolver in his mouth and firing. Ill health was given as the cause of his act. At the time of the suicide, Mr. Wood had been accompanied in his automobile to Flagler Beach by his valet and chauffeur."[34]

8 ❧ FRED ERWIN BEAL

During the nineteenth century, when Boston served as a center of missionary activity, those who chose this calling were generally country boys who had nursed a deep religious sensitivity in their isolation and who found their fellows and vocation in college and the seminary. Fred Erwin Beal (1897–1954) came from a country family, to be sure, but no college or seminary existed to welcome him to his calling of labor missionary. He had to find the word by listening to the street-corner radicals of his home town of Lawrence, Massachusetts, and by learning from his experiences as a worker in the city's mills.

Like Lowell, its near neighbor, and many other mill cities of the province, Lawrence had been planned and developed during the midnineteenth-century Boston textile boom by a corporation that organized the efficient use of a river for power.[1] By the time Fred Beal was born at the end of the century, Lawrence had lost whatever altruism its founders had intended and had degenerated into a harsh city of textile mills and immigrants. After the novelty and expectations of invention left the industry, Lawrence, like so many other mill cities, had become an ugly place, a place where some young people managed to find security, and a very few found wealth, beauty, and hope.[2]

Lawrence's specialty was manufacturing woolen cloth by the new worsted process. Its social order consisted of Yankee, English, and Irish supervisors who directed armies of immigrant French Canadian and European machine tenders. The superintendents lived on the hills overlooking the town or on more distant estates. They also guided, if they did not in fact manage, the local government.

The Beals' move to Lawrence repeated the pattern followed by thousands of provincial farmers before them, and one that millions of American farmers would follow during the first half of the twentieth century. For generations the Beals had been New Hampshire dirt farmers, and as such they were not failures, but as Fred later described it, "They knew nothing of comfort . . . They had plenty to eat but little beyond the simplest wants and no hope of improving their lot. It was this that drove my grandfather to the city, or, as he said, it was my grandmother's social aspirations."[3]

Sometime during the 1880s grandfather sold the farm and with his son and daughter-in-law moved to a "heavily-mortgaged cottage" outside of Lawrence. Fred's father, William C. Beal, secured a job with the railway, but this attempt to establish the family in the mill city failed. After struggling to meet the payments and provide for a family of six growing children for fifteen years, there came "the final surrender which moved us from the fields and the river to the dumps of the city. Our Yankee relatives referred to this neighborhood near the railroad as 'the patch of dirty Irish.' It was a district of ugly crowded tenements with nasty words written in chalk on the clapboards and flies swarming around babies dressed only in smelly diapers. Though we lived there for many years we never thought of it as 'home.' "[4]

In his confession, written when he was forty, when all his millennial hopes had failed him, Fred Beal tried to find in his family's tradition some explanation for his life as a missionary for a millenial socialism. He called his tradition Yankee and Puritan. "My father," he wrote, "never had a radical thought in his head [he supported Theodore Roosevelt in 1912] . . . and though he himself held no strong religious or social convictions, he felt that if you sincerely believed in anything, you were morally bound to preach the word to the people. Historians call this the Puritan tradition. I think that this mixture of zealot and independent, which makes up a Yankee, is something deeper than a tradition. It is born in the blood and bred in the bone. Certainly I found it in myself long before I had ever heard or read of the Puritan tradition. The little schooling I had in my childhood did not include such big words."[5]

Fred Beal's mother died when he was eleven. His father urged Fred to stay in school to learn at least enough to escape the mills through some white-collar job. The father and the two older brothers were working to support the family already, but Fred "did not care much for school." So when he was fourteen, anxious for a pay envelope and for the chance to play a man's role, Fred left school for the mills. There, in factories, on the streets of Lawrence, and in its many ethnic meeting halls, Beal learned his calling.

In 1911 custom and law had not foreclosed all child labor, and in cotton and woolen mills most youngsters were assigned to the spinning department, where they doffed bobbins. Accordingly, the atmosphere of the spinning rooms more resembled the horseplay and turmoil of a suburban junior high school than the concentrated adult world of machine tending in the weaving departments. In one incident Fred's first foreman, after hunting up some absent boys and dragging Fred by the hair, was kicked in the shins for his pains.[6] Such intense conflict, however, was too much for fourteen-year-old Fred, so he walked out of the Crescent Mill and went over to American Woolen's Ayer Mill. Soon afterward he transferred to the giant Wood Mill, where he and four other boys were fired for running down the up escalator.[7]

By December 1911, after brief stints at four mills, Fred had settled down enough to be boss doffer of six fellow teenagers in the spinning room of Pacific Mills. Fred was chosen for promotion because he was a Yankee among immigrants, and his bosses regarded him as one of themselves. Fred encountered the same problems as the other foremen, and he often found it easier to do the absent worker's task than to get him or her back to the frames. The work day was not all business. The boys and girls had adopted names of film and newspaper celebrities, mostly gangsters. One was Slim Jim the Burglar, taken from a character in a popular one-reeler at the local movie house; others were Gyp the Blood and Lefty Louie for notorious underworld characters. Fred himself was called Lobster and Red for his pink complexion and red hair, and his friend, a new immigrant, was Tony the Wop.

The girls took names like Queenie and Little Eva. Little Eva was an under-age French Canadian girl who had to stand on a box when she doffed, and when "Limpy" Fallsby, the state inspector came by, she hid.[8]

Fred Beal discovered his fellowship among the spinners in the Pacific Mills, most of whom were Italians. He remembered them as "warm-hearted, good natured, and excitable," perhaps a welcome contrast to his own discouraged family.[9] The Italians took the lead in the celebrated 1912 Lawrence strike. When Massachusetts passed a law reducing the work week from fifty-six to fifty-four hours, the mill owners of Lawrence, unlike those in some other cities, announced that they would not raise the hourly and piece rates to make up for the lost two hours. On Wednesday evening, January 10, the small Italian local of the Industrial Workers of the World voted to strike if the pay level was not maintained, and the young chairman wired the famous Italian labor organizer Joseph Ettor to come help.[10]

The next day some Italian spinners approached Fred Beal with a strike petition, asking that he sign it first because he was a Yankee. After some turmoil, and despite Queenie's warnings that "those Wops'll get you in trouble," he signed it. So did Gyp and Lefty Louie.[11] At 11:30 the following morning, Friday, January 12, 1912, the paymaster and an armed guard wheeled a truck of pay envelopes to the head of a long line of anxious workers who had queued up on Fred's floor. As the first ones tore open their envelopes to discover two hours deducted from their pay, they were fearful and confused. When the paymaster left, the French Canadians started back to the frames, but someone began shouting "Strike!" "Strike!" like a cheerleader, another threw the electric switch, and a band of Italians ran along the line cutting the belts that drove the machines. Lefty Louie and Fred raced down the frames breaking the threads, while Queenie threw bobbins and Tony the Wop smashed windows. "It was a madhouse, a thrilling one, nevertheless . . . Paddy Parker was at the door as we stampeded for the street. How ineffectual he looked, standing there with the petition."[12]

While the adults struggled to organize the turnout into a city-wide strike, Fred and the kids went skating. "We looked on the strike as a vacation; it would be over and won in a week."[13] But the strike lasted two months. The Italian local's call for the national organizers of the IWW turned a local dispute, an angry Friday walkout that might well have cooled by the following Monday, into a media event. The IWW was the leading evangelist in a large and growing socialist mission. Theirs was the most fascinating appeal—forget the ballot box, forget the trade unions, join us, your fellow workers and be transformed, turn your mill, your mine, your lumber camp, into a workers' institution.

Although the Wobblies were feared and hated by many Americans, they were not in these prewar years thought to be aliens or representatives of foreign ideas or foreign powers. Westerners at first, they were surely Americans, yet another manifestation of agrarian radicalism, like Jacksonian paper money men and free land agitators, Grangers, and Populists, part of the long parade of poor country people's movements that had been cropping up in the United States since Shays's Rebellion in 1786.[14] The IWW was in the news constantly with its revolutionary rhetoric and because of the violent repression of its strikes in the mines of the west. William D. Haywood (1869–1928), leader of the union, rushed to Lawrence after being acquitted of a trumped-up charge of murdering the governor of Colorado. The telegram to Ettor also brought Arturo Giovannitti, the Italian socialist poet. Eugene Debs, leader of the Socialist party and an immensely popular figure, also gave the Lawrence strikers his active support. For socialists of every kind, Lawrence epitomized the new giantism of business and its capitalist exploitation of native and immigrant workers.

Many Americans saw Lawrence in a different light, not in terms of American radicalism, but as a sign of the evils of the old world poisoning the new. They worried about a city, half of whose population had been born overseas, a city of Italians, Syrians, Belgians, Armenians, Lithuanians, Portuguese, and Chinese. As the spotlight of the national magazines and newspapers turned on the city, American Woolen's illegal overseas recruiting of Italian workers came to light. Open immigration and the importing of labor by American business clearly were driving down wages and threatening the unions of native workers. Besides, these Italians with their socialist and IWW leaders were not the loyal Yankees, the English, Irish, and French Canadians who worked so steadily. These familiar immigrants did most of the scabbing and staffed the city and metropolitan police and the state militia. Many provincial Bostonians, along with many other Americans, saw the Lawrence strike as an issue of Americanization and of the necessity for immigration restriction.[15]

Still others saw Lawrence as an exposé of the evils of the new industrial and immigrant cities. A local charitable foundation had just completed a thorough survey of the city, reviewing its severe problems in housing, health, and sanitation.[16] Journalists like Mary Heaton Vorse, writing for *Harper's Weekly*, settlement house leaders like Boston's Robert A. Woods, philanthropists like Max Mitchell of Jewish Charities, liberal divines like Harry Emerson Fosdick of New York City and Adolph Berle of Tufts College all focused on the contrasts between the squalid tenements and the giant mills. Tariff-cutting Democrats campaigned against conditions in Lawrence, calling out that the high tariffs on wool and woolen goods only made mill owners rich and beggared both workers and customers. There were protest rallies and relief meetings in Boston's Faneuil Hall and New York's Carnegie Hall and in Italy and London. The wife of President Taft even came to Lawrence to see for herself, bringing with her the wife of Gifford Pinchot, who had been chief of the U.S. Forest Service under Theodore Roosevelt.[17]

No matter how they viewed the strike—as evidence of a rising tide of western agrarian radicalism, as urban socialism, as a symptom of the destruction of a community overwhelmed by strange, non-English-speaking immigrants, or as an example of the evils of large-scale industrialization—no one thought Lawrence could or should settle its conflicts by itself. Everyone in Lawrence and everyone in the vast audience looking on from the province and the empire recognized that the giant mills built in the name of individual private property were no longer accountable to the citizens of Lawrence alone. The mill owners spoke through their Boston offices. The mayor and the police chief called in officers from nearby towns, summoned the new Boston Metropolitan Park Police, and appealed to the governor, who sent the state militia. The strikers appealed to national unions and sought relief and aid through the national magazines and newspapers.

Because the Lawrence strike of 1912 focused in a few dramatic episodes the intense national anxieties over immigrants, slums, labor unions, socialism, trusts, and big business, it was fully investigated at the time and is still remembered. Indeed, it has become a kind of set piece in our American history texts.[18] Its significance for the Boston province, however, is that it was the first in a series of strikes (1912, 1919, 1921, 1924, 1928) in which the textile workers of the area struggled to win permanent union recognition and collective bargaining. With great pain and suffering the workers ultimately succeeded, yet their effort was doomed to failure. The substitution of union and management bargaining for community action inevitably failed because it drew upon too narrow a set of interests and concerns. The dialogue and conflicts between unions and managers could not sustain the textile industry or mitigate the suffering of its decline.

The fact that the parties in daily conflict in Lawrence in 1912 were not the parties to the labor dispute showed how far community structure had already broken down. The workers and managers, or workers and owners, did not confront one another as they might have in a family quarrel, or in a test of will in a small shop. Instead the mill workers faced the municipal and state police, employees themselves. The 1912 strike was not particularly violent: one morning the strikers broke a lot of windows on the streetcars to stop scabs from going to work, on another day they broke some mill windows and some machinery, and someone stabbed a policeman. To punish these acts of aggression, and to break up their picket lines and parades, the police and state troopers continually clubbed and arrested the strikers. The owners and managers, who controlled the municipal government, steadfastly refused to allow that government to be the forum for discussing and settling the disputes. Instead, while police and strikers fought, management waited in their distant offices in Boston and New York, hired spies, and plotted illegal secret attacks to discredit and confuse their opponents.

William Wood, then president of American Woolen, and perhaps some other men, plotted a criminal action against the strikers. On Friday, January 19, a week after the walkout, John Breen, an undertaker, tipped off the police about the locations of some dynamite caches, one in a dye house, another near where Joseph Ettor received his mail. The discovery of the dynamite momentarily threw the strikers on the defensive. Many townspeople and other Americans imagined that the IWW syndicalists were bomb-throwing anarchists. A few weeks later a local judge determined that Breen himself had been in on the plot. The Massachusetts attorney general joined the case, and in a drunken moment the contractor who had built the Wood Mill confessed to supplying the dynamite. The next day he committed suicide. Although Wood was strongly implicated by the undertaker's and the contractor's confessions, the jury acquitted him.[19]

After two weeks of "vacation" Fred drifted down to the mill gate, where he experienced the police in action against the strikers. Mounted officers charged the picket line, clubbing a pathway for the scabs, and in the melee Fred was almost driven into the frigid mill canal. A man carrying an American flag rallied the strikers and, joining pickets from the Wood Mill, they marched toward the center of Lawrence. Suddenly, up front, someone— Fred thought it was a policeman—fired a shot, and Anna Lo-Pezza, one of the strikers, lay dead in the street. Ettor and Giovannitti were imprisoned on a trumped-up charge of inciting a third man to murder LoPezza. The popular stereotype of the recent Italian immigrant as a person of uncontrollably violent passions lent a cover of plausibility to a police crime that otherwise would have been unbelievable. The Lawrence police and the Lo-Pezza murder, and the local priest's refusal to allow LoPezza to be buried in his cemetery, radicalized Beal and drew him toward the socialist mission.[20]

He found a hero and a message in Bill Haywood. Essentially it was the emotion and message of all strikes—fellowship, unity, and solidarity of all workers. The day LoPezza was murdered, Haywood gave his first speech to thousands of strikers gathered at the Lawrence common. His was an imposing presence. A giant of a man, with one blind eye, he had a deep booming voice and an uncompromising call. Fred remembered that day for the rest of his life. With the other boys, he had wormed his way up to the front of the crowd, next to the bandstand. Haywood looked benignly down at the youngsters in short pants and roared: "These kids should be in school instead of slaving in the mill!" As Beal recalled it, "This was the only thing that Bill said that I wholeheartedly disagreed with."[21]

"Particularly I remember one statement that thrilled and frightened me at that time," Beal later wrote about that day. " 'Only by One Big Union of the working class and by mass action can we hope for the final victory of those who work and produce over those who exploit and sweat us for their profits. The road for us to travel is through industrial unions, not through the American Federation of Labor craft unions nor through the Republican, Democratic and Socialist Party method of voting for 'good men' who will sell us out later. I would *smash the ballot box with an ax!'* "[22]

There followed more police attacks and more arrests, especially during the municipal government's campaign to stop the workers from sending their children out of Lawrence to be cared for elsewhere. But as the weeks passed, the mill orders began to pile up, and the owners agreed to settle with pay raises of between 5 and 25 percent. The workers returned to the mills on May 14, 1912.[23] Fred Beal returned to spinning and in time graduated to the post of shearer in the white room of Pacific Mills. There he led a successful one-week walkout over a special issue of equalizing their piece rates. He seems also to have kept alive his memories of the excitement and fellowship of the strike and his interest in the idea of socialism through one big union.[24]

Fred Beal was twenty years old when the United States entered World War I. An intense surge of patriotism swept over the Boston province, and many young mill workers from Lawrence volunteered. Not Fred. He admired the pacifists and the opponents of the war, like his hero, Bill Haywood, and Eugene Debs. Both faced prison, and their organizations were being smashed by an embryo Federal Bureau of Investigation. Fred considered himself a coward for meekly accepting his draft call in September 1918, but he went. His was a short and nasty tour of duty. Shipped to Fort Devens in nearby Ayer, he worked most of the time as an undertaker's assistant handling the bodies of soldiers who died in the influenza epidemic. The camp YMCA director lectured the soldiers on the dangers of world revolution and the treason of the Lawrence strikers. He called Fred a bolshevik.[25]

The Russian revolution, the turmoil in Europe, and the pains of American inflation and demobilization turned the year 1919 into a time of panic in the empire and the province. Many unions called strikes to get their members' wages caught up with inflation, to secure the shorter work week won during the war, or just to win permanent recognition from management. Radical socialists, excited by the world's first anticapitalist revolution, saw signs of the millenium in the events in Russia, Hungary, and Germany. Anarchists were exploding bombs in public places. The radical rhetoric and the bombs in turn encouraged unscrupulous politicians and propagandists to redirect the hatreds of wartime toward unpopular Americans. The year 1919 began imperial America's decades of red scares, and the Boston province joined the van of the nation's unreason with the police strike in the city of Boston, the deportation of aliens, and textile strikes in the mill towns.[26]

The strike of 1912 had failed to establish any lasting reordering of community arrangements in either Lawrence or the province. The mill managers recognized no unions and refused to deal with their men collectively. Only after workers walked off the job would bargaining commence. Each mill city had its craft unions of carpenters, barbers, and masons, and the city's central labor union council usually included as well as representatives of a few textile craft unions of the skilled men—loom fixers, spinners, and weavers. On occasion these craft unions made demands for their members and even led general actions. During World War I the cotton spinners led a brief strike in Manchester, New Hampshire; Lowell, Massachusetts; and Woonsocket, Clinton, and Mansville, Rhode Island, which was settled for the benefit of all textile workers by a wartime board of arbitration. The liberal shoe manufacturer Henry B. Endicott, of the Endicott Johnson Shoe Company, had been chosen by the union to represent the men before the arbitration board.[27]

In 1919, with inflation, another and bitterer strike began with a debate and call for action by the craft unions of Lawrence, particularly the International Mule Spinners and the United Textile Workers of America (AFL). The issue once again centered on a reduction in hours of work, this time from fifty-four to forty-eight hours per week. Meeting in City Hall under the chairmanship of the Central Labor Union Council, the skilled men called for no pay reduction; in effect, they wanted an eight-hour day with the equivalent of a 12½ percent pay raise. Referring to the generous wartime dividends for the mill owners, one speaker said "It is time they should think of their workers."[28] The Lawrence craft group did not call for a strike but for a walkout each day at the end of eight hours. At this time the eight-hour demand had spread throughout the textile industry. In New York, Governor Alfred Smith had engaged his conciliation machinery to settle the matter.[29] Within the Boston province a number of the mills had already established forty-eight-hour weeks, and the giant Amoskeag Mills in Manchester, New Hampshire, promised to do so soon.[30]

In that climate of flexibility and accommodation it seems as if the Lawrence manufacturers, and American Woolen in particular, wanted to discredit unions altogether. At the very least they seemed to want the workers to absorb the cost of the slack time of postwar reconversion. The workers' hopes for an easy settlement through a call once again for Henry Endicott and arbitration were dashed by management's refusal to talk until the employees had first returned to work. The governor of Massachusetts, Calvin Coolidge, and the Massachusetts Board of Conciliation took that same hostile position.[31]

As in 1912, the force behind the 1919 strike lay with the Italian, Belgian, and Polish workers. During January a number of them had been meeting together and had decided on a strike, not just a job action, beginning February 3. Meeting with them were three radical ministers from a Boston collective.[32] The ministers had all been members of the new Fellowship for Reconciliation, active pacifists during World War I, and they felt that as modern Christians they should lend assistance in the struggles of the working poor. Few on the strike committee spoke English, and some were young men who had been only boys in 1912. They asked the three, Rev. Abraham Johannes Muste, Rev. Harold Rotzel, and Rev. Cedric Long, to take charge of the publicity and fund raising for strike relief and to sit on the strike committee. In time, because other groups could not provide leaders, A. J. Muste became the strike spokesman. Unlike 1912, in 1919 the strikers had to find their way alone. The American Federation of Labor regarded the strike as a wildcat and disavowed all affiliation. President Wilson had destroyed the IWW through the criminal attacks of his Justice Department agents, and the Boston Socialists were too few to do much, although the socialist attorney George E. Roewar volunteered his legal services.[33]

After four bitter months the 1919 strike ended as the previous one had: the owners granted a general pay increase of 15 percent and a forty-eight-hour week.[34] The special quality of this strike, however, lay in the new climate of local and imperial repression and the total loss of the provincial tradition of listening to local voices. Lawrence and Boston had learned just the wrong lesson from 1912 and World War I. Recalling the intense police involvement of 1912, the mayor appointed a citizens' committee to preserve public safety and order. The form of leadership was borrowed from the wartime precedents of local committees for recruiting, stockpiling food, and enforcing loyalty. The commissioner of public safety, Peter Carr, had been a patrolman in 1912, and from that experience he reasoned that the prompt use of force was the key to order. He told a reporter, "It was necessary to prevent organized demonstrations in connection with the strikes and that the presence of outside agitators was not considered desirable."[35] He said, "Lawrence is a city of 100,000 population and thirty-three different nationalities, most of whom are foreign. We feel that this is a fertile field for the implanting of Bolshevist propaganda, and as American citizens it is our duty to suppress it."[36] In trying to prevent parades, stop public meetings, and break up picket lines, the authorities in Lawrence increased the violence of the strike. The local newspaper even called for the creation of vigilante groups to drive out the "outside agitators." One night an AFL organizer from New York and a member of the Lawrence strike committee were routed out of a hotel by a band of twenty armed and masked men, driven out into the countryside, and beaten. No prosecutions followed.[37]

Not only did Lawrence abandon itself to a policeman's war against its own striking workers, but the imperial voice beyond the province buried the earlier worries about trusts, unions, slums, and immigrants beneath a peremptory demand for order above all else. The *New York Times,* in an editorial written after the strike was settled, singled out Lawrence as a case of intolerable labor activity. "As in Seattle," the scene of a general strike in 1919, the editors wrote, "it was seen in time that the preservation of order is more important than the winning of any strike." The editors then went on to praise the AFL for withdrawing its sponsorship of the strike, and quoted with approval the new language of fear and deafness put forth by the Massachusetts Board of Conciliation. The strike was "subversive of the rights of individuals and of private property, and revolutionary in its tendencies, creating terrorism, preventing the resumption of work, disturbing the ordinary business relations of the community, and destructive to orderly government."[38]

Fear and intolerance became dominant elements in the native culture of the American postwar empire and its provinces. In the mill towns of Boston these emotions also included the refusal to listen to and bargain with one's fellow citizens. Instead of mill deputations and petitions, instead of public meetings on town greens and in city halls, communication between mill owners and their workers degenerated into a bizarre theater of aggression and violence between police and strikers. Then, in the Boston and the South Atlantic textile provinces, as the political panic of 1919–20 subsided, it was replaced by the ferocity and narrowness of owners, managers, and workers seeking to squeeze profits or livings out of declining industry and to shift toward new sources of impoverished workers.

Against these waves of anger and bitterness Fred Beal brought little training save what he had gleaned from his own organizing in the mill rooms where he had worked, and from his participation in strikes, parades, and rallies. He had no single text for his gospel of fellowship, no sacred book to fall back upon in times of defeat and confusion, and he had no band of loyal fellow believers to travel with and to lean upon. Abraham Johannes Muste had all these resources, and he lived a long and honored life as a radical Christian. At the end of his days Muste led a delegation of pacifists to Saigon, Vietnam (April 1966). At the end of Fred Beal's life he was living in Lawrence with his brother, who had stuck by him, but he had become a discredited bearer of the bad news that the millennium was not at hand.

To the extent that Beal had anything like seminary training and apprenticeship, his learning came in the years from 1919 to 1924, when he sought the wisdom and example of others. His teachers were the socialists of Lawrence. Thomas Nicholson served as one professor. An Englishman who made his living as an optician and clock repairer, Nicholson followed the tradition of streetcorner speaking. Every Tuesday and Saturday night, when the stores stayed open late, Nicholson would set up his folding chair at the corner of Essex and Franklin streets, unfurl a red banner that said "The Socialist Party, Lawrence Local," and wait for a crowd, which always came. Beginning with the shocking words, "I am a revolutionist!" he gave a scholarly lecture on socialism as the solution to the troubles of mankind. As his argument proceeded he would quote from Shakespeare, the Bible, Jefferson, Lincoln, and Marx. Sometimes he imported guest speakers like Elizabeth Glendower Evans from Boston, who devoted her old age to the defense of Sacco and Vanzetti.[39] Under Nicholson's teaching Beal became "class-conscious" and began reading everything he could get his hands on. Years later he remembered reading the novelists Edward Bellamy, Upton Sinclair, and Jack London. But, he wrote, "I could never understand Karl Marx."[40]

Another of Beal's professors was the English radical Samuel Bramhall, who was active in the 1919 strike and who led the cotton workers of Lawrence during the provincewide 1922 walkout.[41] In that year, in the whole province, except Massachusetts, where state law forbade it, the cotton manufacturers extended the standard work week from forty-eight back to fifty-four hours, and announced a wage cut of twenty percent. The United States Department of Labor estimated that with this last reduction the average weekly wages of New Hampshire weavers had fallen from their 1920 peak of $30.05 to $18.63 for the men, and from $27.60 to $17.11 for women.[42] Where mill owners tried to keep their plants running with nonstrikers, battles broke out between police and strikers. In Pawtucket, Rhode Island, the Jenckes Spinning Company kept operating at the cost of just such a battle, in which one man was killed and six critically wounded when the police opened fire on the pickets.[43]

Fred Beal picketed in front of the Pacific print works, where he had earlier been employed in the white room. Bramhall "walked up to me and asked if I would lead the line. Lead it! Of course, I would lead it."[44] In October 1922 Beal joined Bramhall's Socialist party and under his guidance began to take an active role in the local One Big Union. It was from Bramhall, too, that he learned some of the techniques of defending free speech against municipal and police censorship and repression.

Because Beal was a veteran, the foreman took him back at Pacific Mills after the strike, and during the next two years there he organized the white room and the nearby dye room. "It surprised me," he later wrote of this time, "how easily I could talk people into joining the Union. I believed everything I said. My heart was in the work. I had little trouble in organizing my section. Then I started on the 'dye room' below. I met with success here, too, but only among some of the foreign workers. The Irish and the Americans were too much interested in baseball and prizefights. Some of the Irish were antagonistic and called me names, such as 'King of the Dagos.' "[45]

During his seminary years Beal first experienced the destructive fighting among the radical sects. The socialists of Lawrence in these years had divided into three camps. One group favored advancing socialism through conventional democratic politics; Bramhall and Beal's faction continued to favor the direct action of Bill Haywood's syndicalism; and the Communist party attempted to gain control of all the socialist sects and to lead them together into the American Federation of Labor, hoping that they could thereby capture that national organization.[46]

Fred Beal came into his own in 1924 when called to assist the secretary of the Lawrence One Big Union, Bert Emsley, in leading a failing strike over a speed-up at a mill in Dover, New Hampshire.[47] Emsley was a Lawrence school teacher who had drifted into labor organizing from teaching classes for immigrants in Americanization programs. As Emsley's assistant, Beal learned his own personal style and role. For Beal the millennial message of the coming of a classless society found its reality in the comradeship and solidarity of the striking workers. He himself sought that fellowship, and his response to it constituted his strength as a speaker and as an organizer, and also his weakness. "The strikers were Greek, Irish and French-Canadian. The young people were good fighters. They welcomed the strike, but there was very little discipline. And when I was alone I had difficulty in keeping order. I well remember the strike committee, sitting around on the floor—we had no chairs—telling jokes and discussing sports. When things got dull, the fellows would make motions for certain things that are not fit for print."

" 'Mr. Chairman,' one Irish boy was raising his arm for attention as we used to do at school.

'Yes,'

'I have a *notion* to make a *motion* to cause a *commotion!*'

A chorus of laughs greeted this announcement." By contrast Emsley acted the traditional part of the leader. "He'd never hang around with the boys. He would close himself in a room and make them come to him if they had any business to transact. Yet he is popular as well as respected."[48]

The United Textile Workers Union of the AFL tried to discredit the One Big Union and brought in a Communist speaker to join in the attack. But Emsley and Beal hit upon a successful tactic that rallied the Dover strikers and carried them to victory. With a few strikers they began picketing the mill superintendent's home, rather than the mill, and the police thereupon arrested them for disturbing the peace. A near riot ensued at the police station, and in a panic the police mounted machine guns on the courthouse roof. The judge, however, let the two leaders go after a night in jail and a lecture. The drama discredited the mill management, and the strikers soon won the restoration of the former work rules. Fred Beal returned to Lawrence an established young organizer. That fall he threw himself energetically into the Socialist party's attempt to assist the election of Robert M. La Follette for president of the United States. Beal even put out a weekly newspaper, the *Essex County Workers Advocate*, as part of the campaign.[49]

In January 1924 William Wood had told his employees that "the condition of the country never was more sound and that looking east, west, north and south, there seems to be not even the shadow of a cloud upon the financial and industrial horizon."[50] On June 16, for the board of directors' meeting, he wrote, "Of course there is a letting down in the textile industry in conjunction with the general business hesitation but I and my associates do not think this the proper time to consider a reduction in wages. The demand for goods is here in the country although it may be delayed in reaching the mills."[51]

Finally in December he admitted trouble. "This Christmas above all others is one on which we have to bury the disappointments as we consider present and future blessings. Older men say that the textile depression of 1924 has been the severest since the Civil War. Certainly it has been the worst in all my thirty-six years experience as a mill man."[52] During 1924 the American Woolen Company posted losses to the amount of four million dollars, and the board of directors replaced Wood with Andrew G. Pierce, Jr., of New Bedford, the son of his former patron.

Fred Beal also suffered defeat in 1924. The united campaign of the socialists failed. Instead of La Follette, Governor Calvin Coolidge of Massachusetts, a national symbol of the red scare and the personal embodiment of the new community deafness, was elected president by a substantial majority. That electoral defeat reinforced Beal's direct action beliefs. He quit the Socialist party and devoted himself to all sorts of local labor union campaigns.

In Lawrence Fred's efforts seemed to be leading nowhere. In July he was arrested for violating the local ordinance against open-air meetings when he tried to run a fund-raiser for striking Passaic workers.[53] "For three years I did what I could, through One Big Union, through small local organizations, and through the United Front. Then I gave up."[54]

He gave up to hitchhike to California, but a telegram relayed to him by his father caught him in New Jersey. It was an appeal from the Sacco-Vanzetti Defense Committee in Boston to help them with a last campaign against the impending execution of the two convicted anarchists. Beal rushed to Boston, where the huge crowds, the excitement of leaders converging from all over the nation, and the police attacks on the parades and the picket lines reenacted the 1912 drama of his childhood. For a month Fred Beal handed out leaflets and organized picket lines. It all failed, he believed, because Governor Fuller of Massachusetts wanted to achieve the same sort of national recognition as a stalwart antiradical as his predecessor Coolidge had done.[55] For Robert Grant, reviewing the case with President Lowell of Harvard and President Stratton of MIT, upholding the Sacco-Vanzetti conviction had been an arduous duty that had reaffirmed the necessary forms of the laws of the Commonwealth. Fred Beal considered the two men innocent and saw their execution on August 23, 1927, as a ruthless attack on the "workingman and dreams of the Brotherhood of Man."[56]

The failure and discouragement of the Sacco-Vanzetti campaign drove Beal into the Communist party. "It seemed the most effective radical organization in the field, almost the only one that was really active in behalf of the workers."[57] He began organizing for the party's labor unions, first among the brass workers of Waterbury, Connecticut, and then the Boston office teamed him with another textile organizer, a Scotsman, William Murdoch, from Providence. In early 1928 they toured the province together, trying to establish an industrial union of textile workers. The new organization was called the Textile Mill Committees. Beal and Murdoch hoped to set up committees of all the workers in each mill, and then to join the mill committees in a city central committee and to join all these, in turn, into a new national union. As Beal and Murdoch set about their work, the New Bedford strike of cotton workers broke out, and they rushed to join it in the hope that they could wean the strikers away from their craft unions into the new Textile Mill Committees.[58]

The Boston province's southern textile concentration, with its center in Providence, stretched in a wide arc from Webster, Massachusetts, on the west, eastward to Fall River and the old whaling town of New Bedford, which had turned to the manufacture of fine cotton textiles. By 1928 New Bedford had fifty-six mills owned by twenty-seven separate corporations, which together employed 27,000 workers.[59] As elsewhere, the skilled men were organized into craft unions, which met together in a city-wide

Textile Council. Some unions also were affiliated with the AFL's United Textile Workers, whose headquarters was in New York City. In December 1927 the cotton manufacturers in Lowell began another round of wage cuts, adjusting piece rates downward, speeding up the machinery, and increasing work loads. In January 1928 the mill superintendents of New Bedford posted notices that there would soon be a 10 percent cut in wages. The reduction, the Manufacturers' Association said, was necesary for New Bedford to meet its competition and to counteract the current depression in the cotton trade.

It is a measure of the sickness of the community life of Boston's mill towns that despite at least two generations of walkouts and strikes, the mill superintendents still did not deal with their hundreds and thousands of employees in any organized fashion. They posted changes and dared the men and women to challenge their decision. There was no collective bargaining, either with the craft unions or the Textile Council of New Bedford, before the announcement of the wage reductions or the strike itself. It is a further measure of the sickness of Boston's mill communities that major strikes were lasting longer. The celebrated 1912 strike lasted 63 days; the 1919 strike of the three ministers, 108 days; the New Bedford strike of 1928 was to endure for 173 days, half a year.

On April 10 the local craft unions voted to demand a restoration of pay that had been cut or go on strike April 16. The owners refused to compromise, and 27,000 cotton operatives refused to report to work on April 16. Pickets cheered as the loom fixers carried out their tools. The girls outside the Pemaquid Mills did a snake dance up and down the street, singing "Hail! Hail! the Gang's All Here."[60] Two days later the secretary of the Textile Council of New Bedford warned the strikers against "William Murdoch and professional agitators."[61] There began a three-way conflict: Fred Beal and Murdoch had started by organizing Portuguese syndicalists in New Bedford into the new Textile Mill Committee,[62] and then their ranks grew with the addition of new-immigrant workers who had not been members of the English- and Irish-dominated craft unions. At seven o'clock each morning three groups of combatants appeared at the mill gates:

the Textile Council union pickets, the Textile Mill Committee pickets, and the New Bedford police.

This time there were no violent attacks on the pickets because the mill owners decided not to try to use strike-breakers. Instead the strike settled down to a war of attrition. The local union's strike relief fund soon ran out,[63] and the United Textile Workers raised funds for assistance. The Communist party also raised large sums for the New Bedford relief but, as Fred Beal later regretted, much of the money was diverted to support an army of Communist party missionaries who came to New Bedford to proselytize. Not enough was allocated to needy strikers. Beal reported that at the time he did not realize what was at issue in the decision to use relief funds for political organizers; Murdoch did understand, but he was threatened with a beating if he didn't consent to the practice.[64]

The Textile Mill Committee leaders tried to enlarge the strike by carrying it to neighboring Fall River, but the pay cuts had not been instituted there, and workers in Fall River did not want to strike in sympathy. Little was accomplished save some free-speech battles with the local police.[65] In New Bedford, despite repeated cries of "red," the manufacturers did not attempt any special campaign of repression. The police chief followed a policy of restraint, saying that he considered "a few broken windows better than a few broken heads."[66] Beal and Murdoch, however, endeavored to force the police to make arrests in order to keep their picket lines lively. Many striking workers were arrested repeatedly for minor infractions, and both Beal and Murdoch served short sentences in the House of Correction.[67] If the manufacturers had atttempted to open the mills with imported scabs, New Bedford would undoubtedly have exploded. As it was, one night in July, a rumor passed that scabs had been gathered under cover of darkness at a certain mill. Ten thousand people, according to the police estimate, converged on the mill, throwing stones and smashing windows. The rumor was false.[68] During the summer the manufacturers would open the mill gates from 6:45 to 7:15 each morning, but no more than fifty workers in all the city ever reported to work. At last, in October, the issue was compromised at a 5 percent cut in wages.[69] The New Bedford mills reopened, to fail a bit more before they closed for good.

Although the strike had surely lasted too long to justify settling for a pay cut, and although the Textile Mill Committee had failed to capture the New Bedford mills, Fred Beal had accomplished a lot. He had successfully organized many of the new immigrant workers and held them together in a radical industrial union. Today this may seem an ephemeral accomplishment, but given Beal's recent experience, such work held promise. Had not the textile craft unions repeatedly failed in 1912, 1919, and in 1924? Hadn't the strikes succeeded only when taken over by radicals preaching and demonstrating industrial unions and the unity of the entire working class? Surely, to have opened a major provincial mill city like New Bedford to such a message was an important forward step.

The Communist party thought so. They now regarded Fred Beal as one of their best union organizers. Attorney Albert Weisbrod, who had been active in that strike and earlier in Passaic, New Jersey, now planned a new industrial union, the National Textile Workers Union (1928–1934) with headquarters in New York City. Weisbrod planned a campaign for the northern knitting mills and the southern cotton workers.[70]

In his pride and his enthusiasm Beal did not realize the weakness and dangers of his personal situation. He knew he worked best on the picket line, in the coffee shops, and in the homes of the workers. Living among the workers and sharing their lives, Beal was an effective preacher of his gospel of union fellowship and the coming of the classless millennium. What he did not understand were the dangers of an evangelism that lacked an adequate theology and an appropriate church. Most particularly his hopes for workers' immediate economic gains and his feelings of solidarity with them were not compatible with the contemporary Communist party's goals for forming revolutionary unions. Neither did Beal realize that he had no effective counter appeal against those who sought to exploit anti-Communism.[71] Especially he lacked a message and tactics for the outside community that would observe anti-Communist repression. His experience prior to 1929 had been with the limited violence of the police in divided communities in the Boston province. He had no conception of the unified political, racial, and class repression of the American South.

A more cautious young man might have reflected upon the recent fate of his idol, William Haywood, who had died in a Moscow hospital on May 18, 1928. The IWW had been smashed by President Wilson's agents and Haywood convicted of sedition for his opposition to World War I. Unlike Eugene V. Debs, who accepted his jail sentence, Haywood fled to Russia, where he was received as a revolutionary hero. But an American evangelist for a syndicalist millennium had no role or message appropriate to a war-torn dictatorship. Haywood quickly declined into being a relic and drank himself to death.

In January 1929 Fred Beal arrived in Charlotte, North Carolina, to begin organizing for the National Textile Workers Union. Despite his reputation as a Communist, and the fear of workers that to join any union was to risk being fired, Beal made his way among the millhands, visiting their homes and listening to their special grievances.[72] After several months he found in Gastonia, North Carolina, a mill settlement ripe for action, Loray Village. Here the mill owners, Manville-Jenckes of Pawtucket, Rhode Island, had for two years been stretching out the work, substituting children for men and women, and cutting wages.[73]

Beal led a gallant two-month strike in Loray Village that ended when someone shot the police chief during a vigilante attack on union headquarters. He and six other men were arrested. The subsequent trials of the "Gastonia Seven" became a national cause, but in the end Fred Beal was falsely convicted and sentenced to seventeen to twenty years in prison.[74]

At this crucial moment in his life, Fred Beal faltered, and instead of continuing his mission, he became a prisoner of the Communist party and the state of North Carolina. It is clear from his autobiography that he had no sense of a role as a political prisoner, no idea, as Eugene V. Debs and A. J. Muste had, that serving time in prison might be part of a successful long-term political campaign.[75] Like Haywood, he fled to Russia. But he hated Russia, and secretly returned to the United States, only to be persuaded by his American comrades that his flight from Russia would be bad publicity for the Soviet Union and therefore a blow against the advance of world communism. Once again he returned to the Soviet Union. From September 1931 through Sep-

tember 1933 he served as a labor functionary in the Karkov trac-
tor factory, where he was appalled by the powerlessness of both
Russian and foreign workers. He also witnessed the atrocities
committed against the Ukrainian peasants by which they were
starved into collectivization. In January 1934 he managed to
sneak back into the United States under an assumed name.[76] His
father lent him some money to start out, and he seems to have
worked at odd jobs and to have been passed about by the non-
Communist left. The American Communist party regarded Beal
now as anathema, and through articles in the *Daily Worker* reported his presence in the United States. Beal also believed that
the party assisted in his ultimate detection and arrest on January
19, 1938.[77]

Throughout most of 1934 and 1935 he lived in Los Angeles,
writing his autobiography. Working through the playwright and
screenwriter Sidney C. Howard and the journalist and editor
Isaac Don Levine, he arranged to have his account of his experiences published. The Russian years were immediately in demand
because Beal's account constituted a refutation of the benevolence
of Communist practice. The socialist and anti-Communist New
York newspaper, the *Jewish Daily Forward*, first published
Beal's material in a Yiddish translation during the summer of
1935. The headline read: "Famous American Communist Tells of
His Four Years Living in Soviet Russia." It went on, "Fred Beal,
the leader of several communist strikes in the United States, the
famous martyr of the workers' trial in Gastonia, has left Soviet
Russia and writes his impressions for the *Forward* . . . The division of Soviet society into classes is sharp, deep and astonishing.
The class division is felt in every factory in an indescribable
manner."[78]

Next, perhaps through Isaac Levine, who had been a Hearst reporter, the Hearst press took an interest. Then, on September 4,
1937, the *American Mercury* published the article "I Was a Communist Martyr," simultaneously with the publication of Beal's
autobiography, *Proletarian Journey*. This publicity seems to
have enraged both the Communist party and Governor Clyde R.
Hoey of North Carolina, who had been one of the prosecuting
attorneys in the Gastonia case. Fred, in turn, became bolder and,

in what he later thought was a foolish move, appeared at an anti-CIO union meeting in Lawrence.[79] Some months later, on January 19, 1938, after fleeing his New York City apartment for fear of apprehension, he was arrested by Lawrence police at his brother's house at one in the morning.

A defense committee quickly formed, but Fred Beal decided not to fight his extradition from Massachusetts. What he wanted, but what the North Carolina authorities steadfastly refused to concede, was a full and complete pardon as recognition of his innocence.[80] On February 16, 1938, he surrendered to the sheriff in Raleigh, North Carolina, and began serving his sentence.[81] He kept his health and sanity by working hard on the prison farm. Meanwhile his defense committee continued to work in his behalf. In June 1939, Governor Hoey denied his application for a pardon but did reduce his sentence.[82] By now Beal's position in the United States had frozen. He must be an anti-Communist witness. Accordingly, on October 18, 1939, accompanied by an armed guard, he was summoned before the Dies Committee of Congress to tell his story one more time.[83] Finally, on January 8, 1942, his supporters obtained his parole, and a friend secured him a job in a knitting mill.[84]

Six years later, appearing before the Superior Court judge in Gastonia, Beal won back his forfeited United States citizenship. In making the grant, the local judge said he appreciated Mr. Beal's early warnings against Communism.[85] Fred Beal returned to the province to live out his life in Lawrence and Maine.[86]

The mill town world of immigrant workers and socialist preachers that had first wakened Fred Beal had now perished in economic depression and world war. A cast-off at fifty-one years of age, Beal was an empty husk, like the mill towns of Boston. "A man is a bundle of relations, a knot of roots," the provincial philosopher had said. "He cannot live without a world."[87] Fred Beal died in Lawrence, Massachusetts, November 15, 1954.

IV ❧ THE PROVINCE DIVIDED

ANYONE WHO TRAVELS about the Boston province today can see the signs of the unequal divisions of the culture. Generally, the least powerful elements are the most obvious because the most powerful are invisible. Boston's famous electronic research highway, Route 128, is graded and planted in a manner reminiscent of a turn-of-the-century parkway. Its factories and offices are screened behind remnants of forest or set off on lawns like buildings on a college campus. We find it reassuring to place our rocket factories, insurance brokers, television studios, and computer designers in settings that pretend a link to harmonious designs of man and nature.

The vast new suburban tracts built since World War II are farms for families and children; the more wealthy the farm, the more gardened and forested are the families' settings and the more isolated visually from the motive power of our culture: the commercial strip, the suburban factory, and the downtown office. Today's Boston hero is an incongruous blend of science, business, and sentimentality. He is a scientist who has successfully established a small electronics firm in the remains of an old textile mill; his nearby ranch home has an office retreat with a computer terminal placed so that the young entrepreneur can observe the birds in the forest beyond. These juxtapositions of massive highways, high-technology work, segregated family life, and a restless prodding of nature for emotional sustenance are symptoms of deep cleavages in our knowledge and understanding.

For the past few decades the new culture of reason, science and its manifold applications, has brought prosperity to the Boston province. The American Woolen Company's huge Assabet Mill in Maynard now houses the Digital Equipment Corporation, the company's Shawsheen Mills in Andover contain the new Raytheon Corporation, and the surviving part of the Wood Mill in Lawrence, formerly the world's largest worsted manufacturing plant, has been taken over by the Honeywell Corporation, a midwestern migrant to the province.[1] These replacements, and the many new plants and offices about the province, are signs of the triumph of the scientific culture in research, in teaching, in engineering, and in business. Each year the scientific mode of thought is more dominant, and as it captures more and more of our attention and imagination, what it neglects becomes an ever more menacing ignorance.

These divisions in our culture began in the nineteenth century with the growth of science and social science as special modes of thought and investigation. As they advanced, each subspecialty became an academy in its own right for which special training was required to master its teaching. It is not difficult now, with the benefit of hindsight, to imagine some concerted educational effort that might have counteracted this splintering, but in the past the province lacked the imagination and the power for such reforms. People were imprisoned in the belief in deep separations between science and life, reason and feeling, engineering and art, work and family, women and men. These divisions found social expression in the separate education of women, the isolation of science from art and literature, the segregations of the home, and the isolation of the emotions. As women, Laura Richards and Emily Greene Balch had been brought up in the old literary and romantic culture of the mid-nineteenth century. Then, the one as a married clubwoman and social reformer and the other as a single woman making her way in the new social science of economics had to build upon that cultural base. Their contemporaries, Charles Stone and Edwin Webster, however, trained in electrical engineering, knew nothing of the processes of locating values through human relationships or of how, by attending to emotions, one might find routes to important kinds of truth.

For a time these divisions in the culture seemed not to matter, since the newly educated college women seemed able to carry the old romantic ideas outward into the concerns and conflicts of the modern world. Meanwhile the men explored the new science and its applications in engineering, medicine, business, and administration. In the long run, however, the isolation and political weakness of the women's share of the culture and its institutions proved a fatal flaw, both for the special domain relegated to them and for the ever more powerful scientific culture itself.

Single women, like Emily Balch, had stood at the forefront of women's cultural explorations because they had the time and freedom to develop careers.[2] Their lives advanced from volunteer work to professional training to careers in settlement houses, charity organizations, municipal and state civil service, and college teaching. In such life courses these leaders learned and developed a politics of fact finding, public agitation, lobbying, and electioneering; for them it was possible, as it was not for most married women, to link knowledge to action, and personal values to politics.

Behind these single women leaders came a large army of married women who sought to expand the scope of their lives and who supported the new causes. Their time and loyalties, however, had to be managed within the terms of their households. After some decades of cooperation between the single and the married, the dominance of the politics of family life defeated the women's cultural efforts and reform campaigns of the early twentieth century.

Because women did not vote until 1920, save for an occasional school or municipal election, the power of married women in public life derived in large part from the special prevailing ideology of the turn-of-the-century home.[3]

> Ev'ry sorrow or care in the dear days gone by,
> Was made bright by the light of the smile in your eye;
> Like a candle that's set in the window at night
> Your fond love has cheered me, and guided me right.
>
> Sure I love the dear silver that shines in your hair,
> And the brow that's all furrowed, and wrinkled with care.
> I kiss the dear fingers, so toil-worn for me,
> Oh, God! bless and keep you, Mother Machree![4]

Such sentiment spread thickly over the province from Maine to Rhode Island, from Laura Richards's clubs, to the comfortable family parishes of Edwin O'Connor's Dorchester, to Mary Antin's South End tenements. Hopes for peace, care, and security transformed the house or flat into an imagined Garden of Eden presided over by the Madonna and Child. The goal of an idyllic place for family and children gave married women, especially politically organized married women, a good deal of power and attention when they spoke on issues pertaining to children, health, homes, women, food, schools, and the like.[5] Yet whether we recall these days in anger or in nostalgia, it is important to remember that someone always built a fence about the idyllic garden, just as Samuel Gridley Howe had built a fence about his Julia and his children.

The fence was, and still remains, the essence of married women's life and politics. Within the fence the woman was expected to be totally responsible, a caregiver who offered nurture, support, tolerance, and respect to children, husband, relatives, and the intimate friends of the family. What happened outside the fence she need not be concerned with. Thereby the politics of the home, the politics that every girl learned from her mother and father, was what we would call today the politics of segregation. It was not the politics of conflict and bargaining, it was a method of wielding power by including and excluding. The politics of the home belonged to those with little power save the ability to refuse and ignore. The modern segregated metropolitan region mirrors this social arrangement.

For a time at the turn of the century, married women tried to enlarge the compass of their concern, to break down the fence surrounding their homes and their motherhood. Picking up new ideas of life beyond the Victorian front piazza or the backyard laundry lines, these women saw the possibility of creating wider and richer worlds for themselves and their children. To achieve these ends they employed Laura Richards's tactics. First they organized into all sorts of formal clubs and informal associations to promote the idea that through education and public action the home could be brought into harmony with its environment. They imagined a world in which the home need not be surrounded with such antithetical forces as ignorance, poverty, disease, and the ill use of man and nature. Woman's clubs sprang up in very large numbers at the turn of the century, especially in the new middle-class suburbs. The formal agendas of these clubs nicely stated what married women hoped to find beyond their homes: natural history, literature, art, travel, gardening, nursery and kindergarten education, scholarships for talented high school graduates. They attacked sweatshops, bad sanitation, alcohol abuse, and prostitution. For all their miscellany, these topics were informed by a sensible concept. The club idea was that through self-education in science, art, and literature women could improve themselves and their homes, and as educated women working together they could transform the environment around them to approximate the standards they held for themselves. The only issues unique to women in these agendas were those of suffrage and the special circumstances of women's employment.[6]

As in all clubs, promoting warmth, tolerance, and aid within the group required erecting barriers without. In the Boston province in the twentieth century the most common barriers were the separation of the middle class from those below and the divisions of the middle class along religious and ethnic lines, thereby placing Catholics, Jews, and blacks largely outside the club movement. In many towns and cities the symbol of the barrier was an organization formed around a Revolutionary or pre-Revolutionary theme, that is, the town's heritage before the large-scale immigration of non-Protestants. So in Somerville, a mixed residential suburb and manufacturing satellite of Boston, the local woman's club banner warned off the unclubbable with symbols of colonial times and the days of the Revolution. Perhaps the new and almost all-residential middle-class suburb of Newton, with its dozen recorded woman's clubs, more closely resembled the ideal of a club for everyone who wanted to join, regardless of religious affiliation or ethnic origin.[7] In any case, as in Gardiner, Maine, these urban and suburban woman's clubs were part of a spectrum of local organizations, ranging from committees of both men and women for libraries, schools, parks, and hospitals, to groups of women for suffrage and, later, chapters of the League of Women Voters.

Education is the most challenging expression of family goals, and it was through education that the ambitions of family life were translated into community activities. In the late nineteenth and early twentieth century the list of social inventions sponsored, if not always managed, by middle-class Boston women was quite extraordinary in its richness and variety: the kindergarten and nursery school, the playground and fresh air camp, the settlement house, community school classes for adults, industrial and commercial high schools, and the all-community high school. In the big cities and mill towns these innovations were designed to relieve the narrowness and harshness of daily life and to bring some of the benefits of the middle class to immigrants' and workers' families. In the suburbs, where much of the town could be built afresh and where the intrusions of factory and offices were few, the entire community could be organized as a school. Thus, in a mixed industrial satellite like Somerville, women undertook all the reforms of the day, but their efforts faced continuing conflicts among class and ethnic groups.[8] By contrast, in the new bedroom town of Newton, religious and ethnic divisions could be overcome by a consensus for making the entire town a school for the nurture of families and their children.[9]

Although deeply flawed by the politics of contemporary family life and by its class, religious, and ethnic prejudices and exclusions, turn-of-the-century women's campaigns gathered sufficient power and approval to permanently transform the provincial landscape. These campaigns touched upon the popular sentimental forms of romanticism that have survived in the province, sustained by vague religious and emotional searches for harmony in nature. The popular climate allowed married women's ambitions for family nurture to spread outward from the home into schools and local politics, from suburban front yards and vegetable gardens to campaigns for public parks and the management of the provincial landscape.[10]

A leader of the landscape side of the sentimental movement, Charles Eliot (1859–1897), put the matter this way in 1890. "A crowded population thirsts, occasionally at least, for the sight of something very different from the public garden, square, or ballfield. The railroads and the new electric street railways which radiate from the Hub carry many thousands every pleasant Sunday through the suburbs to the real country, and hundreds out of these thousands make the journey for the sake of the refreshment which an occasional hour or two spent in the country brings to them."[11] This statement appeared in an open letter marking the beginning of Eliot's successful campaign to establish a philanthropic organization of nature lovers to preserve scenic bits of landscape as parks or for the use of visitors and later generations. From this campagn came The Trustees of Reservations, which remains an active and expanding organization in the state and a model for all sorts of preservation and conservation trusts elsewhere.[12]

For his proposals Eliot had enlisted the aid of the Appalachian Mountain Club, an organization of men and women, college teachers of geography and geology, amateur natural history enthusiasts, and hikers. Founded in 1876, the club had over a thousand members by 1900, but more significant, it brought together through its membership men and women, wealthy estate owners and landscape gardeners, suburban putterers and appreciators. Thereby it spoke with power and authority, and throughout the late nineteenth and early twentieth century it was enormously influential as the parent of other landscape and conservation organizations. For example, the Appalachian Mountain Club led the campaign for both Boston's metropolitan park system and the setting aside of the White Mountain National Forest (1911).[13]

For a time during the late nineteenth century the popular education practices of academic science even allowed women's drive for education to be combined with men's scientific research institutions. The now world-famous Woods Hole marine institutions were the product of cooperation among universities, the federal government, private philanthropists, and the Woman's Educational Association.[14]

After World War I all this momentum for social exploration, institutional reform, and public gardening lost its force. It collapsed in part because of the direct attack through a reactionary political campaign by local businessmen and large industrialists who wanted to beat back labor unions and government regulation—reforms that had been sponsored by women.[15] In part the movement died from the closing off of the next generation of recruits through the liberation of girls and young women from family controls, so that young women no longer felt the need for women's organizations.[16] The power and ideology of mother and home, however, was not destroyed by dancing high school and college youth, or high-society partying. The married women's cultural explorations and reform movements suffered destruction from two major causes. The first was the retreat into privatism of middle-class women; the second was the growing power of science, which excluded, confined, and trivialized women's concerns and women's knowledge.

For most married women the clubs, reading, volunteer work, and support for social reforms had been undertaken, as they had to be, in family terms, that is, within the politics of contemporary married life. When married women discovered the world beyond, they could only visit it, at most. Therefore, when they had successfully accomplished their reforms within their own communities, which were becoming more affluent, a good deal of the urgency for continued organization and political action dissolved.

In looking back on these years we often forget that the reforms proposed by the middle classes for the poor were the very ones the suburbanites wanted for themselves. So whatever the failings in the mill towns and slums of public libraries, kindergartens, well-baby clinics, milk programs, visiting nurse associations, hospitals, reading campaigns, or high schools, these same efforts brought excellent institutions to the suburbs. Moreover, in the controversial area of education, the affluent suburban family could choose among ambitious public schools, Protestant nonsectarian academies, and Episcopal and Catholic parochial schools.[17] The automobile also allowed larger suburban house lots and easy access to country and seashore, thereby transforming the whole metropolitan fringe into a potential resort. New fashions added tennis and golf to Victorian croquet, country clubs to garden clubs, radio and movies to card playing, cocktails to tea. Each year during the first three decades of the twentieth century found some major enrichment added to the possibilities and practices of middle-class family life. For many, then, especially in the postwar years, private familial solutions seemed a satisfactory conclusion to the public efforts of previous generations.

If one considers the generations of the past in terms of the ambition of their reach, then surely the generation of the twenties represents a retreat by married women into the confines of family concerns. The former alliances of women across classes, organizations like the Women's Trade Union and the Consumer's League, faltered, and shops and mills disappeared from even the imagined domain of family concern. In space, of course, the middle classes flourished. With the automobile, the new segregated resort and suburban environments extended far beyond the orderly blocks and front porches of earlier times. In schooling each new generation exceeded its predecessor. In every decade of the twentieth century more and more women completed high school, and more and more attended college. Yet in this formal education the women were denied professional training and discouraged from studying the new science. Since the young women also lacked the motives of personal liberation that had driven the collegians before them, they also ceased to press the boundaries of the old literary and romantic culture that they were given.

Romanticism, the conviction that people and objects must be valued according to personal relationships, continued to flourish among the middle-class women of the Boston province, but authentic relationships retreated into the domestic sphere rather than extending outward to the province and the empire. Suburban women in these years could be wonderfully skillful, energetic, and inventive in their activities, but they ceased to be exploring a culture that was of use to the larger world. In Boston one of the most attractive, lively, forceful and good-natured of that generation of women was Louise Andrews Kent, and in her elaboration of the domestic role she demonstrated the married woman's retreat.

The decline of women's cultural explorations and reforms is a matter of far greater concern than just the family inheritance of the daughters and sons of the province. Given the divisions in our dominantly scientific culture between science and human experience, reason and feeling, work and family, men and women, the bottling up of our formerly lively romantic tradition into the leisure-time fantasies of men and the domestic compass of women was a decisive event in determining the present life of the province.

This loss of one important segment of our tradition occurred at the very moment when science and engineering began to cast off their social connections. During the nineteenth century, during the decades of inventors, mechanics, and inspired tinkerers, the application of science had been strongly rooted in the everyday social situation. Power looms took the place of hand weaving, steam forges replaced the blacksmith's arm, railroads took over from horse-drawn wagons and coaches, sewing machines and shoe stitchers replaced needles, thimbles, and awls. Yet as this technology advanced from mechanics to chemistry, from steam pressure to thermodynamics and the physics of electricity, the processes of science began to supersede the immediate discipline of the workshop and the market.

Science proceeds along its own pathways. Scientists, guided by previous training, follow their own curiosity toward questions they think can be answered. It is thus an activity of specialists, the work of loose academies following clusters of questions; its fashions are not dictated by social necessity or market potential. A famous Boston electrical engineer and imperial science administrator, Vannevar Bush, recorded this shift in the processes of invention, which had taken place during his own lifetime. "There are two main ways of going about inventing," he observed. "One is to see a public need, or desire, and scurry about to find a way of meeting it. The other is to develop new knowlege and see where it leads."[18] The first style is the old Boston way of Elias Howe and his sewing machine; the second is the present way of giant offices and laboratories and computers and genetic research.

It was during the twenties that the province of Boston plunged into the unknowns of a world of imperial economies and self-propelled science. As the depth of the depression in the textile and shoe industries grew ever clearer, it became apparent that no one could predict which products or which industries might ease unemployment or bring new wealth. At the same time, such invention as went forward in the province depended more and more upon the uncertainties and indeterminacies of modern science.

Today no one knows where modern science will carry us, just as no one in the past could foretell the course of history with looms, lasters, and stitchers. Yet in prosperity there is a special danger because we imagine that modern research institutions, either in the university or business, have a strategy for mastering uncertainty. But the immediate road to today's success mocks that pride. Our intellectual and industrial achievements have always been highly contingent, and especially as they have grown to depend upon the application of complex science the realms of uncertainty have multiplied. The province's progress from a textile and shoe depression to success in electronics and computing has been a careening course of hunches, gambles and difficult financial choices. Even the giant research institutions and programs of the federal government are guesses and leaps into the fog of uncertainty.

To recall the early years and career of Vannevar Bush and the life of his business partner Laurence K. Marshall is to confront both the unpredictability of modern Boston culture and its ignorance. Although Louise Andrews Kent, Vannevar Bush and Laurence K. Marshall could not be farther apart in their ambitions and achievements—a writing housewife, an imperial science administrator, and a businessman—together they recall the deep flaws in today's prosperous Boston culture. All three lived by a false sense of mastery and control.

9 ❧ LOUISE ANDREWS KENT

Even though Louise Andrews Kent (1886–1969) spent her entire lifetime in the comfortable suburban neighborhoods of South Brookline, various factors, including the fickleness of cotton trading and the early death of her mother, kept Kent during her youth at a slight remove from the settled security of *haute bourgeois* Boston family life. Her father, Walter Edward Andrews, was an immigrant, a Cunarder, who came to Boston soon after the Civil War. The youngest of eleven children in an English country family, he made his way in Boston offices to become a partner in a firm of cotton buyers.[1] For many years his fortunes rose and fell with the firm's trading successes. Since he had no extra capital to invest in a house, his family moved about from rental to rental, and in a bad year, 1899, they stayed in Mrs. Wood's boarding house on Walnut Street, Brookline.[2]

Louise's mother, Mary Sophronia Edgerly, was descended from a long line of New Englanders. Educated in private schools, she married at nineteen and bore three children, Katherine (1884), Louise, and Oliver (1888). She was a natural athlete who became as much of a sportswoman as a Victorian housewife might by playing tennis, shooting, swimming, and riding. At the Country Club in Brookline she won the first women's golf tournament ever played in the United States. In 1899, when Louise was thirteen, Mary Andrews died of influenza. Louise went to live with her grandmother and aunt until 1902, when her father built a fine Queen Anne style–house at 44 Edge Hill Road.[3]

Louise was a near-sighted, bookish girl, not an athlete like her mother, and as a child she "was often dragged to the baseball field or croquet lawn, book in hand, reading until something had to be done about a ball."[4] She was fascinated by words and stories, and her teachers encouraged her to write. In college she sold her first story, and soon thereafter she took up writing a chatty column, "Theresa's Tea Table," for the daily *Boston Traveler*. In time she mastered a style whereby she told brief tales of everyday home life. Her best work was always a dramatization of a domestic incident, told either in the first person or through her popular persona, the middle-aged Mrs. Appleyard. The stories were always reassuring, each one ending happily.

Unlike Robert Grant, whose novels of the previous generation had presented the *haute bourgeois* of Boston as strange creatures whom the reader might enjoy examining, Kent stood close to her readers, offering food. Her tone was hearty, never stuffy, full of fun. She made gentle sport of herself and the follies of extreme fashions in clothes and manners. As the well-educated, well-trained woman of the older generation, she taught a provincial version of good taste in possessions, family rituals, and manners. In her little dramatized incidents the reader was always assured that the well-to-do were just like herself, only they had a bit more money, manners, and possessions. Like the new automobile suburb itself, Louise Kent meant for her style of middle-class family life to spread itself widely across the metropolises of the United States. Like Emily Post, she taught the manners and styles of an older woman of means to a large audience of younger middle-class women who were making their own homes without the guidance of either tradition or wealth.

In her autobiography, written at the age of eighty, she reviewed her life in this same format, rewriting the many stories she had used before.[5] What emerged was a good-natured description of the domestic retreat of twentieth-century married women, indeed a kind of narrative of the steps from the old-style family confinement of girls and young women to the modern, more expressive and free middle-class styles.

In 1892, at the age of six, Louise entered a small private school, Miss Pierce's School (now called the Park School), already knowing how to read and to write. In the fashion of the day she was rapidly promoted from grade to grade. Indeed, the only classwork challenge she reported of her grammer school years was the labor of penmanship, the demand that she copy long sentimental poems in a perfect hand without making an ink blot or stain.[6]

In fourth grade Louise switched to a large public grammar school, the Lawrence School, a forbidding building, a class as big as her entire former school, and a strict, nervous teacher. She was terrified, and her mother was extremely anxious too. Characteristically, Kent later told of her fear and discomfort in terms of the clothes she and her mother had worn. "I clung to my mother's hand . . . My mother helped me hang up my new plaid coat and my velvet bonnet with the ostrich feather curling over my left eye . . . She straightened out my guimpe of muslin and Hamburg lace and my dress of red wool . . . She had on her new bonnet of white roses and bird of paradise plumes. She wore her best cape of dark blue brocade with the red of a bluebird breast"[7] and so forth. Like many novelists and music hall impresarios before her, and like contemporary Hollywood movie makers, Kent offered her readers a detailed tour of the possessions of the rich. At the end of the description of this commonplace incident of a child's terror in a new school, she reported that a classmate took pity on her tears, comforted her, and the two became friends for life.[8]

So the stories proceeded through the memory of childhood. At thirteen she was a tomboy, the biggest in her gang, and she "even knocked down some of those who challenged our group in battle. The Cutler boys who lived further up the street were considered dangerous . . . Yet I had once laid two of them low."[9] At fourteen she was miserable in hand-me-down dresses, but she took the horse cars to Copley Square where, in the hall over S. S. Pierce's Store, a Miss Carroll conducted dancing classes for Back Bay and Brookline boys and girls. It was two-steps and waltzes now, not the sets of Robert Grant's day, and although Louise was not the first chosen, because she "lacked glamour," she was skillful and escaped the tortures of the last-chosen.[10]

In her autobiography Kent did not dwell on the shock of her mother's death. After a short tribute to her mother, she plunged into an account of the friendships of high school and the chal-

lenge and stimulation of the teachers at Miss Haskell's School, a
private girls' preparatory school in the Back Bay.[11] Although
Louise passed the entrance examinations to Radcliffe, her aunt and
grandmother enrolled her in 1902 in the new Simmons College
Library School, just then opening on the Fenway margin between
Boston and Brookline. Kent did not say why she was so passive
and content to follow that course. All she said was that the two
old ladies "remembered that my mother, seeing me with my nose
in a book as usual, had remarked, 'that child ought to be a librarian.' "[12] Most likely Louise wanted to continue her education, but
she also wanted to follow the *haute bourgeois* path of becoming a
debutante and partying around and visiting friends and relatives
as a prelude to marriage.

Her father built the Edge Hill Road house so that his daughters, Katherine and Louise, could present themselves for marriage
and entertain with teas, dinners, and dances.[13] Kent was at her
best retelling the tales of her debutante and courtship days: the
sessions with the dressmaker, the dresses themselves, the gifts of
flowers and candy, the custom of calling cards, the Harvard football game, the wedding gown and ceremony. As she recalled
these scenes, she was at once the insider who enjoyed it all and
the outsider who could gently mock its bygone rituals. In her junior year she dropped out of college to devote herself to serious
partying for three years. She met her future husband, Ira Rich
Kent (Tufts College 1899) at her own coming-out tea, November
23, 1905, but seven years of courtship followed before they married.[14]

What stands out as remarkable to today's reader is not the styl-
ish accessories to a fashionable girl's life, but the degree to which
Louise was still encapsulated within the boundaries of family relationships and acquaintanceships. As a college girl she had come
out into society, but the city that surrounded her and her society
was still, for her, a network of homes and parlors. It lacked even
settlement houses, and it knew nothing of immigrant quarters or
mill towns.

The domestic rounds of her young married friends, however,
did not seem to offer Louise any possibilities; a life filled with
babies, nursemaids, cards, luncheons, and golf seemed a boring

alternative to her single state. Accordingly, when Ira Kent proposed to her by mail after two years of courtship, twenty-one-year-old Louise turned him down. She wasn't ready for marriage, she replied. She finished her college work, graduating with honors in 1909, then began writing her column for the *Boston Traveler*. On Christmas Eve 1911 she was ready for marriage. Fully togged, and following the feints and sallies of a fashionable walk through the park with her young man, Louise Andrews, sitting on a bench beside Jamaica Pond, proposed to Ira Rich Kent, and he accepted her.[15]

It was Louise Kent's genius to make her married life into a public career. She had studied *haute bourgeois* life with intense interest, and she intended as a bride to make something expressive of herself out of that style. As she elaborated and altered the rituals and activities of the style she had inherited, she became a provincial Boston guide to modern suburban life.

It all began with a room full of gifts and an elaborate Brookline wedding in May 1912. There followed a honeymoon on Monhegan Island, Maine, visits to relatives and family friends in New York, Philadelphia, and Baltimore, and settling into a small basement apartment on Chestnut Street on Beacon Hill.[16] Her husband went off to his job nearby as an editor of a children's magazine, and Louise and her young live-in maid, Minnie Wiggs, began keeping house.[17] Having been gently raised, Kent then knew nothing of cooking, she said, but she had inherited a taste for fine food and for table settings of china, silver, and crystal. She was, however, an omniverous reader, indeed she boasted of a lifetime average of one and a half books per day.[18] Guided by inspiring articles in the *Ladies Home Journal* and recipes from the Fanny Farmer cookbook she had received as a bride, she and her inexperienced maid explored the art of cooking. Pregnant by August and depressed by November, Louise characteristically decided to deny her state of depression and put on a cheerful front for her husband's return each evening. She did, however, persuade him that a basement apartment was no place to raise a baby, so in February they returned to her familiar South Brookline and a rented house next to a park.[19] There she bore two of her three children, Elizabeth, called "Kenty" (1913), and Hollister, nicknamed "Sam" (1916). The youngest child, Rosamond Mary, or "Posy" (1922) was born in the house the Kents purchased on Pill Hill, a few blocks from Edge Hill Road.[20] For servants first came young Mary O'Brien, a plain cook who thought "Elizabeth . . . the cutest thing she ever saw,"[21] and then seventeen-year-old Margaret O'Malley, who worked for the Kents for seventeen years before starting her own family

Soon Kent was summering in various places about the province, in Peterborough, New Hampshire, and Pocasset, on Buzzards Bay, Massachusetts, and canning fruits and vegetables for pleasure. Next her husband asked her to test recipes for his magazine. During World War I she served as a block captain for Herbert Hoover's Emergency Food Program, visiting forty families, urging her neighbors to cook whale meat and to substitute eggs for chops. There followed a lifetime of recipe collecting and of providing an ample, and at times luxurious, table for her family and friends. Like her contemporary Irma Louise Rombauer (1877–1962), Kent almost always worked with the companionship and help of a cook. When her daughters married, the cooking ripened into handwritten cookbooks for each. Finally, all this experience blossomed forth as the author's public persona, the good-natured and friendly Mrs. Appleyard, purveyor of recipes and of gentle humor about domestic life.[22]

In her concentration on food Kent followed the wisdom that in serving food, in gathering husband, children, and friends at the table, one could establish domestic rituals, from which many dimensions of a family could grow. As she progressed from the bride's china, crystal, and silver to corn roasts on the lawn and picnics in the mountains, she followed this domestic insight. In *Mrs. Appleyard's Year* she told how at the dinner table the family recognized its special outlook on the world and confirmed its members' roles by repeating family stories and jokes. Husband and wife taught the names and relationships of distant relatives, and the seasons of the year drove the cycle of menus with its repetition of family favorites.[23]

Like Laura Richards's writing, Kent's career paralleled the progress of her children. Her husband was a very successful editor at the Boston publishing firm of Houghton Mifflin, and so neither the provincial textile depression nor the international Great Depression constricted the family.[24] Kent was able to extend her ambitions for her children with a full selection of home activities, private schools, and summer camps and vacations. In the summer of 1915, soon after Dorothy Canfield Fisher had published her influential books on Maria Montessori's teaching methods for young children, Louise purchased a set of Montessori materials and began to instruct her eldest daughter. Elizabeth responded so readily to her mother's teaching that when she later was sent to the Park School, her reading and writing skills carried her immediately to the third grade.[25] Two years later Kenty suffered some sort of eye trouble, so her mother began an elaborate doll house project to entertain both child and mother. The doll house was from Louise's own childhood. Kent later recalled the doll house project with a flash of good-natured perspective on her own interests and ambitions in the convalescent undertaking. "Exactly what the effect on Kenty's eyes was, I can't remember, but we both acquired a sense of scale which has come in handy with my work on my miniature rooms ... No one has more fun than I do."[26]

Later, when her son's teachers complained that he was doing poorly in arithmetic, Kent mobilized her family to create a toy soldier business. Together they cast, painted, and sold lead soldiers, and carried on an elaborate accounting. "When Sam went to Milton Academy, we wound up the affairs of the company. We retired the stock, the only one of my investment list that paid ten percent right through the stock market crash of 1929 and the worst of the depression. The bonds and notes were paid off. We still owned almost three hundred dollars' worth of molds and we had two hundred dollars in cash. With it we bought a canoe ... Sam and I both had slight cases of lead poisoning, but the school had ceased to comment unfavorably on his arithmetic. On the whole the project was a success."[27]

With her children attending three different private schools—the Park School in Brookline, Milton Academy in Milton, and the Winsor School in Boston—Kent's life in the late twenties fell into the modern suburban mother's rhythm of child chauffeuring. In 1927, with her youngest at school, she began a pattern of writing during the mornings, between delivering the children to school and picking them up. Her first book was a re-imagining of her own childhood on her grandfather's summer place at Iron Bound Island, off the coast of the Maine resort town of Bar Harbor. Kent called the formula of this book, *Douglas of Porcupine* (1931), a union of *Treasure Island* and *Little Women.* In the absence of a father the children in the book created a Garden of Eden. Later, confined to bed with a bad back and encouraged by her youngest daughter's questions, Kent began writing *Two Children of Tyre* (1932), a portrait of life in ancient times as seen through the eyes of children. She perfected this theme in a highly successful series of books in which a fictional boy followed a grown-up historical hero. *He Went with Marco Polo* (1935) opened the series, which ended with *He Went with Drake* (1961), published when Kent was seventy-five years old.[28]

During her children's school years Kent also tried her hand at adult novels, writing *The Terrace* in 1934 and *Paul Revere Square* in 1939. As in life, so in fiction: Kent's characters moved about entirely fenced in by families. *The Terrace* was set in a cotton mill town north of Boston, the other in Louisburg Square on Beacon Hill. Where Robert Grant had done his best to explore the relationships among his characters' goals and actions and the larger world of business and politics, Kent's people all maneuvered within the narrow compass of homes. The Great Depression and the war in China set the background, but the subject under study was always the women in the parlor and the dining room. Families inherited fortunes, which were spent or added to, and the various fixed men characters were either family builders or family destroyers. In *The Terrace* World War I crippled a promising son, and the depression turned an old playboy into a conscientious mill treasurer, but these were just the givens the women had to work with. The real focus of the action was two young interior decorators who found husbands and cared for the next generation of children.

In Louise Kent's day the neoclassical revival ruled fashionable taste, especially in the Boston province where many old houses and buildings survived from the past century of colonial and federal designs.[29] When Kent was the head of the Simmons College

Club of Boston, she ran meetings in Boston's West End at the Harrison Gray Otis House, which the newly founded Society for the Preservation of New England Antiquities had purchased and was then restoring. Her own house at 17 Hawthorne Road in Brookline was one of a pair of imitations of large Salem federal-style houses, built in the 1890s.[30]

Actually it was through her husband's inheritance of a family farm in Vermont that Louise Kent found a pattern for uniting all her various domestic interests and activities into a coherent statement. The summer place offered her a chance, as wife, mother, and writer, to participate in the then-popular imagined tradition of the colonial and nineteenth-century Yankee. Ira Rich Kent's family, which had settled in Vermont in the late eighteenth century, owned a collection of houses and barns at Kent's Corner, Calais, in the north-central part of the state, about fifteen miles from Montpelier. The farm was a living antique when Louise Kent visited it as a bride. In time she succeeded to the Vermont place herself, and she devoted much of her life to restoring its early nineteenth-century detail, as well as fitting it out for her many hobbies and collections.

Louise began her historical revival career in the summer of 1918 by scraping and refinishing a set of Hitchcock chairs and by sewing squares for her mother-in-law to quilt. From collecting antique china and furniture, stenciling and refinishing, gardening and arranging flowers, she proceeded to taking color photographs in 1930 and lecturing to garden clubs.[31] These hobbies and lectures received their more finished expression in a children's book on Boston history written with her daughter Elizabeth Kent Gay, *In Good Old Colony Times* (1941), and in an adult picture book of photographs and historical notes, *Village Greens of New England* (1948). The popular version of this mix of suburban crafts and New England historicizing was the very successful Appleyard series that flowered from the 1941 best-seller, *Mrs. Appleyard's Year*, and continued with recipe articles in *House Beautiful* and *The Ladies Home Journal* and some cookbooks written with Elizabeth.[32]

In understanding today's Boston life and culture, the significance of Kent's works is twofold. In her stories and history books she artfully dissimulated the Boston province's failure of community. In her narratives of her own home life and in her prescriptions for the home life of others she demonstrated the exhaustion of suburban domesticity as a successful adjustment to modern middle-class life.

Kent, like all the participants in the colonial revival, such as the Boston architectural firm Perry, Shaw and Hepburn, and the story teller and poet Stephen Vincent Benét, denied the conflicts of the past. In her creations, colonial and nineteenth-century farmers, craftsmen, and merchants dwelt in a harmony that had never existed in reality. Her country square dances, Fourth of July lawn parties, weddings, and Thanksgivings never happened. Indeed they were closer to the sentimental imaginings of the nineteenth-century print makers Currier and Ives than to life in either Vermont or Brookline.

At the personal level she invented Mrs. Appleyard to be "plump, rosy, and cute," while she knew herself to be orderly, hard-working, and even compulsive.[33] In the vague assertion that Mrs. Appleyard "likes people,"[34] she blurred all the class distinctions and ethnic boundaries that marked her own life and those of her circle. The colonial revival was both a retreat to the suburbs by middle-class Boston families of British descent and an attempt to foster their falsely remembered past as a tradition for the entire province. The two great local issues of Louise Andrews Kent's era, mills and immigrants, did not exist in her stories. Mrs. Appleyard, historically isolated and geographically segregated, was a wonderfully motherly, easy-going, adaptable, and witty woman who threatened no one and who seemed always able to cope with the little difficulties of daily life. Her openness and simplicity were supported by the imaginary Vermont setting of folk witticisms, wherein thrifty people, domestic arts, a magic farm economy, and the natural setting found comfortable union. Mrs. Appleyard and her vacation home cut away the artificiality of suburban manners and offered nurture and community without conflict. Both did so, of course, by ignoring the power relationships of modern metropolitan summer resorts and the economies and politics of the metropolitan fringe.

In an earlier generation Jane Addams, after being many times turned away by President Wilson and cornered by her opposition to World War I, took up feeding starving people as a useful activity while the insanity of war followed its course.[35] Kent and Mrs. Appleyard fed everyone who came into the family orbit so that they would not have to be responsible for the world beyond the home. Of course, despite the shelters of modern *haute bourgeois* Boston, neither Kent nor her family were safe from the convulsions of nations or the processes of nature. Her only son was severely wounded in the Italian campaign during World War II, and her husband died of a heart attack in 1945. Looking back in 1968 upon her life since 1941, Kent had perspective enough to sense a world moving on beyond her understanding. "I have never reconciled myself to the idea that the United States of America, the country always counted on for human and humane treatment of people all over the world in time of disaster, is the country that began nuclear warfare. I have heard all the reasons why dropping the bomb is supposed to have been practically a favor to the Japanese people; I know I am showing myself impractical, sentimental and obstinate when I say that I do not agree. In my observation war always makes more problems than it settles. I am thoroughly in sympathy with Senator George Aiken's suggestion that we should announce that we have won the war in Vietnam and go home."[36]

Kent's family life demonstrated the bankruptcy of the retreat of her generation of married women. No woman did more with the domestic role. She fed, she cooked, she nursed, she entertained, she refinished furniture and made miniature rooms, she collected china and lectured on porcelain, she arranged flowers and made photographs, she played the accordion and told stories, she wrote newspaper and magazine columns, children's books, cookbooks and novels, she raised three children, tended a husband, and managed two houses. What more could a woman do? Yet her success in turning this Stakhanovite domestic life into a publishing and lecturing career belies the very formula she and her persona, Mrs. Appleyard, advocated. Even a plentifully financed home like hers could not furnish a full and satisfying life except by allowing the woman's private life to expand outward into some sort of public life. Kent, like many of her generation, found ways to stay within the confines of family life, and yet, through volunteer work and all sorts of elaborate social activities and personal projects, to live a larger life than those restricted boundaries commonly afforded. Given the energy, resources, and ingenuity that Kent had to mobilize to make the patterns of suburban life viable for herself, it is easy to understand why the daughters and granddaughters of Boston's middle-class suburbs later became active in movements for women's liberation.

Kent and her family form a miniature history of twentieth-century Boston metropolitan life. The father, a cotton dealer, bought for the old textile mills; the mother touched the boundaries of Victorian home life with her sports. Louise, a college graduate, married a successful editor who had left rural Vermont for college and a career as an executive in a large trade and textbook publishing corporation. The Kents raised their family in the open, informal, and expansive ways of the post-World War I suburbs and provincial country places. Louise modernized the Victorian role of housewife by her wit in turning the facts of her private life into the public fantasies of a New England tradition for her fellow suburbanites. Her son became an architect, lived in New York suburbs, and followed an imperial business, helping to design the cities of Brasilia, Brazil, and Kitimat, British Columbia. He married twice. Her younger daughter became a philosophy professor and married a Shakespeare scholar. Her elder daughter, a debutante like her mother, also married twice. After writing historical stories and helping her mother with her books and columns, she suddenly abandoned imitation and became a social worker. She made Vermont her home, but she wanted to work in it, not to manufacture it as a by-product of Boston suburban life.[37]

For the Kent men personal history followed the tides of the economy, from provincial cotton merchant to executive in a publishing company to New York architect with an imperial practice. For the Kent women the traverse of generations led from Victorian mother and sportswoman to self-created twenties housewife to married professional.

Such middle-class family sequences were common enough in the Boston province during the twentieth century, but as yet only some of the meanings of this historical progression are clear. The confusing patchwork that constitutes the social geography of the Boston province surely derives from its families' history. The inwardly open, informal, and democratic suburbs and resorts, which are some of the ornaments of Boston, rest upon the strong class, racial, and educational segregation within the metropolis. These new social environments of families and children are clearly the consequence of popular middle-class family politics.

The second legacy of Kent's generation of domestic retreat was the severing of the links between home and the larger world beyond. The grandmothers, Emily Greene Balch's generation, had tried to break down the barriers that surrounded them and to explore the connections among home, neighborhood, city, province, nation, and empire. They never succeeded in gaining much power, but at least they explored the linkages of modern society and tried to find their relationships to the great events of their day—international migration, national industrial economies, and world wars. Kent's generation drew back and settled once more within the boundaries of the home. Although the space they occupied was vastly larger than the scope allowed their grandmothers and mothers, it was a fenced-in space of duties within and no responsibilities without.

It is not yet entirely clear what this past retreat implied for the future culture of women and families in the Boston province. It is clear, however, that the retreat robbed the region of an important cultural force at the very moment when the province desperately needed alternatives to the rising power of science. In the twentieth century, when scientific culture triumphed and the old ways of Robert Grant's merchant and banker families collapsed, the carriers of our major alternative tradition, the women, either were beaten back or faltered or retreated.

10 ❧ VANNEVAR BUSH and LAURENCE K. MARSHALL

Today, in the momentary triumph of computing and electronics Bostonians imagine an orderly historical progress from textile bankruptcy to the building of high-technology businesses. In this past the province is pictured as a hive of universities and banks, of scientists, engineers, and capitalists who know the direction of scientific progress, who can guess the applications of new discoveries, and who can select the right managers for the development, production, and marketing of new products.[1]

The origins of the present culture were quite the opposite. As the pace of scientific investigation quickened during the twentieth century and the possibilities for practical applications multiplied, circumstances did not become more manageable, but less so. As scientific knowledge multiplied, so did the uncertainties and unpredictabilities of life. In 1930 no one knew what products or what industries might offer new employment or fresh prosperity. Now in 1983 all one can say for certain is that the uncertainties are increasing still, racing onward with the rush of modern scientific culture itself.

The lives of two men who were business associates for many years nicely demonstrate both the unpredictable quality of Boston's recent business history and the uncertainty that has accompanied the expansion of scientific culture in the province and the nation. One man, Vannevar Bush (1810–1974), enjoyed a brilliant career, first as a professor of electrical engineering at MIT and as a consultant to industry and government, then later as czar of World War II science and as one of the fathers of postwar imperial science policy. The other, Laurence K. Marshall (1889–1980) was Bush's partner in a small electrical manufacturing firm and later the founder of a giant electronics corporation, one of Boston's first. Today it flourishes as an imperial manufacturing company of many products and services, one of the nation's hundred largest private corporations.

It is difficult to compare the lives of the two friends because Bush, as an academic and an administrator, wrote a great deal and thereby constructed his own history, while Marshall, like many American businessmen, published nothing and conducted his affairs, even those of great public moment, as private, and thereby left only his business as his record. One of his corporate successors, however, had the wit to commission a history of the company while the principals' memories were fresh, and from that work and the perspective of subsequent events it is possible to make a fair estimate of Marshall's progress from the past Boston world of industry to the present world of science.[2]

Vannevar Bush, an only son and the youngest of three children, was born in 1890 in the small industrial town of Everett on Boston Harbor. His father, Richard Perry Bush, was a Universalist minister. Both parents had grown up in Provincetown on the very tip of Cape Cod, which in their day was a dying fishing and coastal trading town. Vannevar was named for his father's boyhood friend, John Vannevar, who followed Perry Bush from Provincetown to Tufts College and the Universalist ministry.[3]

In 1892, after thirteen years as a pastor in Everett, Perry Bush moved his family to the adjacent portside industrial suburb of Chelsea, where he served as minister to the Church of the Redeemer for the next thirty years.[4] His was the middle-class Irish and Yankee side of Chelsea, quite literally the other side of the Boston & Albany and Boston & Maine railroad tracks from Mary Antin's Arlington Street of poverty and new Jewish immigrants.[5] Vannevar recalled his father as a practitioner of the hearty and sociable style; he was a man who could get along with anyone. Perry Bush was an expert pool player, an active Mason and Shriner, an Odd Fellow, and the chaplain of Boston's Ancient and Honorable Artillery Company. A vigorous force in the small city, he joined with the neighboring priest to "tame" Chelsea's saloonkeepers. "His sympathy was never expressed to a woman except with gentleness, or to a man except with forcibleness," his son wrote.[6]

Vannevar admired forcibleness, indeed he felt called upon to deny that he was "belligerent." His autobiography, *Pieces of the Action*, bristles with competitiveness—business, academic, bureaucratic, and social contests proposed, fought, and won. Never an introspective man, he attributed this competitiveness not to his father's example but to a kind of Theodore Roosevelt-like overcompensation for a sickly childhood. He lost a year at Chelsea High School and a half-year of college to rheumatism.[7] Vannevar also had some strong feelings of class and disadvantage. Chelsea had never been a fashionable town, and the minister's son, a public-school boy, was always short of money in college. Just as his father had worked his way through Tufts selling coal to his fellow students, Vannevar paid his way by tutoring in physics and mathematics. A brilliant mathematician, he took the most advanced courses and followed new mathematical articles with two of his Tufts professors. A fellow engineering student, Laurence Marshall joined him in some of these courses, and for a time the two young men roomed together.[8] Recalling their classes together, Bush wrote, "I think I was probably one up on Marshall in regard to the mathematics. But he was certainly several jumps ahead of me in understanding the kind of world we proposed to enter and to challenge."[9] Vannevar seems to have chosen elecrical engineering rather than mathematics as a career because of its better possibilities for making money, but he also took pleasure in the mechanical tinkering side of engineering.

Vannevar Bush admired power; indeed, the trajectory of his life from college to science adviser to presidents shows a relentless, perhaps insatiable, drive for power. He seems to have solved his youthful problems of ill health and genteel poverty by welding together, behind the mask of an old-style Yankee machinist, the characters of imaginative engineer and practical administrator. He distrusted the liberal arts as snobbery, and he frequently spoke of aristocratic Bostonians as "four-percenters" and as do-nothing George Apleys.[10] In later life he was characterized as "a small, keen-eyed, fast thinking, tireless, eloquent Yankee...

whose rustic grin and cracker barrel drawl about engineering conceal an unorthodox scientific mind of whiplash speed."[11] In short, Vannevar Bush was a dominator, not a nourisher, of men.

Upon graduation from Tufts in 1913 Bush tried a couple of jobs to get some field experience as an electrical engineer. He worked for six months for the General Electric Company in Schenectady, New York, and in Pittsfield, Massachusetts, testing electric power equipment. When the entire test crew was fired because the shop needed repairs, Bush worked for some months as an inspector at the Brooklyn Navy Yard. In the fall of 1914 he returned to Tufts as a mathematics instructor, later taking a year off from teaching to get his doctorate in the joint MIT-Harvard engineering program.

At this time MIT, like much of Boston industry, was drifting in the doldrums of past technologies. An old faculty continued to tinker with steam engines and turbines. If any branch of the institute was flourishing, it was chemistry. In these years it was Harvard that attracted students interested in electricity and physics. To improve its position, MIT in 1907 invited Dugald C. Jackson, the founder and head of the University of Wisconsin's electrical engineering department, to come to Cambridge. Jackson had been an early leader in the profession, having worked with the Sprague Electric Railway Company, streetcar pioneers, and as a chief engineer for Edison General Electric Company in the Midwest. His texts on electricity, magnetism, and alternating current motors were widely used, and his consulting firm of Jackson & Moreland flourished. Like Stone & Webster's, Jackson's field was electric power and electric railways. Vannevar Bush became Jackson's ace student.[12]

In the academic year 1915–16 Bush wrote his Ph.D. thesis on some applications of mathematics to problems in electrical engineering. In 1916 he married "the girl next door," Phoebe Davis, daughter of a Chelsea butcher. Subsequently the couple had two sons, Richard, who became a Boston surgeon, and John, who became a successful Boston manufacturer; but family affairs were never the subject of Bush's writings or public speculations.[13]

On the edge of the Tufts campus in Medford, a former wireless operator, the man who had managed the radio on banker J. P. Morgan's yacht, had set up a small company, American Radio and Research Corporation, which manufactured radio equipment for amateurs. Bush, modeling his career on Dugald Jackson's active practice, began consulting for the new firm, and for the next five years (1917–1921) he helped recruit and advise its small research team. When the United States entered World War I, Bush worked full time for the company, trying to develop a magnetic submarine detector. J. P. Morgan hoped the device might become a valuable prospecting device for locating ores in the ground.

It was at American Radio and Research that Bush met a genuine old-style Yankee tinkerer, the machinist John A. Spencer. Al Spencer, born in Maine, was a self-trained man. After his father was killed in a lumber mill accident when the boy was three, the family had dispersed. Al was raised by an uncle and supported himself by working in spool mills. Somehow he got to New York City as a young man, and without formal apprenticeship or much previous schooling, he mastered the machinist's trade. Bush spoke of Al Spencer as "one of the most resourceful and ingenious men I ever knew, and he had a sense of humor which Will Rogers would have cherished."[14] Spencer had invented a thermostatic switch that Bush thought could be a useful electrical device if perfected. The device took the form of a metal disc that snapped in and out under heat, much the way the bottom of an oil can snaps back and forth when you press on it. Spencer had developed the concept, he said, from watching heat change the shape of metal doors of a furnace he had tended in a Maine clothing factory as a boy. After a painful experience of his own, however, Vannevar Bush had learned that Emerson had been dead wrong about the popular response to the invention of a better mousetrap. Bush now knew that "inventions are a dime a dozen . . . Invention is valueless unless it is joined with a number of other accomplishments—promotion, financing, development, marketing, and so on."[15] Despite the Morgan money and an ingenious staff, American Radio and Research was floundering in the postwar years because it was badly managed. Bush felt that Spencer's invention required the skills of a good businessman who could be both prudent and future-oriented. He turned to his old Tufts roommate, Laurence Marshall.

It seems unlikely that either Marshall or Bush anticipated the giant institutional world of science and engineering they later helped create, but Marshall proved to be an excellent promoter of new products, an energetic and enthusiastic man, who had a gift for encouraging others and for carrying groups forward. More than Bush, he was the enthusiast, the gambler, and the visionary. In Marshall's youth and throughout most of his business years, radio was the new technology, the fresh, open field of promise. He saw radio in the widest terms, and as its techniques multiplied he envisioned new worlds of microwave telephone communications, educational television, and accurate high-speed navigation. Many of the extraordinary electronic elements in our daily lives were once pictures in Marshall's fantasies.[16]

Laurence Marshall was the only child of George Francis Marshall and Mary Elizabeth Kennedy. The father had a butcher shop in Newton and later a stall in Boston's Faneuil Hall Market, where Laurence often worked as a teenager. Because George Marshall suffered from Bright's disease, after some years in Newton the family removed to another suburb, Medford, to be near his wife's brother, who was a physician. Mary Marshall had emigrated from Nova Scotia, and for several summers Laurence returned to the Kennedy family farm in Pugwash, where he worked happily on the farm. The Marshalls and the Kennedys were strict fundamentalists, but Laurence revolted against all that and as an adult lived a thoroughly secular life. After Laurence graduated from Medford High School, his widowed mother had no money to help her son, so he borrowed a purse from the Faneuil Hall marketmen and hurried through college in three and a half years. He spent what would have been the spring semester of his senior year inspecting railroad switches because he needed the money. From 1911, when he graduated, to 1917 Marshall worked as a civil engineer. He moved to New York City to work for the general contractor and tunnel builder Patrick McGowan, who was then in charge of drilling a tunnel under the East River for a subway. Marshall soon advanced to night superintendent and then worked for McGowan as an engineer, building bridges and factories.[17] When the United States declared war in April 1917 Laurence Marshall was on a job in Rhode Island. He immediately enlisted and subsequently served as a second lieutenant in the artillery in France. By chance his commanding officer, Major William Gammell, Jr., the son of a Providence banker and cotton manufacturer, was the treasurer of a textile business, the Lonsdale Company.[18]

After his discharge Marshall wanted desperately to get out of tunnel digging and factory construction. He wanted to find a place in the new field of radio and electrical engineering, which he had touched on in college.[19] Even more than a new specialty, he wanted to found and build a business. He returned to Boston and talked with Bush, who had by now become an associate professor of electrical power transmission at MIT. Bush told Marshall about Al Spencer's invention and revealed his lack of confidence in the business management of American Radio and Research. Soon Spencer, Marshall, and Bush set about forming a new company to develop, promote, and manufacture the thermostatic switch. Marshall was very much the right man for the job. He went to work on Spencer's model and modified it so that it would work on alternating current as well as direct current and so it could be used in home electric irons. Marshall then applied to his old major, William Gammell, Jr., who in turn put together a group of Providence investors, which soon included Richard S. Aldrich, whose sister had married John D. Rockefeller, Jr., and Russell Grinnell, a successful manufacturer of fire alarm equipment.

In 1920 the American manufacturers of electric irons were collectively linked in a patent pool; and no single company wanted to incur the costs of changing their design to incorporate the new thermostat because they would be obliged to share their new design with the others with no compensation for start-up costs. Marshall succeeded in overcoming this inertia by stressing the distinction of his investors and mentioning that through their Morgan connections the investors might be able to go into competition, manufacturing electric irons on their own. After a bit of bluffing, Westinghouse Electric capitulated and agreed to purchase the thermostat for a redesigned iron that would not burn itself out. The Providence financiers then joined Marshall, Bush, and Spencer to form a new firm, Spencer Thermostat (now the Metals and Controls Division of Texas Instruments Corporation) to manufacture the new device. The firm was successful, but more important, the Providence investors now regarded Marshall and Bush as winners and stood ready to support their next venture.[20]

The next venture failed, but the failure made possible the future Raytheon Company. In 1921 J. P. Morgan closed American Radio and Research but retained its patents. The retrenchment threw out of work a young Texas physicist, Charles G. Smith, whom Vannevar Bush had hired and whom he regarded as a genius. Smith had only an undergraduate degree and some training in the Harvard laboratory of the Nobel-prize-winning physical chemist, Theodore W. Richards. At American Radio and Research he had been developing power vacuum tubes. Bush had seized upon Smith's ideas and had written some articles with him on the subject. Smith's imagination had also been captured by an idea for a refrigerator with no moving parts. Bush remembered that the scheme depended upon a somewhat obscure physical principal, the Peltier effect, and Bush, Smith, and Marshall all thought the idea might succeed.[21] Marshall and Smith spent several months working on the invention in a bedroom of Smith's house. After investing $720 in materials and a lot of time, they came up with a sufficiently promising model to persuade Gammell and his group to invest in it.

The result was that on July 7, 1922, Marshall, Bush, and Gammell and his group of investors formed the American Appliance Company, with Marshall, Smith, and Al Spencer as employees. Soon afterward the Boston investor, Thomas Jefferson Coolidge joined the list of backers, thereby further expanding Marshall's sources of capital. The new company rented a floor in the Suffolk Engraving Company Building in Kendall Square, Cambridge, amid the foundries, furniture plants, soap and candy factories of what is now being elegantly rebuilt as Technology Square.[22]

Despite several years of work, the refrigerator idea did not succeed and had to be abandoned. In hindsight Bush realized that the Peltier effect could not be developed for commercial manufacture. But the firm's future grew out of Charles C. Smith's earlier power tube experiments. In the fall of 1924 Marshall arranged to purchase the old American Radio and Research patents for

Smith's tubes from J. P. Morgan, who accepted $10,000 in cash and $40,000 in stock. Thereafter the Morgan interest continued to be an important element in the business, represented in the beginning years by Thomas Nelson Perkins of the Boston law firm of Ropes & Gray. Later that role was assumed by Charles Francis Adams, Jr., an investment banker from Paine, Webber, Jackson & Curtis.[23]

In 1924 there were two and a half million radios in the United States, all battery powered. Smith's rectifier tubes could transform alternating current to direct current, making it possible to dispense with batteries and plug the radio into an electric outlet. Here was a "public need" and a "way of meeting it," as Bush defined the old-fashioned mode of the inventing process.[24] The tubes proved an instant success, the very thing Marshall had been searching for, a major new product in the new radio industry. The Champion Lamp Company of Salem blew the glass and assembled the tubes, and the Cambridge shop tested and packed them.

In 1925 the young men discovered that a company in Indiana already owned The American Appliance Company name, so they adopted the name Raytheon, coined by their new sales manager. The word was a composite taken from the French *rayon*, "a beam of light," and the Greek *theon*, "from the gods." In 1926, with sales of $1 million, Raytheon made a profit of $324,000. In July of that year the firm moved to larger quarters at nearby Carleton Street.

That same year the thirty-seven-year-old Laurence Marshall married Lorna McLean, a Radcliffe College graduate student in English, who also had relatives in Nova Scotia.[25] Indeed, the two had met first through family acquaintances in Bridgeville, Nova Scotia. Lorna Marshall's father had been a mining engineer in Arizona, and she had graduated from the University of California at Berkeley. After teaching at Mount Holyoke College, she moved to Cambridge to work for her Ph.D. For the next few years the Marshalls traveled frequently to Europe, where Laurence worked out patent agreements with European manufacturers and sought new products for Raytheon. He also began a lifelong interest in painting, and as he prospered he joined the list of Boston's collectors of Impressionist and Post-Impressionist painters. The Marshalls had two children, a daugher and a son, both of whom were later involved in another of their father's adventures.[26]

At this moment of initial triumph the small provincial firm collided with an unexpected stream of formerly separate events whose force and magnitude threatened to drown all of Laurence Marshall's hopes for building a successful company. Raytheon suddenly found itself on the lethal side of a radio patent pool of America's imperial corporations. The situation was quite beyond anticipation and not brought on by any misadventure of the little company. The threat to Raytheon's existence arose from the internal affairs of the patent pool itself.

This pool had originated in the confusion of patents that accompanied the first rush of radio invention. In 1895 Guglielmo Marconi invented a sytem of wireless telegraphy, and a British firm, with the encouragement of the Royal Navy, set about exploiting Marconi's inventions and patents. In 1899 the British firm established an American subsidiary, which offered wireless service to ships along the Atlantic coast. At once, independent inventors rushed into the field and began filing patents on a variety of devices for radio broadcasting, radio telephony, and the amplification of telephone and telegraph signals. The most important cluster of patents centered about Lee De Forest, who had recently graduated from Yale with a degree in electrical engeineering. De Forest's three-element vacuum tube, the audion amplifier of 1907, opened the whole field of electron tube design. Impressed by the new possibilities of radio and fearful of losing its monopoly on the transmission of voice signals, the American Telephone and Telegraph Company established a large research department in 1911. Soon it had 900 men at work on fundamental and applied research; it was the beginning of the famous Bell Laboratories. In 1913 the phone company purchased De Forest's inventory of patents and began internationally to transmit voice signals, the most spectacular achievement being a telephone message that was transmitted intelligibly from Alexandria, Virginia, to the Eiffel Tower in Paris.

Other American electrical corporations, equally impressed by the possibilities of radio, hastened to secure basic patents. By the time the United States entered the First World War, AT&T, Western Electric, Westinghouse, General Electric, American Marconi, De Forest Radio, and two Boston-based companies, United Fruit (banana growers and Caribbean ocean shippers) and Wireless Specialty Apparatus Company, a local manufacturer, held the major radio patents. But the patents had been issued in an overlapping and conflicting fashion. The General Electric patents conflicted in particular with those owned by the AT&T and its affiliate Western Electric. For the duration of the war the government staved off legal conflict by guaranteeing protection against infringement suits to all manufacturers. During wartime all the companies manufactured radio parts without regard to patent ownership.[27]

Peace in Europe in 1919 spelled the end of the radio patent truce. The conflicts could no longer be avoided; as each company pursued its own research and development, it quickly found its path blocked by a competitor's already filed patent claim. Military ambitions further complicated the management of patent boundaries. Toward the war's end General Electric offered to sell its important patents to the British-controlled American Marconi, but the Department of the Navy feared the sale would prevent the United States from developing its own international broadcasting system. With President Wilson's approval, two admirals visited General Electric to request that they not close the sale. The corporation acceded to the patriotic call and broke off negotiations with American Marconi. Instead it began working with the U.S. Navy to set up a unified private transmission company. Secretary of the Navy Josephus Daniels, however, soon cut off this effort because he believed that all American radio broadcasting facilities should be publicly owned and operated. Perhaps stimulated by what it had learned in these discussions, General Electric aggressively entered the radio field in 1919 by setting up a subsidiary, the Radio Corporation of America, to which it assigned its patents. RCA, in turn, purchased American Marconi. By the end of 1919, General Electric and its subsidiary RCA, along with AT&T and its subsidiary Western Electric, stood as the dominant antagonists in America radio patents.

The giants settled their differences by forming a patent pool in which they attempted to divide the new industry into telephonic and nontelephonic hemispheres. The telephone group of AT&T and Western Electric agreed in 1920 to let the electrical and radio group—General Electric, RCA, Westinghouse, United Fruit, Wireless Specialty, and Tropical Radio and Telegraph—use their radio-related patents, and those companies agreed to let the telephone pair use all their patents for message communication. This first division, however, did not establish hard and fast lines, and for some years the pool members competed with each other while sharing patents. AT&T did some entertainment broadcasting, and Western Electric manufactured broadcasting equipment, movie sound equipment, and electrical appliances in competition with RCA and the electrical group. RCA, in turn, leased telegraph lines from the telephone company's competitors in order to establish its own network.

After much debate and some attempted arbitration, in 1926 a fresh agreement was signed in which the telephone group abjured all broadcasting and all manufacture of electrical equipment, except movie sound equipment; in return they received exclusive control of all message transmission, including lines to carry radio programs and television. This second agreement, with its carefully divided industrial realms, carried with it a provision of exclusivity. Patents granted by one of the pool companies to another could not be let to third parties without the consent of the company whose specialty required the patent.[28] In the fall of 1926 the pool members announced that they would refuse to sell the rights to any of their patents to any outside manufacturer who used parts or tubes other than those purchased through the pool. Simply put, no American radio manufacturer could use Raytheon tubes unless he was willing to forego the use of any of the patent pool's equipment. And that was impossible.[29]

Raytheon counterattacked by commencing a lawsuit against the pool, thereby holding at bay any actions by the pool against other manufacturers while the case was pending. Meanwhile Raytheon went into the tube business in a big way; it leased the old Saxony Textile Mills in suburban Newton and began making all kinds of tubes, even those covered by the pool's patents. The

Raytheon lawsuit and the pool's answering lawsuits dragged on in the courts for twelve years. While they did, the threat of antitrust action by the Department of Justice forced the pool corporations to abandon their exclusive practices. This modification altered Raytheon's position from the danger of sudden death if its lawsuit failed to the likelihood of demise through atrophy. In the long run Marshall could not build and sustain a company manufacturing radio tubes and parts, because offering a full line of tubes would require him to join the pool in some fashion. As a pool member, he would be required to share Raytheon's inventions with his giant associates. So positioned in the industry, his tiny research and sales organization would be unlikely to compete successfully against RCA or GE or Westinghouse.[30]

During the lawsuit, however, even before the pool had relaxed its exclusive rules, an imperial opportunity arrived, a chance for Raytheon to break out of its confinement and reach a wide national consumer market.[31] The National Carbon Company (a subsidiary of the Union Carbide Corporation), which had established a lucrative market with its well-known Eveready batteries, thought that radio tubes might be a good complement to its line. The corporation had accumulated a lot of surplus cash, so it negotiated a joint venture agreement with Marshall to test out its tube ideas. National Carbon agreed to advertise and to market Raytheon tubes under a dual Eveready-Raytheon label, and it even took an option to purchase the provincial company. Attractive wooden and glass display cases containing tube testers were prepared and distributed to drug, hardware, and radio stores throughout the country, but the idea failed. The American public regarded radios as complicated, mysterious, even dangerous appliances, and they would not test and replace radio tubes as they did flashlight batteries. Then the Great Depression struck, and to conserve its capital National Carbon withdrew from the agreement.[32]

Raytheon was saved by the cash it received from National Carbon in payment for forfeiting the contract and by Laurence Marshall's seemingly limitless fund of energy and encouragement. The firm shrank to 338 employees in 1932, and some weeks the crew didn't work at all. It lost $163,000 on sales of $1.2 million. Marshall desperately searched for new products to add to his line of power tubes and resistors. He bought up a small firm of MIT engineers who had invented the "excito tube," which translated the visual track on the edge of a movie film into electrical impulses for sound reproduction. The group was supporting itself by building police radios, and they had ideas for an electric welder. Marshall, noting the big price spread between the Raytheon test model and the current electric welders on the market, leapt at the chance. When he announced his new welder, however, the competition lowered its prices. Raytheon never succeeded in profitably breaking into the welding business. There were other attempts, and some small successes, but no new profitable line like the power tubes appeared. Nevertheless, Marshall's doggedness held a talented staff together. The firm's skill in making tubes, and the continued expansion of the radio industry, allowed it to regain, after a decade, its 1920s sales level, if not to recover its earlier level of profit.[33]

While Marshall scurried about to keep his small firm alive, the wealth of the electric power industry and the rapid development of electrical engineering was carrying MIT and Vannevar Bush forward on a wave of expansion. By 1932 Bush had achieved a national reputation as a professor of electric power transmission and had just been appointed dean of the School of Engineering and a vice president of MIT. A frequent consultant to electric power companies and contractors, Bush had just completed a large version of his differential analyzer, a mechanical species of analog computer, and he and his colleagues had constructed a network analyzer for simulating the performance of electrical distribution systems. He was often called upon to give speeches, and in these lectures he began to develop his ideas about the proper way to stimulate invention. Most of Bush's experience in academic research and as a consultant to large firms lay beyond the small-firm problems of Laurence Marshall and Raytheon. In contradistinction to the old respond-to-a-need, or inventor's-breakthrough method discussed by Marshall, Bush's belief was in a new and better way to advance technology.

In 1932 Bush chided a group of textile manufacturers for not investing sufficiently in research. Thereupon he offered his new recipe for success. Do not tie a laboratory to the detailed problems of the shop floor, he said. Don't bother the lab with broken threads. Instead, hire a well-trained young scientist as research director and let him assemble a competent staff. Give the team generous funds. Let the research director set the research goals, and in time current science would produce profitable new products. In general Bush urged the supporters of research to loosen the ties between science and social need. He expected that the incremental growth of scientific knowlege would suggest products whose uses would prove beneficial to both businessmen and their customers.[34]

The process that Bush imagined as the ideal relationship between science and industry was just then receiving dramatic affirmation in the research of Wallace H. Carothers and his associates. Carothers was then leading a team of organic chemists who were investigating the polymerization of large molecules. As the group came to understand the logic of polymers, they found that both a rubberlike substance which they named neoprene, and a tough filament, nylon, could be made. In time Carothers' breakthrough became, along with the discovery of penicillin, a classic argument for the new way: pursue the openings of science itself and let the uses fall where they may.[35]

In such exhortations and favorite case stories Bush and other academics were recording and fostering a fundamental transformation of the Boston culture. Unwittingly, perhaps, Vannevar Bush was undermining the values and the institutional fabric that had nourished Alexander Graham Bell, Stone & Webster, and Laurence Marshall. Boston's goals and values were being shifted from the ideals and traditions of commerce to the ideals and traditions of universities and of corporate, philanthropic, and governmental bureaucracies.

In the subsequent triumph of his own career and in the enthusiastic sweep of big scientific establishments, Bush forgot the older setting of science and invention and turned his back on the consequences of his cultural and institutional transformation. After the boom of World War I no Boston textile manufacturer could afford the kind of large research laboratory Bush envisioned. Only a few of the nation's largest corporations, like Du-

Pont, which had hired Carothers, could establish and maintain such facilities. Only the nation's imperial businesses could persuade talented researchers to leave academic positions, as Carothers had left Harvard in 1928. Even Raytheon, situated next to a thriving academic research center, could not afford to maintain a fundamental research lab. The best Laurence Marshall could do was to hire professors as consultants and thereby keep in touch with university research. Even though his firm worked in a new technology, its small size limited it to seeking opportunities in what was already known and to improving what was already in use.

While Marshall and Raytheon were struggling in the stiff competition of the radio business, fresh opportunities opened up for Vannevar Bush. In 1938 he took on the presidency of the Carnegie Institution in Washington, D.C., which was the the nation's largest nonuniversity private research institution. Carnegie's projects were scattered across the globe and addressed all manner of subjects, from astronomy to embryology, from terrestrial magnetism to botany and nutrition. At the time the institution's Mount Wilson Observatory and its new giant telescope had captured the most public attention. Funded by Andrew Carnegie in 1902 with a generous endowment, the institution was established to encourage "investigation, research, and discovery, and the application of knowledge to the improvement of mankind."[36] Both the position, which he held until 1955, and the charge matched Bush's personal goals and philosophy. He soon transformed the role of president of the Carnegie Institution into that of director of American wartime science by anticipating the necessity to mobilize engineers and scientists for military purposes.

In Washington Bush immediately set about restructuring the organization of weapons development. Since 1924 he had served as a consultant to the U.S. Navy, and now, in 1939, he assumed the chairmanship of a panel of experts called the National Advisory Committee for Aeronautics. Bush regarded this panel as a model institution. It had power and funds because it reported directly to the president of the United States; it was not merely an advisory committee outside the federal budget and bureaucracy, as many of the technological committees had been during

World War I. Moreover, because it was composed of civilian experts and a few military men, the panel could set its own agenda, free from the field demands of the military commanders. When war resumed in Europe in 1939 Bush, along with his friends James Bryant Conant, a chemist and president of Harvard, and Frank Baldwin Jewett, then president of Bell Telephone Laboratories, worried about America's lack of preparedness for war. The three men were especially concerned about the possibility that the Nazis might possess an atomic bomb. With President Franklin Roosevelt's special approval, Bush established the National Defense Research Committee (later called the Office of Scientific Research and Development), modeled on the Aeronautics Committee and presided over by Bush himself. Divided into functional groups, the institution enjoyed notable success in the development of the atomic bomb, radar, proximity fuses, and all manner of antiaircraft and antisubmarine devices.[37]

It was Vannevar Bush's settled policy, and the basic charter he received from President Roosevelt when he approved Bush's initial memorandum, that the federal government would conduct as much of its research and development as possible through grants to existing research teams in the nation's business and university laboratories. The government would not, as it had in World War I, attempt to build new laboratories and staff them with drafted scientists and engineers. Instead, it would nourish and expand what already existed. This grant-in-aid strategy worked so brilliantly during World War II that it has become the pattern of American policy ever since.[38] Like the idea of pursuing fundamental research as the best strategy for the multiplication of useful knowlege, Bush's grant-in-aid policy has worked to the advantage of large, well-established institutions and to the disadvantage of the individual and small groups.

Just prior to the German invasion of Poland in September 1939, British physicists had developed a high-powered, high-frequency signal system for detecting airplanes—what we now call radar. The British were well in advance of American experimenters, but they faced very serious problems in the manufacture of their equipment. The magnetron, which generated the energy for the radar device, was cumbersome, complicated, and exceedingly difficult to make. In September 1940 the British brought the device to the United States and showed it to Vannevar Bush and his committee. They also requested that Jewett's Bell Laboratories, the largest and best-known electronic research group in the United States, take on the problem, which they did.[39]

At this time Bush had severed all his ties with Raytheon. He made no attempt while he was in Washington to direct new business toward his former associates. Since 1938 Raytheon had continued along is restricted path, with Laurence Marshall still seeking a new product like the power tube that would enable his firm to find security outside the radio tube business. Marshall knew nothing of the English radar developments. Then one day in 1940 he received a draft of a patent exchange he was negotiating with AT&T. A paragraph in the draft excluded Raytheon from making high-frequency tubes. This exclusion was especially disagreeable to Marshall because by supplying tubes and some assistance to one of his MIT consultants, Edward Linley Bowles, Marshall had been endeavoring to keep in touch with new developments in high-frequency radio. Bowles was a former student of Vannevar Bush and a patent consultant. At the time he was experimenting on Cape Cod with high-frequency waves to guide airplanes. Bush had appointed Bowles to the microwave committee of his Office of Scientific Research and Development, and there Bowles had learned of the British radar. Marshall telephoned Bowles and asked him to intercede for Raytheon at AT&T, urging the idea that during wartime once again American companies must share their ideas and inventions. Bowles went further. He persuaded the British and the microwave committee to let Raytheon also try to manufacture the magnetron. He argued that it would be a wise policy for rapid development to pit a small firm like Raytheon against a large one like Bell Laboratories: the small firm just might have an advantage in flexibility and imagination.[40]

At this moment in 1940 another old-fashioned Yankee machinist entered the story, Percy Lebaron Spencer (1894–1970), older brother of Al Spencer, the thermostat inventor. After the death of his father, Percy had been raised by an aunt, an itinerant weaver who moved from one Maine mill town to the next, seeking the factories that were hiring. Percy therefore received little formal schooling. He went to work in a machine shop and was introduced to electricity by a contractor who hired him to help electrify a pulp mill. When he was eighteen, radio captured his imagination. It was 1912, the year of the sinking of the *Titanic* and young David Sarnoff's broadcast of the signals and rescue operations from his radio key in a New York city department store. Percy, seeking the poor boy's education, joined the Navy and served from 1912 to 1915 as a radio electrician. During World War I he worked as superintendent for the successful Boston radio firm Wireless Specialty Apparatus Company (later absorbed by RCA). After the war a new Boston company that had been formed by local yachtsmen and bankers, Submarine Signal Company, hired him as its manager of field engineering. When the company wanted to transfer him to Norfolk, Virginia, he quit, and in 1925 he joined Raytheon.[41]

At Raytheon Percy Spencer's first job was to supervise the manufacture of radio tubes at the Champion Lamp Company in Salem. He did so with distinction, making important inventions and improvements in the tubes. Over the next ten years he rose in the firm as its leader in tube development. Percy Spencer's achievements owed a good deal to Laurence Marshall's ability to work with and to encourage a wide variety of men. Percy had his demanding, self-righteous side, but he had been blessed with an agile mind and a knack for getting things done. It was Spencer who figured out how to mass produce the radar magnetron.

At the outset he visited the Western Electric plant to observe its methods. There they were using very elaborate milling machines and highly skilled machinists to fashion the copper cores of the magnetron, but they were having difficulty turning out even eight per day. Spencer realized that Raytheon could not command the necessary priorities to obtain such machinery, nor could it probably find the machinists to run the tools even if he could purchase them. Instead of reworking a solid block of copper, Spencer proposed to stamp out thin sheets of metal to conform to the changing contours of the magnetron's pattern. That could be done by unskilled operators running available punch presses. Next the sheets would be coated with solder, piled one atop the other, and baked in a oven until they fused into a solid unit. In this last step Percy was able to draw upon Laurence Marshall's experience with ovens at Spencer Thermostat. The scheme proved to be a breakthrough, and Raytheon's production zoomed, reaching a peak of 2,600 magnetrons in one day.[42]

The magnetron triumph saved Raytheon. It was the major new product line Marshall had so long been seeking. As a military contractor specializing in radar, antiaircraft, and related naval equipment, the company took off. At its 1945 peak the number of employees had multiplied sixteen times to 16,000, its sales had soared to $173 million, its profits to $3.4 million.[43]

Always a man of vision, and fearful of being cornered once again by a narrow specialty, Marshall plowed all his surplus cash into the development of new products. In 1945 he purchased a successful Chicago company that had profited for years by making radios and phonographs for Montgomery Ward and other brand marketers. Captured by the potential of high-frequency wireless transmission, he purchased a line of hilltops from Boston to New York City, planning to mount a microwave tower on each. Unfortunately, the technology for such a project had not yet been perfected, his designs were faulty, and he had not secured an agreement with the telephone company for links to its exchanges. In another attempt he personally baked hundreds of batches of gingerbread, trying to perfect what in time became Raytheon's successful microwave oven. Everything he attempted either required much more time and money for commercial development than Raytheon could afford, or it faced stiff competition from large, entrenched companies. Bendix already dominated the automobile radio field, and RCA and others defeated Marshall's attempts to break into the manufacture of phonographs, radios, and television. Although there continued to be a civilian demand for radar and sonar and other navigation equipment, the markets came nowhere near their wartime levels. Soon Marshall and Raytheon were cornered again.

Worse still, the cash that Marshall had used to find new directions was now taken from him. During the war Raytheon, like most military contractors, had taken on more jobs than it could complete, on a cost-plus basis and for indefinite time periods. No one knew how long the war would last. After the war was over and a full accounting was made, the United States government renegotiated these contracts. The wartime profits Marshall had pledged to future development melted away, and in 1947 the company faced bankruptcy.

The First National Bank of Boston provided a large loan, and the Morgan group maneuvered to protect their interests. Henry S. Morgan, son of J. P. Morgan, persuaded his brother-in-law, the investment banker Charles Francis Adams, Jr., to take over the management of Raytheon. Marshall was forced aside by the directors in 1948, and he formally retired in 1950.[44]

Adams inherited a large and competent laboratory staff, but systematic development of existing products could not save the company in this time of need. Nor could Adams's new cost accounting or his careful management practices generate new business. Instead, what saved Raytheon, and made it the giant it is today, was war and one more of Marshall's wild hunches. During World War II, when he could at last afford all the talent he could find, Marshall hired three disgruntled young scientists from RCA, Royden C. Sanders, James Ludwig, and William Mercer. The trio had invented a fine airplane altimeter at RCA, but the research director would not allow them to follow this lead. Marshall told them to go to work on their ideas. Later he recalled that he didn't fully understand what they were about, but they seemed to be full of fire and promise. In 1945 he found an assignment for them.[45]

During these years Marshall had the habit of prowling the corridors of Washington, looking always for fresh contract possibilities. His reputation had soared with the magnetron triumph and with the brilliant execution of a U.S. Navy radar contract. Military procurement officers now welcomed him. During 1945 low-flying Japanese kamikaze planes were successfully escaping radar detection and breaking through the antiaircraft defense to destroy a number of ships. The planes were obscured by echoes on the radar screen created by ocean waves. Marshall offered Raytheon's research services to solve the problem and set Roy Sanders and his team to work. Five years later, after a tangled series of development contracts, Raytheon's research group succeeded in perfecting a test rocket that intercepted and destroyed low-flying aircraft. The Korean War in 1950 and the ceaseless arms race of the cold war against the Soviet Union put Raytheon on its feet once more as a military contractor. The development and manufacture of low-altitude and short-range missiles, as opposed to intercontinental rockets, became the company's specialty. Raytheon won a succession of government contracts to perfect and supply such missile systems: Hawk and Sparrow antiaircraft and antimissile missiles, Sidewinders to be shot from aircraft, and Dragons to be fired by troops facing tanks.[46]

To avoid becoming a prisoner to government military procurement, Adams embarked, with the money accumulated from these huge military projects, on a policy of purchasing companies having civilian specialties. Today the Raytheon Company is an imperial conglomerate, sixty-second on the *Fortune* list of American industrial firms. It employs 74,000 people around the world, 30,-000 in the province of Boston itself. This provincial payroll is just a few thousand smaller than that of the American Woolen Company at its post-World War I peak sixty years ago.

Half of Raytheon's business is military, half civilian. It publishes books under the name D.C. Heath in suburban Lexington, and manufactures Caedmon and Arabesque phonograph records in New York City; it makes Beech private airplanes in Wichita, Kansas; it manufactures Caloric, Modern Maid, and Glenwood stoves in Delaware, Ohio, and Topton, Pennsylvania; in Ripon, Wisconsin it makes Speed Queen washers; and in Amana, Iowa, it purchased the land and the name of an old German utopian community to build Amana refrigerators. It still makes tubes, transistor chips, switches, connectors, cables, and all manner of electronic gear. One division prospects for oil, another builds heavy construction equipment, and one branch designs and erects industrial plants in competition with Stone & Webster.[47]

Raytheon began with three young engineers who were fascinated by a new technology. They sought in that new set of ideas inventions that would "meet a public need," and they found and marketed a few. But it was war that made Marshall's provincial company into an imperial military and industrial corporation. The complexity of electronics, the proximity of Boston's many university laboratories, and the military demands of war and international arms competition transformed this Boston firm into one of those peculiar, but typical, midcentury American institutions: an organization of men and women who are at once master chefs of human destruction and providers of the appliances of domestic life.

During World War II Bush and Marshall carried on a long fight over the proper assignment of patent rights on subcontracts undertaken by Raytheon through MIT for Bush's Office of Scientific Research and Development. After the war the two men did not patch up their old friendship.[48] Marshall began an entirely new career after he was forced out of Raytheon. Like many a successful Boston businessman, he had settled his family in a large, comfortable suburban house. Family vacations were spent either canoeing and fishing in Nova Scotia, or on a small dairy farm in Peterborough, New Hampshire. Never a club man, Laurence Marshall on vacation picked up threads from his own childhood summers on the Nova Scotia farm and also a bit of the wilderness experience so many Americans seek.

In 1950, when Marshall was sixty-one and officially retired from Raytheon, his son John was eighteen years old. The war and postwar problems of the business had kept Marshall away from his family, and he fixed upon the idea of a long trip, some sort of shared adventure with his son before the young man grew up and left home for good. During the winter the two imagined all kinds of journeys, but in the end they settled on Africa because it was the site of John's favorite children's story, *Jock of the Bushveld.*[49] Lorna Marshall recalled having a large map of Africa spread out on the living room floor. Near the veld, on the western edge of the Kalahari Desert, was a large open space, the sort of empty white spot on a map that has tempted Americans for centuries. The Marshalls' Cambridge home was near Harvard's Peabody Museum of Archeology and Ethnology, so they could easily find out what was known about the area. The director of the museum encouraged them and suggested that the two would-be explorers seek evidence of an iron-working people who had been enslaved during the Bantu invasions, some of whom might still live at the edge of the desert.

Laurence and John Marshall traveled to South-West Africa during the summer of 1950. As they drove their jeep about the desert they found no evidence of lost peoples or lost settlements, but they did encounter some Bushmen, people who lived independently in the desert by hunting and gathering food. Excited by the beauty of the country and by the possibilities of anthropological study, Laurence Marshall energized his family with the same sort of enthusiasm that earlier had inspired the Raytheon staff. The Marshall family began seriously studying anthropology and making regular trips to the Kalahari. In time their daughter, Elizabeth Marshall Thomas, wrote a best-selling account of the Bushmen *The Harmless People* (1958); John became a successful documentary film maker and African specialist, and Lorna Marshall undertook systematic anthropological reporting.[50] Laurence Marshall, the visionary man of machines and business, made his retirement into a search for ever-widening fields of human understanding.

Nothing except the inexorable processes of old age altered Vannevar Bush's path or forced him to ask for new ways to truth. Always a man of action, he had moved toward the applied side of mathematics, toward the engineering side of physics, and toward the administrative side of science. He was a man who wanted power, and he found it in his contemporary world of science, especially in his fifties when he served as a wartime administrator in Washington. Thereafter much of his thought and reflection turned around his experience with power, especially the management of power in the setting of imperial business and imperial government.

The splendor of World War II armaments and the triumph of Bush's scientific role in their development blinded him to other aspects of the world. He was a wonderfully successful manager in a war that had been won in part through a complex organization of the nation's scientists and engineers and their laboratories and businesses. This was his skill and his outlook. Both before and during the war Bush's experience was entirely restricted to bureaucratic hierarchies: consulting for private businesses and sitting on boards of directors of corporations like Raytheon and American Telephone and Telegraph; serving on academic committees and climbing the rungs of MIT management; or working with research foundations and the federal government. He lacked familiarity with electoral politics or bargaining by conflicting groups, such as management and unions or various coalitions of nations. What he had no experience with, and what he did not know, was how he might orient himself when the goal was not to manage or to win but to accommodate to groups over which one has no real control. He never understood the multiplicity of forms of human conflict, and he could not imagine the wide range of possible modes of settling conflicts. He knew only two modes of institutional behavior: the bureaucratic mode of managing and the military mode of threats and war.

As a young man he had paid little attention to politics of any kind—local, national, or international, and when he turned his attention to these matters he proved to be very much the child of a World War I outlook. He saw the political affairs of the Boston province merely as rivalry for public office.[51] International affairs he structured into a simple world of violent antagonisms. The Bolshevik Revolution, totalitarian Communism, and totalitarian Fascism stood in direct opposition to capitalist democracy. His experience with World War II and the ensuing Stalinist cold war years convinced Vannevar Bush that the world was divided into two parts: Soviet totalitarianism and American democracy. Bush wrote his most popular book, *Modern Arms and Free Men* (New York, 1949), to urge his fellow Americans to see the world in this way and to accept a permanent cold war with Russia. He could not then imagine a more complex process of change in the world or a more complex system of conflict and bargaining.

As the cold war dragged on, and as its absurdities of ceaseless armaments and false divisions of peoples revealed themselves, Bush gave up the urgent issues of immediate government policy.[52] He began to sift through his speeches and writing and to rework those he judged to have the most enduring significance. He turned his attention toward the universal goals of science and to examining the processes of science as he knew them. Though Vannevar Bush would never admit that emotion and reason were inextricably bound together, he did speak in his last book of collected essays, *Science Is Not Enough*, of what he deeply cared about, revealing some ways in which his heart and mind had been fused. In these essays he is still a scientist, and thus he tells those who have followed him in high-technology Boston a geat deal about the core ideas and values driving our present-day culture and institutions.

At the heart of these ideas and values is the contest of science. Like all human activities, science can take many forms—cooperative teams, teaching and production hierarchies, lone searches and fantasies—but what Bush really cared about was the contest form. He spoke often of the young men who pursue scientific knowledge with the energy and devotion that only youth can squander. These young men pursue science because they too love the contest; its meaning for them is personal triumph in the game. The successful young men are, or should be, Bush thought, generously rewarded with money, honors, and responsibility.[53] The only social controls in this vision of science are the elders and the peers, the formerly successful and the young contestants themselves. It is wholly conceived as a man's contest, not just because in Bush's lifetime most scientists were men, but because he and his contemporaries could not imagine gender as being a significant element in the ideas of science itself.

From his core beliefs there stemmed much good sense and useful public policy. Bush reinterpreted the egalitarian tradition of America so that it would serve his contest—science. Egalitarianism for Bush meant a meritocracy; he did not focus on the issues of equality of being, the rights of citizens. He and his associates proposed a national system of science fellowships based on open competition and designed specifically to exclude all considerations of "race, color, creed, sex, or need."[54] In addition, his experience in business, universities, and government had taught him that science must be protected from fraud, bribery, and manipulation and that the safest way to secure that protection was to have science policy controlled and supervised by committees of elders and peers. These experts, being subject to open criticism within the scientific community, would be forced to maintain adequate professional standards.[55] Expert panels and the self-direction of science informed Bush's science politics, and the success of his convictions lives on in the form of the National Science

Foundation (founded 1947) and in many U.S. government practices.

These shared beliefs made a consistent faith and fitted well with Bush's life experience and others'; what is startling is that in their view science was isolated and insulated from the larger society in which the scientists themselves dwell. No thoughtful person today can set forth with Bush's certainty a prescription for an adequate science policy for a democratic nation. Never has a democracy had to exist in a climate of so much scientific activity and so many scientific institutions. We do, however, know the absurdities of our position, and we know that Bush's prescriptions no longer answer our needs.

In his vision the vast majority of mankind have no voice. All those experiences that at any given moment lie beyond contemporary scientific capabilities receive no acknowledgment. Vannevar Bush had faith that in a democratic society science would produce benign knowledge that would advance the well-being of all citizens. Indeed, that has been true. Today provincial Boston is at least three times as wealthy as it was in Bush's childhood, and even the poorest are in many ways better off.[56] But people have learned that the gains of science and engineering carry destructive elements: wonder drugs bring on wonderful addictions, awesome weapons create awesome slaughter. Even Bush had to acknowledge the growing complexity of the social problems attending technological advances.[57] Instead of confronting these inevitable limitations and evils of science, instead of seeing science as a human social process and therefore full of conflict, Bush liked to imagine science to be a building in continuous construction. In this metaphor the young men added new walls and rooms, and the old men offered advice and wisdom.[58] His building images focused upon the cumulative aspect of science, the addition of one piece of knowledge to the next, science building more science. Such a view, however, denies any social meaning beyond the activity itself. The meaning of science becomes once again the contest, the race of scientists toward anywhere their theories take them. Bush pursued science for the joy of the game itself, as heedless of consequences and as irresponsible to mankind as academies have always been.

There is an extraordinary pride and an extraordinary blindness in all of this. The pride is in placing at the pinnacle of human striving the figure of man thinking. Like many of Boston's religious thinkers, Vannevar Bush relegated mere creature comforts and social well-being to the level of lesser virtues. Like Thoreau, he worshiped the cold and the hard. "They who come to this world as to a watering-place in the summer for coolness and luxury never get the far and fine November view of heaven."[59] "Soft utopias" Bush called the visions of comfortable human societies.[60] Man thinking was his farthest view, and all he could imagine was man thinking according to the reasoning and conventions of science. With so blinded a captain at the helm, ours has been a dangerous voyage.

V ❧ MERITOCRACY AND ROMANTICISM

SHOULD VACATION or business bring a visitor to Boston, or should curiosity carry an old resident out into unfamiliar parts of the province, neither one will find plaques or signs commemorating the birthplaces or the works of the men and women in this history. Only Laura Richards and Edwin Arlington Robinson have been the beneficiaries of local pride. The rest, neither politicians nor generals, exist only in the memories of families and friends and in the books of the library, where a reader like myself may come upon them.

There are, to be sure, as many histories of Boston as there are people who recall the past. Most of these histories join one fragment of time to another to form a pattern whose meaning is only personal. A few, however, carry you outward from experiences you recognize to landmarks you didn't know existed. To me, the men and women of this history stand out as guides, each one pointing to different corners of the dimly lit places that are my present. One tells of the continuing flow of overseas migrants, another of the imperial worlds of business, a third of the inadvertent communities of modern technology, still another of the isolation of the homes and the segregations that carve up the province. In the flow of time from past to present, each one stands squarely in the middle of some aspect of my own experience.

The city of Chelsea does not celebrate Vannevar Bush Day. It does not honor the triumphs of its most distinguished citizen, nor does it contemplate his limitations. There is no Fred Erwin Beal Junior High School in Lawrence, nor do the employees of Stone

& Webster know their history. The Jamaica Plain branch of the Boston Public Library is not the Emily Greene Balch Branch Library, although she is the only winner of the Nobel Peace Prize the city of Boston has ever known. Neither does the large Hispanic community in Jamaica Plain know of Rev. Charles Fletcher Dole and his opposition to the Spanish-American War. Like their fellow Bostonians, they do not appreciate the sad turning away that that little war meant for the ideals of the province. Fred Allen's homes in Allston and Dorchester survive, but he is remembered for his least interesting qualities—his generosity and his success.

A good deal of our forgetting comes from the insistence of the present. The twentieth century has presented itself as a series of crises demanding our immediate attention, crises that have turned us away from a concern for the diversity of life and for the courses of individual lives. Class and religious warfare, revolutions, economic collapse, military aggression, the democracies of tyrants—all these spread rapidly across the globe after World War I, amplifying all the local prejudices and panics of the Boston province.

Many leaders, elected politicians, owners of businesses, and heads of social clusters sought to gain personal popularity and power by organizing their followers into cohesive blocks of racial, ethnic, religious, and class prejudice. The helplessness of the United States in a world turning away from liberal capitalist oligarchies toward military tyrannies was matched by the helplessness of the province before economic depression. Bostonians defended themselves under the narrow banners of American, Yankee, Irish, Catholic, Protestant, Jew, white, black—established against newcomer, local against outsider, respectable against needy. In all these familiar reductions of the human condition the people of Boston fought to preserve some private advantage or to get a little piece of the province's shrinking wealth, power, and prestige.

The most generous and optimistic people sought to quiet popular fears and to allay popular prejudices by stressing an alternative tradition, that of an America open to all citizens. Just as Mary Antin had characterized the new Jewish immigrants as repeating the experiences of the Puritans, so liberal leaders after World War I once more called up the old goal of preserving the province and the nation as a place that would reward all citizens of talent, hard work, and economic utility. Deeply conservative themselves, these postwar leaders believed that private property was ultimately the most important defense against tyranny. They viewed with alarm the introduction of many social democratic reforms, like public housing and social insurance, in European democracies, and they confused democratic socialism with the spread of tyrannies in Russia, Germany, Italy, and Spain. Fairness, equality before the law, equal opportunity for education, jobs, and promotion, and a minimum of social security against the worst hazards of local and national economic failure—this was their message.

In the long run the liberal leaders triumphed. Secularization dampened denominational animosities, and the economic achievement of the Irish and other immigrants drew off the class sediments in the prevailing ethnic snobberies. The slaughter of millions of European Jews discredited anti-Semitism as a social conceit, and discredited as well the respectability of antagonisms between whites and blacks. Indeed, the political and social victories of leaders like Henry Dennison, Owen Young, Leverett Saltonstall, Louis Brandeis, and David I. Walsh have probably done as much to make the province a pleasant place to live as the wages of the new technology.[1]

Yet this liberal victory was such a negative victory, a nineteenth-century defense against twentieth-century antidemocratic attacks, that it could hardly provide nourishment in its own right. Like all partial truths, liberalism carried its own antisocial tendencies. By necessity it stressed keeping education, business, and government open to all citizens, and by doing so it fixed upon attainment of power and wealth as the proof of virtue. By defining life as a race for success, the liberal campaigns divided our people into winners and losers, the successful and the unsuccessful, the deserving and the undeserving. As the twentieth-century decades unfolded, the ideal of equality of being was increasingly neglected before the triumphant self-satisfaction of the strong of all groups.

These days two people keep coming to my attention as exemplars of continuing tendencies of the recent Boston past. James Bryant Conant, a chemist, college president, science administrator, ambassador, and educational reformer, typified many of the strengths and weaknesses of the liberal and scientific traditions. Rachel Carson, a summer visitor to the province, a zoologist, minor government official, and nature writer, captured the public imagination with her blend of the romantic tradition and modern science. In her writing the uncertainties of modern science and the significance of the relationships among people and between people and nature became once again fruitful social and political possibilities.

11 ❧ JAMES BRYANT CONANT

James Bryant Conant (1893–1978) was at the peak of his powers during the succession of crises that swept over the province and the world during the twenties, thirties, and forties. He was one of Boston's very best men, and the province honored him with its most distinguished office, the presidency of Harvard University. An organic chemist like Vannevar Bush, Conant enjoyed a brilliant career in the newly imperial roles of academic and science administrator. As president of Harvard from 1933 to 1953, he inherited that office's license to preach, and following the Boston tradition of Increase Mather, William Ellery Channing, Phillips Brooks, and another Harvard president, Charles W. Eliot, he assumed the robe of moral guide and schoolmaster to the nation.

Blessed with a quick, inquisitive mind, Conant prided himself on his ability to find the facts and to invent workable solutions to social and institutional problems. He had enormous self-confidence, and he sought out the largest conflicts of his day: the international threats of German fascism and Russian communism, the pressures of the new scientific culture, and the divisions of American society into classes of wealth and education. International diplomacy, war, universities, foundations, and public schools were his arenas.

Trained in the province's best schools and associated with its leading men, Conant in many ways mirrored in his life the progress and failings of Boston itself. He served as a leader in the triumphal expansion of science and technology, and within his own institution and in his political role he fostered the liberal program for an open society. More exceptionally, he wrestled with the conflicting goals of universal education and training for a meritocracy. Yet because of the very divisions and weaknesses of the provincial culture he was raised in and lived in, he proved unable to master the choices of war and international conflict, and even, perhaps, unable to realize the choices open to science itself. It was as if Boston sent forth from the province one of its best knights, half-armed.

James Bryant Conant rose to eminence from the most commonplace provincial circumstances. He was born and raised in Dorchester, a then new residential section of Boston. His names signify the urbanization of two mill village families. The move to Boston of the Bryants and the Conants added one more ripple to the tide of the century; the Antins, the Woods, the Beals, the Marshalls, the Bushes, the Kents—all had followed the same powerful current.

His mother's relatives, the Bryants, were once the prosperous side of the family. Grandfather Seth Bryant had been a shoe merchant in Boston, but he had removed to East Bridgewater, Plymouth County, twenty miles south of Boston, where he owned a small shoe factory. His pride had been furnishing 200,000 pairs of boots to the Union Army.[1] A veteran of the Revolutionary War had told Grandfather Bryant of the ill-fitting shoes of that army, and he determined that the men and boys of his troops would have the best.

James's father's father, Grandfather Conant, had worked as a shoe cutter in Grandfather Bryant's mill, and the Conants lived across the village road from the Bryants. But there were still closer ties between the two families. Grandmother Conant had died while giving birth to James's father, James Scott Conant; when Grandfather Conant remarried, the second wife did not get on well with the son. He had a hard time in his own house and took frequent refuge in the Bryant home across the way.[2]

When he grew up, James Scott Conant left his unpleasant family life and his village to learn the trade of wood engraving in Boston. He opened his own shop just after the Civil War, mastered photography as an adjunct to his business, and in the 1880s, when photoengraving became common, he expanded into the new process.[3] From his Boston success he returned to East Bridgewater to marry Jennett Bryant, the daughter of the neighbor who had befriended him.

When James Scott Conant married, he purchased a large pre–Civil War farm house and barn and some fields near the Ashmont railroad station in Dorchester. When the horsecar lines were electrified during the late 1880s he gave up his horse and carriage as an unnecessary luxury, tore down the barn, and built on its site a two-family house. From this first venture came more, and throughout the next decade James Scott Conant cut up his fields into streets and lots and erected strips of two-family houses and three-deckers. That was how the city grew in those days. Seventy years later Conant recalled his father's pride in his building investments. "The twentieth century, they said, would certainly bring more streets and more electric cars—possibly things called automobiles as well, though I had never seen one. No one suggested that the two- and three-family houses my father was building were, in fact, rather unattractive dwellings crowded too close together. My best friend lived in the one next door. I would have been amazed to hear anyone say a word against his home."[4]

A slump in the shoe business during the eighties cost Grandfather Bryant his fortune. When the factory closed and the home had to be sold, the remembering and grateful son-in-law took the old couple into his ample Dorchester home. Little Jim, like his father, was the youngest in his family, the only boy, with two older sisters. Grandmother Bryant became the boy's constant companion, reading to him and mothering him as she had his father.[5]

Both families' religion had been Swedenborgian since the 1820s, when revivals had swept through Bridgewater and East Bridgewater. Grandfather Conant had read aloud the passages at the New Jerusalem Church, and Grandfather Bryant had given money. For many years the Conant parents traveled to Roxbury on Sundays by streetcar to attend the Swedenborgian Church there.[6] Schism, however, split the congregation, the parents shifted to a Unitarian congregation, and James Bryant Conant was raised as a nonattending Unitarian. His mother combined Swedenborgian mysticism, and its belief in a spiritual realm that infused everything, with Unitarianism. As James remembered it, however, her outstanding characteristic in religion, politics, and all things was dissent. He said he learned from her that "dissent was not only respectable but usually morally correct,"[7] and he often praised dissent as a source of social insight and innovation. Never an angry name caller, Conant later became known for his careful sizing-up of extreme positions in public debate and for his settled administrative technique. From the fragments of his auto-biography, it is hard to guess whether his mother's Swedenbor-gianism and Unitarianism held for him the same romantic images and social outlook as Rev. Charles Fletcher Dole's beliefs held for his parishioner Emily Balch. It seems likely that Conant and Balch shared a common tradition, but James's political outlook did not develop from his family's religious associations.

Like many fathers, James Scott Conant encouraged his son's mechanical skills by building him a small workroom of his own. He also showed the boy his photoengraving plant, where young James was fascinated by the intricate chemical processes that created the copper printing plates. Soon the boy fell into the role of local wizard, repairing the neighbors' new-fangled electric doorbells and exhibiting chemical explosions. James attended the elementary grades in the nearby public school and when he was eleven, he was enrolled in a six-year college preparatory course at Boston's ancient private academy, the Roxbury Latin School. There he proved an adequate student of the classical curricu-lum—five years of reading French and Latin, three of German, and sufficient English literature and ancient history to pass the College Board examinations. In later life, when he wrote on edu-cational policy, Conant ridiculed Roxbury Latin's sort of classical curriculum as narrow and undemocratic, as training for snob-bery.[8] Some of this attack derived from his study of the modern public high school, but some seems the schoolboy residuum of resentment at having been forced to read authors whose language and messages held little meaning. Looking back from the 1980s one can say that the ancient authors, Victorian poets, and literary authorities might have been interpreted in ways that would have helped Conant in his later life, but such speculation forgets the era. At the turn of the century the classics had lost their relevance for most teachers and students, and the discovery of their important meanings was then as heroic a task as teaching the history of the Ottoman Empire or the botany of the abandoned city lot would be for today's teacher. Important subjects all, but beyond the reach of a provincial Boston teenager and his instructor. Chemistry and physics were what captured Conant's imagination as a schoolboy. Under the sponsorship of a young science teacher, Newton Henry Black, Conant was given special preparation in chemistry, and with special examinations and Black's recommendations he was admitted to advanced standing in the Chemistry Department at Harvard College in the fall of 1910.[9]

Conant entered Harvard only a year after the end of Charles W. Eliot's forty-year presidency, and the college was still being run on Eliot's free-wheeling elective system. A brilliant, and enthusiastic student, Conant earned his degree in 1913, after only three years. His advanced standing allowed him some free time from the laboratories, so he was able to compete successfully for a position on the college paper, the *Crimson*. Being on the *Crimson* staff in turn gave him admittance to the Signet Club where, Conant recalled, he received his general education from lunching with the literary-minded students. Though working hard to keep up with the upperclassmen and graduate students in chemistry, Conant also enjoyed himself in college. A fellow resident at Mrs. Mooney's boardinghouse, an engineering student named John P. Marquand, who was having a miserable time, recalled Conant's being the leader in such games as throwing paper bags filled with water or racing on the new subway to a bar on Essex Street in downtown Boston to drink two beers and return to the boardinghouse in the shortest time.[10]

Conant continued on at Harvard as a teaching assistant and graduate student, earning his Ph.D. in organic chemistry in 1916. He was a student of Harvard's Nobel-prize-winning (1915) physical chemist, Theodore William Richards, and of organic chemistry professor Elmer P. Kohler. From these professors he learned one model for the way a scientist could and should work. At the core of the beliefs of the chemistry department in those days stood the sharp division between science and the rest of the world's activities; within their own academy the division was between pure and applied science.

Before World War I, chemistry, like most other disciplines in

American private universities, was German and thoroughly academic. President Eliot had brought the German academic style to Harvard, and many of his professors had studied at German universities. Indeed, Richards had gained his appointment as a full professor at Harvard in 1901 only after he had been offered a post at Göttingen. Richards and Kohler refused to do industrial consulting because it was not appropriate for men who wanted to contribute to theory. Such practical work belonged to the chemical engineers, the sort of physical chemists who were just then making great strides at MIT. The Harvard professors and their laboratory assistants pursued current problems that they hoped would lead to advances in theory. Their goal was to elaborate the grand logical systems of science itself. As in Germany, the pursuit of knowledge was assumed to be an unmitigated good; but, unlike Germany, America had not yet developed extensive industrial and academic networks for the application of academic science.[11]

All of James Conant's fellow students expected to become college teachers, and they expected that the very best among them would ultimately become university research scientists. These were Conant's first expectations as well, and he followed them successfully for many years. He found a set of theoretical questions in the current work on the structure of organic compounds, and he carried on this line of research in his dissertation and in his later professorial career. He worked on the chemistry of chlorophyll in plants, of hemoglobin in blood, and on the polymerization of molecules, the topic that Wallace Hume Carothers, the sometime Harvard instructor, so brilliantly transformed for industrial purposes.[12]

In his autobiography Conant did not speculate as to why he was not content to be a wholly academic person. Power and the pleasures of getting things done seem always to have attracted him. He recalled that when he was courting his wife in 1920 he confided in her a triad of ambitions. "The first was to become the leading organic chemist in the United States, and after that I would like to be president of Harvard; and after that a Cabinet member, perhaps Secretary of the Interior ... I did not aim at world-wide recognition such as that enjoyed by Prof. Richards. I only hoped to be the leading American organic chemist; I did not contemplate staying with chemistry for a lifetime. Even my administrative targets were those not of a committed man but of a restless soul."[13]

Whatever his early personal ambitions, it was a summer job during graduate school that began Conant's training in what would become an increasingly important part of American science and of his own life—applied industrial science. A former Harvard instructor invited him to spend a summer at the laboratories of Midvale Steel, where he learned of the widening possibilities for research-trained scientists in modern industry.[14] The next year, 1916, he and two fellow Harvard chemistry graduates formed a company to manufacture organic chemicals that were then in short supply because the British had sealed off the German trade. Their first experimental plant caught fire and burned down as Conant and a partner tried to start it going. Before they could construct a second plant with the fire insurance money, James was offered, and accepted, an instructorship at Harvard. The second plant subsequently exploded, killing one partner and a plumber because, as Conant later admitted, the preliminary laboratory work had not been sufficiently thorough.[15] Although a subsequent sale of the patents paid off the investors, the disaster must have been a painful memory. It seems likely that Conant retold the story fifty years later because he wanted to stress the difficulties and the importance of applied science and to defend what he came to call the "American way," the concentration of scientific funds and energy in applied research.[16]

Neither the pure science of Professor Richards nor the applied science of Conant's American way, however, joined science and scientists to the general processes of society. Academic scientists pursued questions of their own making; if a human being should appear in the problem, he would appear as an object only. In commercial and industrial research, humans were customers or employees; in medical research they were patients, doctors, or nurses; in military research they were our soldiers or the enemy. In none of these cases would the scientist's technical knowlege or intelligence take responsibility for, or inform, his relationships, and those of his scientific investigations, to human beings or society. As a result a well-trained and gifted young scientist like Conant had to find his values and his approach to human problems in some other source. The material he devoted his most earnest attention to was held to be irrelevant to human relationships.[17] Here was not just the old divisions between mind and heart, power and morals, but a division within the trained mind itself. Science, with its reach out into the processes of nature, had a great deal to teach Conant, and in his lifetime science became increasingly involved in immediate questions of human affairs. Yet he and many others of his generation steadfastly endeavored to keep their scientific academy isolated from the problems of human relationships.

Prepared in this divided way by the best provincial scientific training, but unprepared, as all Americans and Europeans were, for the consequences of the First World War, Conant first stumbled as an industrial researcher for the United States Army. Unlike the later conflict, World War I did not mobilize the nation's scientific talent. The army and navy decided on a few tasks for scientists, put the researchers in uniforms, and assigned them to research posts. The chairman of the MIT chemistry department persuaded Conant not to enlist as a general combat officer, but instead to use his talents and training in tasks closely related to his advanced scientific knowledge. Conant joined the professor and accepted the leadership of a group charged with doing research on poison gas. Soon he was trying to start up a pilot plant to make a supposedly deadly and burning gas called lewisite, an improved version of the mustard gas then being used on the western front. Although he pushed hard, sleeping in the plant in Willoughby, Ohio, and driving his men, he was not able to get the pilot plant into production before the November 1918 armistice.[18]

In Conant's very long autobiography he ably reviewed and defended his many activities and accomplishments. Then in his mid-seventies, with a lifetime of great tasks and important administrative positions, he was nevertheless crowded by the climate of the times. A supporter of the Vietnam War, writing in the midst of peace protests and student challenges to university authority,[19] Conant did not use the occasion of his book to explore the possibilities that might be uncovered by the wisdom of hindsight. Instead he reiterated his fixed beliefs, and his autobiography immediately struck the rock of scientific isolation. His defense of his participation in poison gas research, like our defense today of continuing atomic bomb development, was that of a common private peering out of his foxhole. Conant reviewed a list of reasons for using poison gas as an additional weapon, but the list did not consider the possibility that there were choices in wartime other than the multiplication of weapons. Writing as an old man, he found no alternatives to his intellectual and emotional prison; he twisted and turned in his discomfort.

The Germans started it, it was the enemy's fault, Conant began. Besides, everybody was doing it. By the time the United States entered the war, the British, the French, and the Germans were all spraying troops with phosgene and mustard gas. "All of us involved in this secret undertaking were thankful when the armistice was announced. We were now through with this strange adventure in applied chemistry, which was tied to the highly unattractive task of producing poisons to be used in combat. With a great deal of relief, we proceeded to demobilize and re-enter civilian life." The work was secret, they hated it, but somebody higher up had made the decision, and no debate on arms policy was possible during wartime.

Later Conant learned that "there had been doubts as to whether lewisite was, in fact, effective," so perhaps the work didn't matter, they couldn't have hurt anyone if they had tried. Besides, the Chemical Warfare Service had its beneficial peacetime spin-offs; "Tear gas for the use of police forces was a gift to the forces of law and order." But if lewisite had been deadly, and if the plant had succeeded in producing it, what then? "I did not see in 1917, and do not see in 1968, why tearing a man's guts out by a high-explosive shell is to be preferred to maiming him by attacking his lungs and skin." Killing is killing, "all war is immoral."[20]

These are the arguments of a cornered man who accepts the narrow vision of the enemy rifle pointed at himself. James Bryant Conant, however, was not a draftee in the infantry. His experience in two world wars and in international diplomacy could have taught a wider vision, yet he persisted in reducing the conflict between nations to its narrowest proportions.

Immediately after this argument, his autobiography turned toward possible alternatives in international law, and he concluded the discussion with a saddened review of the course of history since his youth. Gas and submarine war were condemned by many, he wrote, because they attacked noncombatants, civilians. "To those of us who have lived in intimate contact with the development of aerial bombing in World War II, such an argument sounds old-fashioned. Civilian casualties become not only a necessary consequence of bombing, but one might almost say an objective in the fleets of bombers directed by the British, the Germans, and the Russians, as well as the Americans."[21]

In 1917 Conant had not yet begun to think of himself as a social inventor. This role, which he later discovered and in which he took justifiable pride, never extended to the human activity of war itself, however.

The immediate consequence of Conant's wartime service was that he met a group of talented scientists from other universities and from DuPont and other chemical companies, and these men later helped him organize programs to build the atomic bomb and to produce synthetic rubber during World War II.[22]

After returning to Harvard as an assistant professor of chemistry Conant, in 1921, married the daughter of Professor Theodore Richards. Grace (Patty) Richards was then an amateur painter, presumably encouraged in her art by the example of her grandfather, William T. Richards, a successful painter of seascapes. The young couple settled for the next dozen years in a house on Oxford Street,[23] next to the university laboratories. In addition to their active life in Cambridge the Conants spent a year in Germany (1924–25) and a semester in California, where James canvassed the possibility of joining the new group then starting up the California Institute of Technology in Pasadena. His research and teaching prospered, and he rose by quick stages to be chairman of the chemistry department in 1931. He and Grace had two sons, James and Theodore. Then in 1933, in the depths of the Great Depression, when Abbott Lawrence Lowell retired, James Bryant Conant, aged forty, was appointed president of Harvard University.[24]

As president, Conant, the young man trained to think in terms of the international community of science took a relentlessly cosmopolitan position, thus completing the process begun decades earlier by Charles Eliot. The Great Depression, however, raised an immediate obstacle to this approach; indeed, it fostered the most serious internal crisis of Conant's twenty-year administration. Opposed to cutting salaries in order to balance the budget, Conant proposed instead to lay off faculty. In the mounting tension, only a quick administrative invention by the president saved the university from an ugly faculty rebellion.

The difficulty stemmed from his predecessor's reworking of Harvard College. President Lowell had constructed a series of dormitories (the Harvard "house" clusters, such as Lowell and Eliot), and had hired many tutors to give personal instruction to the undergraduates in the manner of English colleges. As a consequence the faculty had expanded rapidly. The reduced resources of the Depression made it impossible for the university to keep a large staff. Besides, Conant objected to the scholarly standards of many of the tutors. He insisted that as far as it was possible to so choose, Harvard faculty should be scholars of national and international reputation. The university's wealth and its ability to pay scholars to do research, he thought, was a national resource, one to be carefully husbanded, Depression or no. Accordingly, he instituted a review system whereby all young faculty were to be examined for tenure after six years, and he ordered these examinations to be conducted by national committees of scholars, not by the resident faculty alone.

The invention of this review process solved the problems of weeding out faculty in a fair manner, but inevitably it hastened the transformation of the Harvard staff into a nationally and professionally oriented group with little concern for undergraduate life or provincial Boston affairs. On the one hand, the Conant reform has proved over the years to be an excellent one for maintaining the reputation of Harvard scholars; on the other hand, it has brought with it a rootlessness and irresponsibility that is now characteristic of today's large Boston institutions, both new corporations like Raytheon and long-descended ones like the First National Bank.[25]

Conant was a quick and inventive president who faced opportunities with an undogmatic outlook, and his administration fostered a number of successful additions to the university: the Littauer School of Public Administration for the academic training of civil servants; the Nieman Fellowships for journalists; the competitive national scholarship program of four-year college fellowships; improved ties with western and midwestern alumni; university professorships; coeducation; and the General Education curriculum.[26] All these enlargements transformed an excellent provincial university "designed to serve the northeastern upper class" into a "national university drawing on young men and women of all classes, colors, and creeds."[27] The innovations show Conant's wonderful ability to learn quickly, but he could never learn fast enough to keep up with the expanding realms of the powerful positions he was asked to fill.

Conant's positions as president of Harvard and later as Washington science administrator taught him much, but they also obscured his ignorance and isolation. As a Roxbury Latin School boy from Dorchester, a prize Boston scholar who had begun to make his way in the international world of organic chemistry, he inherited the deep divisions and blind spots of his culture. Nothing in his academic training or his Harvard situation informed him of conditions in Fred Allen's parish, St. Margaret's in Dorchester, or the hard times in Mary Antin's Chelsea and Fred Beal's Lawrence. Nothing brought him news of Boston's Irish, blacks, and Jews, or its country Yankees and mill-town Italians and French Canadians. The Harvard Tercentenary sermons on man and tradition and culture passed over most of humankind in the Boston province, just as they omitted most of the peoples of the globe. As Conant later recognized, his call in 1936 for "a unified, coherent culture suited to a democratic country, in a scientific age" used a platitude to hide the deep chasms of ignorance that beset his university and his culture.[28]

Yet for all the narrowness of his background and training, and despite his isolation as Harvard president, Conant did learn a great deal. At the outset of his term in office, personal goals and the accident of an inherited crisis carried him directly into the issues of creating an open society. James Bryant Conant had made his way by personal gifts, good training, and hard work. That was the way of international science when it was not blocked temporarily by seniority and privilege. In 1933 Conant was a convinced liberal, deeply committed to the idea of a meritocracy as the proper goal for American society.

For policy reasons he wanted at the outset of his presidency to announce an important fund drive to accompany the Tercentenary, in hopes of capturing the momentum of that celebration. He proposed a scheme of national fellowships, initially to be offered to bright students from the midwest who wanted to come to Harvard. The fellowships were to be awarded solely on the basis of academic promise, to be determined by competitive examination, high school grades, and special interviews. The size of the stipend would be determined on the basis of need; the maximum award could pay for four full years of college tuition and expenses.

The midwestern pilot program proved immediately successful, and as the idea gained popularity it helped Conant transform Harvard College into one of the top academic training centers in the United States. In conjunction with Princeton and Yale, which had carried out the first national scholarship experiments, Harvard under Conant's leadership helped the idea grow into the present National Merit Scholarships and the Scholastic Aptitude Tests, which today sort out all the nation's high school graduates.[29]

For Conant this success commenced a lifetime campaign. Following his own logic of open educational mobility, and pursuing the Jeffersonian goal of a national aristocracy of talent, he discovered how many barriers there are to the realization of human skills.[30] At first he thought that the national tests were measuring raw intelligence, but soon he realized that no such quantity existed and that the scores reported the ability of students to use trained verbal and mathematical skills. This more sophisticated understanding was bad news, even for a man concerned only with the fairness of the competition among young people who wanted to be trained for the professions. If competitive examinations for college entrance reflected the quality of schooling, then a scholarship program could only redress the family income disadvantages of talented high schoolers; it could not provide them with the good precollege instruction they required. The scholarship program thus led Conant to consider high schools, and there he confronted the conflicts and black holes of American culture. Should college preparation dominate high schools? If so, what academic culture should be taught? If not, what subjects and what culture should be taught in place of the academy?

On the eve of World War II Conant had just discovered these questions of cultural conflict, but he had not yet thought seriously about them nor proposed any research. He credited the discovery to his association with a Harvard professor of education, Francis Trow Spaulding.[31] Conant and Spaulding had been thrown together by the financial crisis at the Harvard School of Education. The Depression and poor educational policy had driven off the school's students, mostly teachers working part time for advanced degrees and credits. Conant had to decide whether to close the school, turn it into a small research institute, or continue it as a place for training secondary school teachers.[32] He ultimately decided on the last alternative, but in terms of one of his social inventions—a new program in which the departments of Harvard College and the School of Education would collaborate in training teachers. Students in the program would fulfill departmental requirements for subject-matter competence and then be given instruction in pedagogy by the School of Education faculty. Their degree was to be called a master of arts in teaching. Conant's plan reflected university professors' distrust and dislike of professional pedagogy, their demand that formal academic subjects be the prime fare of teachers, and also their lack of interest in, even dislike of, schools and teachers. The MAT degree was an uneasy compromise that failed in the end, but in the process Conant and Spaulding spent a good deal of time touring to raise money from alumni and foundations and discussing educational policy.[33] Ominous news from Europe, however, drew Conant's attention away from schools toward the military defense of England, France, and the United States.

In the fall of 1939 Conant started speaking on the radio and writing public letters urging that the United States send aid to England and France.[34] As an admirer of German science and later as Harvard president, Conant had followed the rise of the Nazis.

He was shocked by the xenophobia and anti-Semitism of the new regime and frightened by the stories told by refugee scientists. At the same time he tried to keep open the channels of scientific communication between the two nations. By 1940 he thought of the Nazis in terms of "gangster rule, the suppression of individual freedom, ruthless anti-Semitism and armed aggression."[35] After the defeat of French, English, and Norwegian troops and the fall of Norway and Holland in May 1940, he feared "the shadow of a totalitarian state sweeping over ... Europe."[36] Urged on by the Harvard alumni of New York City, some of whom were bankers with offices in Europe, Conant gave a strong radio speech in behalf of American intervention on May 29. From his Harvard pulpit, he soon proved to be an eloquent opponent of American isolationists.

In June Vannevar Bush asked Conant to join his fellow scientific administrators in setting up a presidential committee on weapons development, the National Defense Research Committee. Along with Bush and Conant, the core group included Karl T. Compton, president of Massachusetts Institute of Technology; Frank B. Jewett, director of Bell Laboratories and president of the National Academy of Sciences; and Richard C. Tolman of the California Institute of Technology. As a leading member of the National Defense Research Committee, and after 1941 its chairman, Conant became more and more isolated. He concentrated upon the urgent issues of weapons development, and his circle narrowed to that small, select group of scientists, industrialists, corporate lawyers, and generals who shared those tasks with him. The conflicting demands and voices of American democracy ceased to be Conant's teachers. Instead, as is true for all men in such roles, his enemy, Nazi Germany, became his disciplinarian.

June 1940 was the time when the Germans overran France and drove the French and British into the sea at Dunkirk. In July the continuous air offensive against Britain commenced. A few months earlier the Germans had succeeded in terrorizing French refugees by making air attacks on the roads behind the French lines. They had pounded the Dutch into submission by wiping out a sixteen-block section of Rotterdam with saturation bombing. From these and similar examples the Germans reasoned that bombing was the way to subdue Britain. After all, modern warfare was a clash of armies supplied with machines. If the factories that made the machines could be destroyed, if the workers lost their homes, and if men, women and children were terrorized by incessant bombardment, then surely bombing civilians and houses was the key to victory on the military front. The Battle of Britain raged through the summer of 1940 and continued until the German invasion of Russia in June 1941.

Conant spoke even more urgently of the necessity for U.S. aid, and as he listened to the London radio reports of the Battle of Britain he desperately wanted to visit England, to see for himself what Harvard and the federal government could do to help. The NDRC's desire to establish a liaison office with British scientists provided him with the excuse, and in February 1941 he sailed for England.

"The trip to England in 1941 was the most extraordinary experience of my life," he later wrote. "I was hailed as a messenger of hope ... I saw a stouthearted population under bombardment; I saw an unflinching government with its back against the wall. Almost every hour I saw or heard something that made me proud to be a member of the human race. Courage I had always admired greatly; tenacity and loyalty to avowed aims I place high among the attributes of a civilized person."[37]

In this emotionally charged climate, where ordinary people daily showed the possibilities of benevolence, both Conant and his English hosts failed to learn the lesson of commonplace heroism.

Despite heavy casualties and enormous losses of property, the British population was not terrorized and the output of war materials did not decline. Why then, in these months and in later years, did the British government and the American government think that a similar bombardment of German civilians would bring submission? Did the bombing of Coventry teach the efficacy of the destruction of Dresden?

What Conant experienced, but what he could not master, were the exhilarating passions of war. The bomber airplane gave new reach to the anger and aggression of fighting men. It allowed revenge and retaliation to gorge on piles of high explosives. The bombing of cities became the careless modern equivalent of the rape, pillage, and fire of former sieges.

Conant returned to Washington and the NDRC in April 1941, urging that everything possible be done to improve the manufacture of radar and pressing for the rapid development of useful weapons. Others, however, were pressing Vannevar Bush for research and development of an atomic bomb. At first the debate centered on the feasibility of such a bomb; then the argument among the scientists turned to issues of time and use of scarce resources. At the beginning Conant suspected that Arthur Holly Compton of the University of Chicago wanted to use the passions of war to finance abstract research in physics, which Conant thought should be postponed to peacetime. Refugee physicists cited the advanced state of French and German physics and reported that the Germans were already at work on developing a uranium bomb. Further study that summer and more memoranda by the Chicago and California physicists convinced Conant that an atomic project could succeed. On December 6, 1941, on the eve of the Japanese attack on Pearl Harbor, Conant, Bush and the NDRC decided to undertake the development of an atomic bomb. In Conant's mind the overwhelming justification for such a gamble with money, manpower, and materials was "the terrifying thought that the Nazis might make an atomic bomb within the next year or two."[38]

For the next four years, as chairman of the NDRC, Conant served as Vannevar Bush's lieutenant, at once a supervisor of many weapons research contracts and an insider on the development of the atomic bomb. Conant kept the president and a few Cabinet officers posted on the progress of the bomb, he shared with these few in making the decisions for its use, and with them he took the lead after the war in proposing international control of atomic weapons.

James Bryant Conant steadfastly advocated using the atomic bomb and doing so in the manner of the times—dropping it on an industrial city where war material was manufactured so that the bomb would simultaneously destroy factories, workers, and their houses.[39] In 1968 he wrote in his autobiography, "My own misgivings have never been about the use of the bomb. I think the decision was correct."[40] His only regret was that construction difficulties delayed its use from May until August, thereby, he thought, costing America its heavy casualties of that summer's campaign against the Japanese-held Pacific islands.

There were other options, of course, in the spring of 1945. On April 12 President Franklin Roosevelt died; eighteen days later Adolph Hitler committed suicide as the Russians fought their way into Berlin; and on May 8 Germany surrendered unconditionally. The United States now faced but one war and one enemy, an enemy too distant to ever be able to bomb American cities. The earlier Yalta Conference and the forthcoming conference in Potsdam seemed to promise that soon the Russians would join in the war against Japan.

On May 31 Conant met with the interim committee for top-level atomic policy. They resolved unanimously to recommend to President Harry Truman that the bomb be used without warning on a Japanese target.[41] In June and July the Japanese began seeking peace terms with the United States. Simultaneously, American physicists, led by a core group in Chicago, urged the exploration of alternatives to dropping a bomb on a Japanese city. On July 16, 1945, the first atomic bomb test at Alamogordo, New Mexico succeeded. On August 6, without warning the Japanese or consulting with the Russians, the Air Force dropped the first atomic bomb on Hiroshima. Two days later the Russians attacked the Japanese in Manchuria. The second atomic bomb was dropped on Nagasaki on August 9, and the next day Japan offered to surrender.

Today, after thirty-five years of arms competition, the number of atomic weapons has multiplied by the thousands, and the lethal power of each of the big bombs has similarly multiplied. The Boston province lives each day beneath the cloud of atomic annihilation. Should some of these weapons be used there as they were in Japan, the province would cease to exist.

As a people, we Americans do not agree among ourselves in our judgment of this past. Some applaud Conant's and Bush's initiative and skill in directing the atomic projects and support their recommendation to use the bomb against Japanese cities. The war ended quickly after that. Others curse the two men and their confederates as narrow, ignorant, evil people who cast all living things into jeopardy.

In the years after August 1945 the atomic bomb was never far from James Bryant Conant's thoughts. He referred to it in his lectures on science, and he dealt with it directly as chairman of the Atomic Energy Commission's General Advisory Committee (1947–1952). There he voted against the development of the much more powerful hydrogen bomb on the ground that such a weapon was an intolerable threat to mankind, "a weapon of genocide."[42] After September 1949, when the Russians announced their own atomic bomb, the atomic arms race became part of Conant's politics of cold war competition with the Soviet Union and national Communist parties everywhere. In these postwar years his defense was not the wartime unleashing of human passions for death and destruction but a Boston philosopher's assurances about the enduring equilibriums of the universe. He called upon his fellow citizens to take courage, "to walk boldly along the tightrope of the atomic age," because he hoped that Ralph Waldo Emerson's faith would protect us all."[43]

"The natural tendency of many people to recoil with horror from all thoughts of further scientific advance," he wrote, "because of the implications of the atomic bomb is to my mind based on a misapprehension of the nature of the universe. As I watched the secret development of the atomic bomb through four years of war I often thought of the work being done at the same time . . . of the then secret research on penicillin, on DDT, on antimalarial drugs, on the use of blood plasma, and realized how much these scientific advances meant for the future welfare of mankind. I often thought of Emerson's famous essay on the Laws of Compensation. '. . . with every influx of light comes a new danger . . . There is a crack in everything God has made. It would seem there is always the vindictive circumstance stealing in at unawares . . . this back stroke, this kick of the gun, certifying that the law is fatal; that in nature nothing can be given, all things are sold.' "[44]

This theme of the necessary mixture of good and evil was one Conant often returned to, but Emerson's definitions could not shelter him, nor will they shelter us. Today our science does not see the world as ordered by the divinely linked human souls that had secured the Boston philosopher's universe. Conant's science and our culture of reason take no cognizance of the many dimensions of human life that made Emerson's steelyards balance. We are ignorant of our science, and our science is ignorant of the world. Ignorance, not mastery, was the important lesson the two world wars had to teach, but Conant, despite his quickness and unease, could not quite master it. He measured the piles of human death and suffering correctly, and he thereby estimated that firebombs were equal to atomic bombs, but his reason could not direct him toward calculating the multiple paths of alternative choices to either weapon.[45]

During the spring of 1945, while American physicists and statesmen secretly debated the use of the atomic bomb, city dwellers in Japan continued to be slaughtered by paltry applications of modern physics and chemistry. The World War I invention of incendiary bombs did not trip any American consciousness of alarm and neither did a small improvement on the World War I flamethrower. A team of Harvard chemists applying the techniques of making automotive greases conceived of adding an aluminum soap to gasoline to make a jelly that would burn, napalm.[46] So armed with new models of the last war's devices, the American Army Air Corps set about burning up Japan during the spring of 1945. One night in March a fleet of American planes attacked a twelve-square-mile section of Tokyo, where over a million people dwelt. That night fourteen American planes were lost, sixteen square miles of Tokyo burned, 84,000 Japanese died, 41,000 wounded. No fire in the history of the West ever caused so much human suffering and devastation as the one that night—not Nero's burning of ancient Rome, not the Great London Fire of 1666, not the burning of Moscow in 1812, not the Chicago Fire of 1871, not the San Francisco earthquake and fire of 1906. General Curtis LeMay thought that if he kept at it he could have Japan burned down by October, just in time for the planned United States invasion.[47]

The Tokyo carnage shocked Secretary of War Henry L. Stimson. He recorded his discomfort, but his understanding of the world failed to help him find alternatives. "I told him [President

Truman) I was busy considering the conduct of the war against Japan," Stimson wrote in his diary, "and I told him how I was trying to hold the Air Force down to precision bombing but that with the Japanese method of scattering its manufacture it was rather difficult to prevent area bombing. I told him I was anxious about this feature of the war for two reasons: First, because I did not want the United States to get the reputation of outdoing Hitler in atrocities, and second, I was a little fearful that before we could get ready, the Air Force might have Japan so thoroughly bombed out that the new weapon [atomic bomb] would not have a fair background to show its strength. He said he understood."[48] Emerson concluded his list of proverbs and wise sayings about compensation by jotting down, "The Devil is an ass."[49]

The immediate postwar years were a time of intense activity for James Bryant Conant, and perhaps his most creative period. At the height of his powers, enriched by the experiences of being a university president for more than a decade, and now with five years as a national science adviser as well, he rushed from committee to lecture platform to writing desk, trying to ease major public problems. The scientists deserved a reward for their wartime services, so Conant joined Vannevar Bush in setting up the National Science Foundation. The bomb threatened to escape both international and American imperial control, so he journeyed to Moscow, and he served five years as chairman of the Advisory Committee of the AEC. When political confusion, weakness, and inflation threatened the liberated states of western Europe, Conant campaigned for President Truman's policy of aid to Europe and for Soviet and Communist containment. Seeing that Harvard's professors were teaching ever more narrowly to their college students, as if each student were destined to follow the professor's particular specialty, he empaneled a blue-ribbon committee to make recommendations. The liberal capitalist cultures of the West seemed to have crumbled before tyrants speaking the words of democracy and practicing terror, so Conant began a personal campaign for the ideological reform of America's schools.

A scientist, an imperial leader of bureaucratic politics, a recognized statesman of American education—who could have done more? Surely none of his contemporaries attempted more. Conant tried to find in the practical world of daily affairs solutions to the deep cleavages in twentieth-century American and European society. He failed, inevitably, because he himself was divided by those same cleavages. Boston, America, and Europe had lost their way well before World War II. What emerged from Conant's tireless efforts was not a discovery of alternatives but an endless defense.

His hopes for atomic control failed utterly. Like many of the insiders of the wartime project, he hoped that atomic arms might be controlled and proliferation stopped through a United Nations agency that would have broad powers of international inspection. The Russians' unwillingness to allow America's atomic monopoly to continue unchallenged, their total prohibition of any outside inspectors, and the mounting tensions between the former allies and Stalin's USSR soon foreclosed any possibilities for control and management by the UN.[50]

Meanwhile, when Conant was chairman of the AEC Advisory Committee, he was outvoted by those seeking safety and power through an arms race.[51] In January 1950 President Truman called for building a hydrogen bomb; on November 16, 1952, the United States exploded its first; on August 20, 1953, the Soviet Union did the same. Not only had all international restraints on atomic weapons failed, but reactionaries within the United States had seized upon the popular fear of modern weapons and Soviet armies to fasten the nation to the never-ceasing labors of imagining and responding to Satan. The Red Scare of Senator McCarthy and his many supporters, in which both Conant and Harvard University figured as minor targets,[52] permanently fixed the Boston province and the American empire to the task of responding to what we imagined our enemies intended. The common private's imprisonment by the rifle of his enemy became the official orders of the empire.

Conant suffered from fears of atomic weapons as much as anyone. In 1969 he recalled the ambivalence he had felt in 1945 after the success of the first Alamogordo explosion. His disquiet grew with the invention of better bombs, better bombers, and missiles.[53] As the atomic negotiations with Moscow broke down during the spring of 1946, Conant seems to have begun reformulating his earlier expectations of disaster for the United States. This time, instead of imagining the empire isolated in a world overrun by Nazi armies, he imagined an ideological threat that would swallow up the democratic and capitalistic states one by one. His was a kind of Marxian projection, a prediction that the world would suffer periodic economic disorders accompanied by political turmoil. In such moments national Communist parties would seize control of their governments, perhaps at the same time inviting the aid of friendly Soviet troops. As he imagined these events repeating themselves over the years, spreading from one country to the next, he could foresee a future time when the United States would stand alone, its economy and its society threatened by a ring of hostile tyrants. The Prague coup of February 1948 seemed to confirm this fearful prediction.[54]

Conant worried that the western European governments and political parties might not be strong enough to resist such ruthless forces. The previous spring, in 1947, Truman had announced his military and economic intervention in Greece and Turkey, and in June, when General George C. Marshall came to Harvard to receive his honorary degree, he used the occasion to announce his proposal for a European economic recovery program, the Marshall Plan. The favorable response of all but the Soviet-controlled nations of Europe won Conant completely over to Truman's policies of cold war and rivalry with the Soviets.[55] Thereafter, working once more with a citizens' committee, as he had on the eve of World War II, Conant spoke and wrote in behalf of the Endless Defense.

America's military commitments to the North Atlantic Treaty Organization, as well as the sudden outbreak of the Korean War in 1950, unexpectedly threw two of Conant's major concerns into conflict—his goals for an active U.S. imperial military policy and his lifelong campaign in behalf of fair practices in the youthful race for position. In the debate over the terms of a new draft law Conant was surprised by the force and the new source of the demands for privilege. Instead of coming from the old, wealthy preparatory school families, the insistent demands now came from middle-class suburban families in behalf of their college-bound children.

During World War II certain professions and certain categories of students had been exempted from the draft on the grounds of wartime necessity. The long-run and military needs of the society required that some scientists remain civilians and some students continue in medical school.[56] Conant had been uneasy with this compromise, which proffered safety to the experts and front-line duty to ordinary Americans; as he watched the list of exemptions grow by the intervention of special-interest groups, he realized that exemptions were entirely improper for peacetime or for a long-standing draft. All young people should serve, he believed, or at least all should be equally liable to selection. He and his citizens' group proposed a draft and lottery for all eighteeen-year-old boys, with no exemptions. No genius would be blighted, he observed, by the loss of a year or two between high school and advanced training. Congress, however, voted him down. Middle-class parents of college-bound children insisted on exemptions for their boys, and later, in 1961, when the Vietnam War came along, all the evils of a rich man's war and a poor man's fight were revealed.[57] For Conant in the 1950s this selective service defeat gave warning of the new threats of metropolitan segregation to his most cherished ideal of open social mobility through education.[58]

The insatiable wartime demand for academic engineers and scientists—and the contrasting wartime unemployment of historians, classicists, literary scholars, and many social scientists—convinced Conant that the traditional academic subjects needed revision. In his 1936 Tercentenary oration, when he called for a "coherent culture suited to a democratic country in a scientific age,"[59] he did not yet appreciate what he was saying. The wartime collapse of European nations before the advances of fascism suggested to him a profound cultural crisis. At the same time the excitement and example of wartime mobilization encouraged making the largest plans for the peacetime future. Perhaps a committee of Harvard scholars, nonscientists mainly, with plenty of time on their hands because students had deserted the campus, perhaps they could formulate a plan whereby the universities, with Harvard as the model, and the schools could work together to modernize and revive the culture of the nation.[60]

Accordingly, in January 1943 Conant appointed the Committee on the Objectives of a General Education in a Free Society. After consulting many high school teachers, educators, and college professors, the committee issued its report at the war's end in 1945. The authors were worried about the increase of specialized knowledge of all kinds. They attributed the current lack of unity and understanding across specialties to the bankruptcy of Christian beliefs. Formerly Boston schoolmasters and college professors had employed a general Christian faith in the unity of all God's works to bind together the miscellany of the liberal arts curriculum. Now, the schoolmasters having lost their faith, the fragmentation of knowledge stood fully revealed. The Harvard committee deplored the fact that today's poet did not, and probably could not, read modern astronomy, while his Romantic predecessor of a century earlier could and did so. As a remedy to the fragmentation and as a secular replacement for the earlier schoolmaster's faith, the committee urged a revival of reading the classics of the Western tradition as an important means of teaching young people values and ethics. The definition of classics, however, was to be modernized to include relatively recent works in science and social science, Einstein as well as Marx. Using these books, the schools would interpret the moral conflicts of the modern world according to a secular version of the Judeo-Christian tradition.[61]

In his introductin to the committee's report Conant pointed especially to its first chapters, which reported the results of the extensive conversations between the *schoolteachers* and the professors. He regarded this colloquy as the heart of the report, because the reforms he envisioned would improve both high school and college. He repeated his philosophy: general education was "for the great majority of each generation." It was not merely a reform of college liberal arts, such as the curriculum of the University of Chicago or the St. John's College western civilization curriculum.[62] Because Conant had commissioned the report and because he frequently used the words "general education," the report came to be associated with his name. The urgency of his political experiences, however, had already driven him beyond the report's cautious modernization of academic tradition. For the moment he remained silent.

For the moment, the report and the reforms at Harvard that stemmed from it gave Conant a chance to experiment with teaching science to nonscientists. For three years, 1946–1949, he taught a course, Natural Sciences 4, at Harvard, following his historical case method. To his mind it made little sense to teach the rudiments of a specialty, like elementary chemistry or elementary physics, to nonscientists. It set them to solving problems whose answers would not help them enjoy science as outsiders or appreciate how scientists went about their work. As an alternative he proposed a careful working up of a few cases, like Nicolaus Copernicus's analysis of the solar system or Robert Boyle's reasonings about the behavior of gases. In presenting such cases Conant hoped to give the student a sense of how a scientist might proceed even with bad data and ignorant or incorrect speculations. What Conant prepared and taught was a kind of science appreciation for nonscientists. He admired the case method used by the law and business schools, and he thought it could be used to show how science had advanced by accidents and by reasoning from one problem to the next. From this experience in teaching, Conant later advocated a historical approach as a way to reach nonspecialists in all fields, in literature no less than science and social science.[63]

At the time many scientists doubted that Conant's historical cases would make science more generally available. J. Robert Oppenheimer thought the exercises would fail because they insufficiently represented the experience of ignorance and the climate of error in which scientists must work.[64] Conant's enthusiasm for his project, however, and his vigorous advocacy in behalf of better science teaching undoubtedly added much to the general push for reform and to the National Science Foundation's development of a new high school physics course in 1956 and a new mathematics in 1958.[65] In all of these reforms and experiments, however, Conant held to his belief in a division between scientist and nonscientist. He did not believe, as some do today, that a thorough grounding in what might be called scientific literacy could be given to American adults or children.[66]

It was not school politics or Harvard politics that drove James Bryant Conant to write his educational platform. The cold war lent the impulse to gather together all his lectures and ideas into one coherent call for the reform of America's schools. *Education in a Divided World, The Function of the Public School in Our Unique Society*, written during the spring of 1948, was intended as a program to make "public schools . . . instruments of democracy."[67]

He began his text with a call to the defense: "The international situation which to many appeared ambiguous in the fall of 1945 has become alarmingly clear again . . . Whatever may be one's political views, it seems hard to deny today that the relation of the United States to the struggle between the Soviet Union and the democracies has overriding significance for our national planning. The relevance of this struggle to our American system of free schools seems also clear."[68] He had seen European nations crumble from within, and he wanted to make sure it would not happen here. The schools could be agencies of both political maintenance and social repair. In the forthcoming long years of an armed truce with Russia, Americans "must look increasingly to our free schools for the effective demonstration of our answer to totalitarian ideologies." Like many Boston preachers before him, James Bryant Conant hoped that by reminding the parishioners of the perils of Satan he could awaken in their breasts the motives for good behavior.[69]

Conant generally took pains to present his proposals as a middle way, a reasonable compromise between political extremes and between necessarily conflicting goals. This 1948 educational platform followed his favorite style. In politics he noted that radicals spoke as if "human society were possible without diversification of employment and without concentration of responsibility and authority in a relatively few people."[70] A modern society could not function without a hierarchical structure. "Eventually within the limits imposed by public opinion decisions of far-reaching importance are made by relatively few."[71] But he considered conservatives just as wrong in thinking that the present methods for determining who shall rule and who shall be rewarded are the only and the best ones. A better compromise between equality and hierarchical structure can be struck.

A second compromise must be found, Conant continued, in order to balance the need to train all children in a common democratic cultural tradition and the need to adequately prepare gifted youth for higher education and positions of leadership. His book then reviewed the current balance of these political and educational compromises and concluded by setting forth Conant's middle way.[72]

Conant associated his goals with the nineteenth-century frontier period, a time when rapid settlement and economic expansion not only gave many a chance to get ahead, but made the society appear to be without fixed classes because so many were in motion economically, socially, and politically.[73] He hoped that an adequate public school program could approximate this earlier condition even in a complex, hierarchical, industrial civilization. The possibilities for mobility through the school system would, he expected, provide fluidity and changing status from generation to generation, while democratically managed schools with common core curricula would simultaneously reduce the visibility of the nation's class ladder.[74]

As he wrote in 1948 he had gathered a deal of educational wisdom from Harvard social scientists and from his experience as a member of national educational boards. By now he appreciated the strength of the obstacles to the sort of educational meritocracy he wished to foster. One of the oldest barriers to fairness was the conflicting desire of families to find noncompetitive ways to advance their children and to find privileged positions for them.[75] Another barrier he named educational Toryism, the insistence that a particular curriculum be taught always and everywhere, regardless of the nature of the local community and the interests of its families and children. What makes a curriculum satisfactory or unsatisfactory is often "not due to discrepancies in the intellectual capacities of students, but the social situation in which the boys and girls are placed."[76]

Another barrier rested on the deep racial oppressions and ethnic antagonisms of American society, which closed out many talented youngsters. Finally, Conant noted some of the obstacles formed by the varying environments of schools. His book was freighted with the vocabulary of social ecology and euphemisms for the nasty words in the American vernacular. There are no

slums in this book, but "congested areas"; no poor, but "low income groups"; no working class, but "neighborhoods where 90
percent of the families have union cards." There are "those concerned with running machines or distributing machine products," and there are "well-to-do residential suburbs."[77]

Conant located his middle way between pairs of alternatives.
He accepted the current political balance and concentrated instead upon adjusting the educational one. He cautiously skirted
the responsibilities of local school politics for the class, racial, and
ethnic barriers to the education of American children. Instead of
attacking localism, he associated local control with the continuation of America's historic democratic traditions. Later, for these
same reasons, he became an ardent proponent of the comprehensive high school.[78] For the moment he stressed that despite all
manner of segregations and all kinds of differences among local
schools, those schools promoted a common American culture by
at least holding together the children who enrolled together,
regardless of family backgrounds or future aspirations. He
added, in passing, his hopes that "younger social scientists" might
be of service by designing ways to help the nation shed its prejudices.[79]

His educational compromise attempted to harness the two conflicting poles of America's tradition of equality. Conant's cold war
fears and his growing awareness of the children who were not
college-bound led him to stress the need for schools that could
refresh the empire's democratic ideology by reaching out to all
children. "Within the limits imposed by the heterogeneity of our
population, we are trying to develop a program for the general
education of all American youth."[80] The equality of children, the
equality of being, at least in school, was at one pole of his educational compromise. At the other pole stood his lifelong devotion
to social mobility—the race of the talented, the advancement of
the American meritocracy. The local high schools must offer adequate training for those who can go on to higher education, those
who can compete for the limited positions of authority.

Conant's suggestions for the reform of the common curriculum
combined things he had learned from Dean Francis Spaulding
with his own personal restatements of the concept of general
education. Following John Dewey, he insisted that regardless of

subject matter the school could best teach democracy by practicing it. Snobbery must be rooted out, and the schools of the nation must exemplify the values "we extol." Moreover, the schools must offer counseling to help each child choose a career that would match his or her interests and talents. High school students must no longer drift on the waves of fashion. They deserved help in finding careers in which they could succeed. Guidance was Conant's answer to the European tradition of early separating the academically gifted from others, an economical practice that exacerbated class tensions and injustices.[81]

Finally, the common curriculum should impart a universal democratic culture. This ideological task was Conant's reason for introducing general education, and in presenting it he labored hard with all the timeless difficulties of school subjects. He found the humanities most at fault for being too bookish and too snobbish. He wrote impatiently of humanists as the agents of upper-class fashion, instructors in class nastiness. In an open democratic society, Conant attacked, "you can no longer entice pupils of any age with appeals to the higher snobbery. For if we can all have knowledge for the asking, its snob value is very small. So 'we the people' say to the humanists, you will have to 'sell us' on the value of your understanding and appreciation of the past before we will even enter your classrooms, your museums, or your libraries. The social and parental pressures that once brought you humanists your well-clothed and well-born pupils no longer hold."[82]

Having demolished the old literary ways, Conant took an aggressively contemporary stand. Modern society, the world around the pupil and the school, should be the starting point. Curiosity about this environment and how it came to be should lure teacher and pupil toward serious study of their cultural heritage. Modern society, Conant explained, perhaps unguardedly, presented an "amazing picture," and the commonplace "social bewilderment" of most Americans could perhaps goad students' interest in the art and literature of the past.[83]

Conant wanted to focus social studies, what he called "the study of man," upon the teaching of democratic ideology. He felt that each school should determine its own blend of civics, history, and social sciences, but like his Harvard professors, he suggested that teachers draw upon a secular interpretation of the Hebraic-Christian tradition. This tradition, he thought, represented the root of Americans' national cultural consensus. So that the courses could be simple and comprehensible to all, they should be taught descriptively and historically. Philosophical questions should be postponed for college. Again Conant hoped curiosity about contemporary society might carry teacher and student toward an inquiry into its traditions and origins.[84]

James Bryant Conant did not think science could play an important role in the common curriculum of general education because he believed its ideological content to be very limited. Historically, he viewed science as having developed apart from the general culture until the nineteenth and twentieth centuries, when it began to merge with it. He imagined that science did not contribute to the democratic tradition he wanted children to master. Yet, in spite of these reservations, the contemporary world was filled with science, so some science should be taught. Again he recommended the descriptive and historical method.[85]

The other side of his educational balance, the training of gifted children, Conant found easier to specify. In keeping with his political sensitivities he stressed a minimum competence that any high school might successfully undertake. Local schools need not launch ambitious college preparatory programs for their academic youngsters. Foreign languages, philosophy, and specific sciences could wait for later. The essentials for the gifted were few: skill in writing English, the ability to handle mathematics through algebra, and the habit of concentrated reading. Stated another way, gifted children of seventeen must have been intellectually stimulated in some subject or subjects, they must have a belief in the efficacy and relevance of book learning, formal study, and rational analysis, and they must have good work habits. College, graduate school, postdoctoral research and training could do the rest.[86]

Conant's 1948 educational compromise proved immensely popular. Its acceptance of local control of schools insulated it not only from the immediate battle over federal control but also from the searing battles of the later civil rights movement. Its stress on education for all children lent support to the nation's harried school boards and teachers, who faced the task of keeping pace with the baby boom. Its modest demands for the gifted dampened class conflicts at a time when suburbanization and increased college attendance made education an ever more forceful contributor to misunderstanding, antagonism, and conflict among classes.

Clearly his platform was the handiwork of a gifted educational statesman. The popularity of this book and his later ones testified to his skill and judgment. As he continued in the field, however, he reluctantly abandoned the goal of a common core culture, a single ideological tradition that could be translated into a multiplicity of locally appropriate curricula. "As I write these words [in 1969], I find it a painful necessity to admit . . . that I have silently thrown overboard my assumption that a unified coherent culture was possible in a democratic country . . . I long since became convinced that a pluralistic ideology must be the basis of a democracy."[87] His acceptance of the politics of localism for his 1948 platform prefigured such a retreat.

Nevertheless, his basic proposals were strange ones for 1948 and remain peculiar today. Their inappropriateness resides not in Conant's educational theory or in the balances of his educational statesmanship, but in his isolation of science from the realms of common knowledge. Although he was a scientist living in a "scientific age," he sharply circumscribed science in his proposals for popular education. He was either unable to master or unwilling to apply his own experience. It was a matter of the utmost urgency, he said, for children to master civics, American history, and the common voice of the Judeo-Christian tradition—but why not include science and its values?

The isolation and minimization of science in Conant's educational platform is all the more striking because during these same years his lectures on science to college audiences presented an extremely accurate and potentially useful portrait of our modern culture. His science lectures offered the Boston province of high technology and the American empire of machines much better keys to self-examination than what later triumphed as the fashionable outlook.

The fashionable mode was to hide behind the excuse of two cultures. C. P. Snow came to Harvard in 1960 and popularized this conceit with his stories of English universities and British civil servants.[88] And because the two-culture fiction allowed the powerful and the famous to choose either screen to hide behind, the fashion persisted. A distinguished provincial physicist, Gerald Holton, recently spoke of the social and political evils he thought attended the academic conventions that divided our culture into two parts, scientific and nonscientific. "The exlusion of most of us from the mode of thought which informs scientific advance," the physicist said, "the painful awareness that its operative conceptions are alien to the mass of educated persons: these are the wounds of intellectual deprivation, of being denied the knowledge without which some of our best cannot be sure they have a sane hold on the world. This intellectual deprivation feeds the sense of helplessness concerning the social and political decisions which science directly or indirectly helps to propel."[89]

No one knew of the isolation and of the barriers between scientists and nonscientists better than Conant. But he also knew there were not two cultures but one: the culture of reason and science. Of course, within, beneath, and beside this dominant culture there were fragments of all kinds, the sets of value clusters that had forced him to accept pluralism in school politics. But pluralism or no, the culture of reason and science dominated all the other, lesser ones.

In a series of lectures given at Columbia University in 1952 James Bryant Conant carefully set forth his understanding of modern science to a general college audience. In the Brampton Lectures, published as *Modern Science and Modern Man,* Conant tried to tell educated laymen what they ought to know about their new cultural circumstances. He first cleared away the common misunderstanding that because scientific knowledge is cumulative it must therefore provide a more and more complete and consistent guide to nature. Science, Conant said emphatically, does not resemble a map, it is not a diagram that becomes increasingly finished. Instead, science is closer to an art gallery, an ever-growing museum in which the collection of portraits, landscapes, and still lives encourages artists to paint still more. Each one of the pictures in the museum offers a different outlook upon nature. Some of these outlooks have given rise to whole schools of painting, others have not led any artists to further exploration. Each painting, or school of painting, examines its own material, is consistent unto itself, and is useful to the viewers for some purposes, but never for all. As a whole the museum's collections do not make a unified portrait of nature.[90]

The culture of reason and science is thus multiple, or plural, and Conant thought the culture would become more complex and increasingly multiple as scientific reasoning and investigation continued.[91] In reviewing this process he was keen to warn us, as Vannevar Bush was, that a scientist does not work on problems because they might have practical application, but because the scientist's curiosity and knowledge and the scientific climate lead toward a problem.

But to say that science is an academy, and that it is abstract, that it follows the enthusiasms of scientists is not to say that it exists apart from the general culture. On the contrary, Conant strongly argued that "we must regard scientific theories as guides to human action and thus as an extension of our common sense."[92] Today's common sense may lag behind the latest developments, yet in time it always incorporates yesterday's science. For those who live in a province of computers, laboratories, and missile factories it is impossible to deny Conant's understanding. Bostonians live among the hypotheses of recent science, just as their grandparents accepted as common sense Pasteur's new hypothesis about fermentation.[93]

Conant summed up his lecture as follows: "Literally every step we take in life is determined by a series of interlocking concepts and conceptual schemes. Every goal we formulate for our actions, every decision we make, be it trivial or momentous, involves assumptions about the universe and about human beings. To my mind, any attempt to draw a sharp line between common-sense ideas and scientific concepts is not only impossible but unwise . . . The common-sense ideas of our ancestors before the dawn of modern science were the foundation of all their value judgments. If scientific concepts are now part of our common-sense assumptions, and who can doubt they are, then to that degree at least, the consequences of the actions of previous scientists now affect our value judgments."[94]

Surely such an outlook better describes the life and circumstances of our province today than the dodge of two cultures. But if Conant believed in the unity of science and society, why did he give so little of his general educational reform to science? As Gerald Holton concluded, "How can we think of ourselves as capable of self-government, and therefore of freedom in such a world [of scientific ignorance]?"[95]

Perhaps James Bryant Conant, the educational statesman, feared that it was asking too much of American schools to undertake scientific literacy. Perhaps he realized that neither his Harvard professors, nor the schoolteachers, nor the parents were yet willing to identify the science in their common sense, their modern literature, and their current values. As a leader of World War II and the cold war, perhaps he feared that science had destroyed the old tradition he wanted so desperately to prop up. Perhaps he hoped that what he knew to be true was mistaken, and that somewhere, somehow, beyond the province of reason, perhaps in the knowledge of the common people, or in their memories of the past, there was a residue of wisdom that would keep science safe in human hands. Whatever he believed, the best he could offer his audience was the bleak comfort of the Book of Job.[96]

12 ❦ RACHEL CARSON

The death of seven robins in Duxbury, Massachusetts, during the summer of 1957 was the proximate cause of a new political movement that has since endeavored to end the isolation of science and some of its ignorant applications. Like many towns with marshy places in Massachusetts, the seashore resort of Duxbury embarked on an ambitious DDT spraying program during the summer of 1957 in the hope of controlling its mosquitoes. The book editor of the *Boston Post*, Olga Owens Huckins, then a resident of Duxbury, observed with horror that the spraying killed the robins in her backyard. The following winter she wrote to a friend, the marine biologist and nature writer Rachel Carson (1907–1964), to tell her what had happened.

Carson had long been worried by what she regarded as the dangerous abuse of the earth by those in charge of modern industry. When she received Olga Huckins's letter, she decided to undertake the task of revealing this new scientific crisis. This was not the heedless slaughter of thousands of men, women, and children during a war but the greedy, short-sighted, and ignorant behavior of millions of men, women, and children, whose small actions began countless little chains of destruction, with incalculable long-term consequences. Here, in a new guise, had arrived the indeterminacies and infinities of our modern culture of reason.[1]

Rachel Carson was a familiar sort of figure in the Boston province, a visiting scholar who became an enthusiastic summer resident. As a college girl in Pittsburgh, Pennsylvania, she had discovered a fascination for the ocean, but she did not meet her lifetime subject until the summer of 1929 when, just out of college, she spent six weeks studying turtles at the Marine Biological Laboratories in Woods Hole, Massachusetts.[2] Thereafter the Atlantic coast and ocean became her focus of study and exploration, and the granite coast of Maine her special delight.

From 1946 until her death in 1964 she came each summer to stay at the edge of the Sheepscot River, in Boothbay, Maine. In a letter to a friend in Washington, D.C., during her first summer there, she concluded, "From all this you will know that I don't have brains enough to figure out a way to stay here the rest of my life. At least I know that my greatest ambition is to be able to buy a place here and then manage to spend a lot of time in it—summers at least."[3] Seven years later, with the royalties from her book *The Sea Around Us,* she was able to buy a small shore lot and to build her own cottage at West Southport.[4]

Rachel Carson was born in the small town of Springdale in the Allegheny River valley, sixteen miles north and east of Pittsburgh. In 1900 her father Robert Warden Carson, had purchased sixty-five acres of land and had set out an apple orchard hoping that as the town grew he could prosper by cutting his woods and orchard into streets and house lots. Springdale, however, grew very slowly and Carson received only small profits on occasional sales of his lots. He supported his family mainly as an operator at the local electric power station.[5]

Rachel's mother, Maria, was a Presbyterian minister's daughter. She had graduated from a Pennsylvania female seminary and had taught school before marrying in 1894. Her first child, Maria, was born in 1897, and the second, Robert, in 1899. Rachel, the youngest by eight years, was kept close to home during her early school years. Her mother seems to have watched over Rachel's education very carefully and to have keenly identified with her ambition to be a writer.[6] An excellent student in the local public schools, Rachel in 1925 enrolled in the Pennsylvania College for Women (since 1955, Chatham College). Always short of money and shy by temperament, Rachel followed a common path of the scholarship student; she became the engrossed scholar. She first triumphed in English literature and composition, and then, in a

required course in biology, she discovered the fascination of scientific research. Under the guidance of an inspiring teacher and
later close friend, Mary Scott Skinker, Rachel Carson became a
zoology major, graduating in 1929 *magna cum laude.* Her college
distinction won her a scholarship to the master's program at
Johns Hopkins University in Baltimore and a six-week summer
study session at Woods Hole.[7]

Back home in Springdale the Great Depression apparently had
destroyed her family's economic situation. In January 1930, when
Rachel rented a house at Stemmer's Run, Maryland, thirteen
miles northeast of Baltimore, but only two miles from the Chesapeake Bay, her mother, father, and brother moved there with
her. The following summer Rachel began a seven-year stint as an
assistant in a summer general biology course at Johns Hopkins.
She also found a half-time job for three years as an assistant in zoology at the University of Maryland. In June 1932 she completed
her master's essay, a study of the development of the larval kid-
ney of the catfish. Then in July 1935 her father died of a heart attack, and Rachel was forced to find full-time work.[8]

Because of her interest in fish, she went to the U.S. Bureau of
Fisheries in Washington where, to her good fortune, the head of
the Bureau's Division of Scientific Inquiries, Elmer Higgins, was
just then struggling with a writing task. The bureau had con-
tracted for a fifty-two-week series of seven-minute radio programs entitled "Romance Under the Waters," but Higgins had
run out of ideas, and the professional script writer knew nothing
of marine biology. Higgins hired Carson to finish the series. That
summer she took the highest score in the federal civil service
examination and joined Higgins's staff as a junior aquatic biologist.

The job proved a happy arrangement for all. Higgins gained a
bright, energetic biologist who was also a fine editor and a brilliant writer. For the next sixteen years Rachel Carson worked at
Fisheries,[9] in time becoming head of a small information office
that handled publications, answered inquiries, and wrote bro-
chures and manuals on everything from fish recipes to wildlife
refuges.[10] On Carson's side, she found a sympathetic boss who
encouraged her to write books on her own. The job gave her ac-

cess to Fisheries' Atlantic stations in Florida, North Carolina, and Massachusetts, where she carried on her own examinations of the life of the shore and the ocean. Articles and books on what was slowly developing as the modern specialty of ecology crossed her desk.

Secure in her government job, Rachel Carson and her mother moved to Silver Spring, Maryland, just outside of Washington. There they raised the two school-age daughters of her older sister Maria, who had died at forty. Later, when the younger of the two children died as a young adult, Rachel adopted her five-year-old grandnephew, Roger.[11]

In 1935 Carson's work was far removed from the fashions in academic chemistry and physics that had then captured the imagination of most American scientists: Conant's polymers, the radio of Bush and Marshall, Arthur Holly Compton's X-rays. In fact Carson and her fellow biologists were in a far room of the museum of science, following a line of questions whose popularity had passed. Their work, however, could not have been of greater social significance. They inherited Charles Darwin's evolutionary and genetic revolution, which in the late nineteenth and early twentieth centuries had been dangerously misapplied as prescriptions for human behavior and rules for ranking human beings. Many states were enacting laws for the compulsory sterilization of the "unfit," and American social science, politics, and popular culture spilled over with hereditary and racial imaginings. In Europe the extermination of the Jews was about to begin.[12] The marine and wildlife biologists, by keeping their studies fixed upon plants, animals, and insects, bypassed these social issues and in time were able to make the study of evolution and ecologies more reliable. Their work made it possible for a gifted writer like Rachel Carson to translate science into a more accurate portrait of the place of humans in nature.

The U.S. Fish and Wildlife Service, like the Forest and Park services, was a product of the United States' first conservation movement. For a generation, from 1880 until World War I, this fusion of sport hunters and fishermen, foresters, and wilderness enthusiasts constituted a powerful political movement. The threats then perceived came from lumber and mining companies, whose methods exploited the land and threatened the nation with the loss of its forests, threatened the arid West with loss of its water resources, and brought floods to the Midwest and South. Intellectually the movement drew its strength from American geological studies, from English and German forestry practices, and from a chain of nature writers, including Henry David Thoreau and John Burroughs in the East and John Muir in California.[13]

The first conservationists' success in setting apart vast tracts of timber and wilderness lands brought unexpected scientific complexities. Quite without preparation, the wildlife managers became the engineers of Darwin's evolutionary processes. Questions about the proper management within the reservations soon came up, and a number of disasters revealed the naturalists' ignorance. For example, when the elk of Yellowstone National Park and the Kaibab deer of the Grand Canyon were carefully sequestered in the 1920s, both species nearly died off from subsequent overpopulation and lack of predators.[14]

The man who most quickly learned from these early mistakes was Aldo Leopold of the U.S. Forest Service, and Leopold's writings strongly influenced Carson. His message was a challenging one. It demanded a set of attitudes that are not common in the drive to win in science, business, or politics. It demanded that Americans and their scientists take a long view of human time, that they assume a wide geographical focus, and that they be willing to see human beings as enmeshed in extremely complex biotic systems. Leopold's outlook, though today often mentioned with reverence in conservation circles, is still far from commonplace either in the Boston province or the empire. He asserted that if man was to survive on the long time scale of the earth itself, he would have to maintain a series of biological steady states. That is, human societies would have to conduct their affairs so that the large biotic communities to which they belong could change slowly enough to be able to maintain their balance. The sudden reduction in the numbers of different species and the also-sudden multiplication of a few species through urbanization and high-technology agriculture Leopold understood to be a grave danger to man and to the earth's steady states.[15]

Rachel Carson in time found ways to translate this ecological value system into terms by which it could be connected to popular tradition and general understanding. She began her career as a nature writer in 1935, turning out short pieces for the *Sunday Baltimore Sun*, stories like "Chesapeake Eels Seek the Sargasso Sea" and "It'll Be Shad-Time Soon."[16] Then in 1937 she sent an evocative article on the cycles of the sea to the *Atlantic Monthly*, which published it as "Undersea."[17] The article caught the attention of several nature writers, and, encouraged by them, she enlarged her article into her first book, *Under the Sea-Wind* (1941). The book had the misfortune to appear on the eve of the United States' entry into World War II, but it did enable Carson to practice her technique and to develop ways of translating modern biology into readily intelligible narratives and descriptions.

Her writing was always a joining of the insights of modern science with a literary outlook. She inherited from the Romantics the style of the first-person relationship to nature. Thoreau's sermons on Walden Pond had been of this type, and the form continued for many years thereafter. Miss Carson particularly admired Henry Beston's *Outermost House* (1928). In his book Beston recounted his responses to a year spent on the edge of the Atlantic Ocean, on Cape Cod. Beston's outlook repeated the provincial moralism of Thoreau and Emerson. He was a city dweller who sought restoration by distancing himself from a debilitating urban society. "The world today is sick to its thin blood for lack of elemental things," he began, "for fire before the hands, for water welling from the earth, for air, for the dear earth itself underfoot. In my world of beach and dune these elemental presences lived and had their being, and under their arch there moved an incomparable pageant of nature and the year."[18]

Rachel Carson gave up the outworn convention of city versus nature and expanded her consciousness to as many subjects as the ecology demanded. In *Under the Sea-Wind*, about the coast of North Carolina, the subjects were the rat, the turtle, the heron, the skimmer, the sandpiper, the eel, the shad, and the crab. All were seen as subjects in their own right, each species acting according to its own necessities. They were also described as parts of the shoreline ecology and of the cycle of ocean seasons.

In this first book Rachel Carson was still unsure of how to locate herself. Having abandoned the naturalist's "I," she sought safety in the conventions of nineteenth-century fiction. For each of her main subjects she devised a principal character—Rynchops the black skimmer, Scomber the mackerel, and Anguilla the eel. Each character was accompanied through the activities of a year's cycle by an all-seeing author, much as Charles Dickens had shepherded Mr. Pickwick through London.

In her later books, *The Sea Around Us* (1950) and *The Edge of the Sea* (1955), Carson adopted a more straightforward decriptive style. Both the naturalist's "I" and the novelist's main character disappeared, and she spoke directly to her reader. She persisted, however, in her special relationship to nature—never subject to object, but always subject to subject. Here she drew on the best of the romantic tradition, which recognized forces and purposes other than man's in all human settings. The subjects for Miss Carson were always plural, indeed as multiple as the science of ecology demanded. The expectation behind the style was that as science discovered more and more interactions, they too would be added to future descriptions of the relationships of nature.

Modern science also required abandoning the conventional time scales of the past. The life of the single individual and the millennial clock of Judaism and Christianity could not possibly describe the modern world with any accuracy. These traditional measures neglected the time frames of the many creatures of the earth and their particular rhythms, and by so doing falsified the position of man within the many ecologies of the world. Even in the early "Undersea," Carson insisted upon multiple time frames: the rapid cell division of the mackerel embryo, the high-speed change of the crest of a wind-blown dune;[19] the slower clocks of the year's cycle of seasons, and the fertility of birds, fishes, and mammals; the even slower cycle of predation from diatom to fish to man; the very long times of the forces of evolution and geology.[20] One of Carson's gifts was her ability to present a moment's observation or a description of an ongoing phenomenon, such as ocean waves, in a manner that either mentioned directly or implied the multiple time scales of the creatures and forces in interaction.[21]

Often in her descriptions she spoke of imagining the long time frame from the evolution of early sea creatures to the present. She referred to this sensation as "the sense of creation."[22] She wrote at the opening of *The Edge of the Sea* that "there is a common thread that links these scenes and memories—the spectacle of life in all its varied manifestations as it has appeared, evolved, and sometimes died out. Underlying the beauty of the spectacle there is meaning and significance. It is the elusiveness of that meaning that haunts us, that sends us again and again into the natural world where the key to the riddle is hidden."[23]

She continued the provincial and American religious concern in nature writing. In this genre the position of God has always been crucial, as it is still in our popular approach to nature, whether it be as viewers of scenery, watchers of birds or weather, gardeners, mountain climbers, hunters, or fishermen. In all these activities there is an element, unspoken or spoken, of religious feeling. Boston's philosophers and divines in the past drew upon the ancient tradition of Plato and his formulation of the Great Chain of Being. In this construction it was imagined that God required the existence of all the beings in nature, so out of his generative powers He created all the living things that populated the globe. For Plato, as for later Christians, God did not spread his grace about equally, but chose to bestow it in a hierarchical fashion. God's plenitude flowed first down to man, then spilled over on the higher mammals, and so forth, down to the lowly and ubiquitous plankton.[24]

Charles Darwin blasted this hierarchical concept, and the Great Chain of Being is no longer credible to an informed mind. Yet science did not destroy, indeed it fed upon and augmented, our desire for order and harmony in nature. These were the feelings that Rachel Carson expressed in religious terms as a "sense of wonder." It was an outlook that celebrated life in all its multiplicity, a religious point of view drawn from the writings of Albert Schweitzer (1875-1965), the missionary physician to Gabon (French Equatorial Africa), Bach scholar, organist, and theologian. Schweitzer, like Gandhi, had become a secular saint for many Americans, who saw his life as an alternative to the narrow science, petty business, and barbaric politics of the twentieth century. Like most theologians, Schweitzer wrote to reconcile modern knowledge with religious belief. He found his affirmation in what he called "reverence for life."[25] Like Carson's sense of wonder, his reverence for life was both an adjustment to modern existence and a continuation of nineteenth-century religious trends.

Carson's *Silent Spring*, which attacked the contemporary uses of pesticides and herbicides, was dedicated to Schweitzer. When she accepted the Schweitzer Medal from the Animal Welfare Institute in 1963, she acknowledged her debt to him and spoke of her religious feeling. "From my own store of memories, I think of the sight of a small crab alone on a dark beach at night, a small fragile being waiting on the edge of the roaring surf, yet so perfectly at home in its world. To me it seemed a symbol of life, and of the way life had adjusted to the forces of the physical environment."[26]

Rachel Carson was planning to write another book somewhat like *The Sea Around Us* when the letter from her friend in Duxbury on the robins killed by DDT convinced her that she must turn to politics. From 1958 until 1962 she sifted through the scientific literature to assemble her attack on the ignorant, shortsighted, and often dishonest use of pesticides and herbicides. In *Silent Spring* she managed, as Emily Greene Balch had before her, to translate her private feelings and her extensive study of the contemporary world into effective public action. Upon publication, the book immediately caused an explosion of public opinion. Since that time debate over the management of the earth and its environments has become open and public, a fitting subject for politics at all scales of human organization.

The specifics of the reception of *Silent Spring* do not require retelling in a history of the Boston province. Bostonians proved to be as divided and ambivalent in their willingness to restrain their pollution of the air, land, and water as other Americans. For the province, however, the special meaning of Rachel Carson's last book lay in its thorough revelation of a cultural crisis. By 1962 the dominant culture of reason was gaining ever more popularity as the electronics industries began to flourish. It was a flash of engineering triumph in the midst of scientific bankruptcy.

In the behavior of the agricultural and chemical companies, all the dangers that Vannevar Bush and James Bryant Conant feared manifested themselves. Bush and Conant had insisted upon the isolation of science and the insulation of academies managed by peers because they feared the corruption of science under the control of business or government. Now, in the business and politics of agriculture and chemicals, information was being suppressed, faulty data used, and campaigns launched to promote public ignorance and prejudice.[27] If scientific knowlege could bring wealth and prosperity by invention, so it must also bring the wealth and power to control and to corrupt.

Thoughtful scientists had long realized that as knowledge multiplied and science more and more intervened in the interactions of man and nature, the outcomes of these interactions would multiply and their consequences would become indeterminate. *Silent Spring* documented that process. Once DDT had been offered for sale nationally and worldwide, the actions of millions of people became significant. Their millions of uses of DDT changed the interactions of local biotic systems and food chains. And the sheer numbers of actors and events soon became so great as to defy prediction of the outcomes. What seemed an intentional, reasoned event—the manufacture and sale of a chemical—had become irrational and indeterminate.

Emily Greene Balch, studying the scale of international economies and migrations, had come to see the modern human condition in similar terms. Her approach to the immigrant city, to industrialization, and to international wars stressed humane processes, not just because they were desirable methods for improving health, economic justice, or peace in the short run, but also because such processes offered the best chances for safety in a world whose outcomes could not be predicted. It seems no accident that both Balch and Carson drew their values from the same romantic tradition, which stressed the relationships between the observer and the observed and found in these relationships the source of value. Those values, however, are not those of the province of reason. Our values have become those of Bush and Conant, of open competition and success. These are important half-truths, but they are far too limited and feeble to teach us about science, life, or war.

At the time of the publication of *Silent Spring*, Rachel Carson was already being overtaken by cancer. She spent a year on public platforms, testifying, arguing, and accepting honors, then retired for a last summer at her cottage on the Maine seashore. On April 14, 1964, she died at her home in Silver Spring, Maryland.

NOTES

CREDITS

INDEX

NOTES

INTRODUCTION

1. Albert E. Stone, ed., *The American Autobiography* (Englewood Cliffs, N.J., 1981); Marc Pachter, ed., *Telling Lives, The Biographer's Art* (Washington, D.C., 1979).
2. Sam Bass Warner, Jr., *The Way We Really Live: Social Change in Metropolitan Boston Since 1920* (Boston, 1977), pp. 6–16.
3. Cleveland Amory, "Boston in the 'Proper' Spirit"; Alan Lupo and Caryl Rivers, "Changing Boston," in *Boston: The Official Bicentennial Guidebook* (New York, 1975), pp. 11–43.
4. Alfred Kazin, "The Self as History: Reflections on Autobiography," in *Telling Lives*, pp. 75–89.

1. ROBERT GRANT

1. Grant was born at 62 Mount Vernon Street, raised at 5 Chestnut Street, and spent his collegiate years at 14 Commonwealth Avenue. His own first home was at 104 Marlborough Street, and his final home at 211 Bay State Road.
2. Robert Grant, *Fourscore, An Autobiography* (Boston, 1934), p. 71.
3. Grant, *Fourscore*, pp. 21–23.
4. Grant, *Fourscore*, pp. 24, 110.
5. Grant, *Fourscore*, p. 42.
6. Grant, *Fourscore*, pp. 28–36; Henry Cabot Lodge, *Early Memories* (New York, 1913), pp. 67–72, 83–90.
7. Grant, *Fourscore*, p. 42.
8. Grant, *Fourscore*, pp. 27, 30.
9. Grant, *Fourscore*, pp. 56–61.
10. Grant, *Fourscore*, p. 75.
11. Grant, *Fourscore*, pp. 80–96.
12. Robert Grant, "Harvard College in the Seventies," *Scribner's Magazine*, 21 (May 1897), 554–566.

13. The Grant family house at 14 Commonwealth Avenue has been torn down and replaced by an apartment house built in 1927.

14. Grant, *Fourscore*, pp. 103, 110–111, 127–132.

15. Grant, *Fourscore*, p. 112.

16. Grant, *Fourscore*, pp. 113, 116–117.

17. Grant, *Fourscore*, pp. 118, 125.

18. Grant, *Fourscore*, pp. 125, 157–159.

19. Grant, *Fourscore*, pp. 132–133, 145–148, 151–152, 163, 391.

20. The house at 104 Marlborough Street, which still stands, is an ordinary Back Bay house of the 1866 mansard type, five stories, with a parlor bay on the sunny side facing the alley. Patrick Grant died in 1895. Grant, *Fourscore*, p. 216.

21. Grant, *Fourscore*, pp. 194–196. The Fred and Josephine stories were published in book form as: *The Reflections of a Married Man* (New York, 1892), *The Opinions of a Philosopher* (New York, 1893), and *Convictions of a Grandfather* (New York, 1912).

22. Grant, *Fourscore*, pp. 191, 352.

23. Robert Grant, *The Chippendales* (New York, 1909), pp. 307–308, 498, 532.

24. Robert Grant, *Dark Horse, A Story of the Younger Chippendales* (New York, 1931), pp. 84, 227.

25. Grant, *Fourscore*, pp. 366–374; Francis Russell, "America's Dreyfus Case," *New York Review of Books*, 28 (Nov. 5, 1981), 15–18; *Sacco-Vanzetti: Developments and Reconsiderations—1979*, Conference Proceedings, Boston Public Library, October 26–27, 1979 (Boston, 1982).

26. Grant, *Dark Horse*, p. 93.

27. Grant, *Fourscore*, pp. 220, 283.

28. See especially the attack on Selma White by Flossy Williams. Robert Grant, *Unleavened Bread* (New York, 1900), pp. 243–244.

29. Grant, *Dark Horse*, pp. 85–86, 99; *Fourscore*, pp. 263–267.

30. Robert Grant, *Law and the Family* (New York, 1919), pp. 21–22.

31. Grant, *Fourscore*, pp. 360–363.

32. Grant, *Fourscore*, pp. 268–272.

33. Grant, *Fourscore*, pp. 199, 211, 250–251, 260–262; Nathan C. Shiverick, "The Social Reorganization of Boston," in *A Social History of the Greater Boston Clubs*, ed. Alexander W. Williams (Barre, Vt., 1970), pp. 128–143.

34. Grant, *Fourscore*, pp. 258–261.

35. Grant, *Fourscore*, pp. 253–254, 314–322. Like his friend Theodore Roosevelt, Grant enthusiastically supported the United States' entry into World War I, even though he saw it as a conflict of imperial rivalry for economic supremacy and world domination. *Fourscore*, pp. 305–306.

36. Grant, *Fourscore*, pp. 290–291.

37. Avery's invention was based upon the actual work of a local inventor, William W. Jacques of Newton. Jacques patented a process for generating electricity from carbon in an iron pot filled with caustic soda (U.S. Patent no. 55551, March 3, 1896). The engineering firm of Stone & Webster tested the

idea and found it to be "a deceptive *ignis fatuus.*" L. B. Buchman, "Stone and Webster in the Field of Electro-Chemistry," *Stone and Webster Public Service Journal,* 1 (September 1907), 151.

38. Grant, *Chippendales,* p. 308; *Fourscore,* p. 290.
39. Grant, *Chippendales,* p. 204.
40. Austin Warren, *The New England Conscience* (Ann Arbor, 1966).
41. Grant, *Chippendales,* p. 257.
42. Grant, *Chippendales,* pp. 334–335.
43. Grant, *Chippendales,* p. 343.
44. Grant, *Chippendales,* p. 600.

2. MARY ANTIN

1. Mary Antin, *The Promised Land* (Boston, 1912), pp. 202–205, 207.
2. Antin, *Promised Land,* pp. 209–217.
3. Antin, *Promised Land,* pp. 209–217, 249–250, 274–275, 317, 338.
4. Antin, *Promised Land,* pp. 237, 240; Alvin H. Rosenfeld, "Inventing the Jew: Notes on Jewish Autobiography," in *The American Autobiography,* ed. Albert E. Stone (Englewood Cliffs, N.J., 1981), p. 138.
5. Antin, *Promised Land,* pp. 252, 265. Wheeler Street no longer exists; its houses have been thrown down and its land incorporated into a housing project, Turnpike Towers, on a triangular plot bounded by Shawmut Avenue, Tremont Street, and Corning Street, next to the Massachusetts Turnpike.
6. Antin, *Promised Land,* pp. 264, 314.
7. Antin, *Promised Land,* p. 273.
8. Antin, *Promised Land,* p. 271.
9. Antin, *Promised Land,* p. 279.
10. Antin, *Promised Land,* pp. 276–277, 292.
11. Antin, *Promised Land,* pp. 295–296, 341–342.
12. Antin, *Promised Land,* pp. 288–291.
13. Antin, *Promised Land,* pp. 291, 314.
14. Antin, *Promised Land,* pp. 277–278, 297–299, 338, 349.
15. Antin, *Promised Land,* pp. 339–340.
16. Antin, *Promised Land,* pp. 344–349, 360–361.
17. In the anguish of the Jews since the World War II slaughter of millions, Mary Antin's, and many American Jewish immigrants' adjustment to the modern world has come under attack by those who assert that a return to the observance of Jewish ritual and tradition is the only proper mode for modern American Jewish life. Rosenfeld, "Inventing the Jew," pp. 146–156.
18. Oscar Handlin, "Foreword," in Mary Antin, *The Promised Land,* 2nd ed. (Boston, 1949), p. viii.
19. Zangwill was later the author of the popular play, *The Melting Pot* (1908). Josephine Lazarus wrote a laudatory review of Mary's book in *The Critic,* 34, old series (April 1899), 295, 317–318.
20. Antin, *Promised Land,* pp. 325–326, 330, 335. Hale House stood on Gar-

land Street, a short block between Shawmut Avenue and Washington Street, near Dover Street. It has since been demolished for the ill-advised Castle Square urban renewal project, and the street has been replaced by garages.

21. Antin, *Promised Land*, pp. 330–331, 335.
22. Mary Antin never graduated from Girls' Latin School. The Boston School Department records do not report her finishing with the class of 1901, and her biography lists her only as "attended." "Mary Antin," *The National Cyclopedia of American Biography*, 39 (1954), 40.
23. "Amadeus William Grabau," *National Cyclopedia*, 34 (1948), 89.
24. *New York Times*, May 18, 1949.
25. Josephine Lazarus, "Emma Lazarus," *Century Magazine*, 36 (October 1888), 875–884.
26. Josephine Lazarus, *The Spirit of Judaism* (New York, 1895), pp. 20, 25–27, 39–40, 52–53.
27. Lazarus, *Spirit of Judaism*, pp. 183–184. In terms of Jewish religious history, Josephine Lazarus's work seems most like that of the English radical reform leader Claude Montefiore (1858–1938), whom she often quoted.
28. Antin, *Promised Land*, pp. xii–xiii; *New York Times*, June 30, 1912.
29. Handlin, "Foreword," p. xii.
30. Antin, *Promised Land*, p. xiii.
31. Ellery Sedgwick, "Mary Antin," *American Magazine*, 77 (March 1914), 64–65.
32. Handlin, "Foreword," p. vi.
33. Mary Antin was a Theodore Roosevelt enthusiast, although she did not share his endorsement of woman suffrage. Mary Antin Grabau, letter to Theodore Roosevelt, Aug. 2, 1913, Papers of Theodore Roosevelt, Library of Congress (microfilm ed.), series one, reel 179; "Mary Antin," *National Cyclopedia*, 39:40.
34. Mary Antin, "They Who Knock at Our Gates, A Complete Gospel of Immigration," *American Magazine*, 77 (March, April, May 1914); published as a book with illustrations by Joseph Stella (Boston, 1914).
35. Antin, "At Our Gates," *American Magazine* (April 1914), 12, 19; (May, 1914), 46.
36. *New York Times*, July 20, 1916; Oct. 11, 1916.
37. "Mary Antin," *Twentieth Century Authors*, ed. Stanley J. Kunitz and Howard Haycraft (New York, 1942), pp. 33–34.
38. Letter to author from Rose L. McKee of Gould Farm, Jan. 2, 1982.
39. Rose L. McKee, *"Brother Will" and the Founding of Gould Farm* (William J. Gould Associates, Great Barrington, Mass., 1963), pp. 3, 11, 46, 67, 73.
40. Mary Antin, "The Soundless Trumpet," *Atlantic Monthly*, 159 (May 1937), 565–566.
41. Mary Antin, "House of the One Father," *Common Ground*, 1 (Spring 1941), 41.

3. FRED ALLEN

1. Edwin O'Connor, *The Edge of Sadness* (Boston, 1961).
2. *New York Times*, Mar. 18, 1956.
3. *Boston Globe*, Aug. 17, 1976.
4. The house was on Bayard Street, now well kept and comfortable, between Franklin and Weitz streets, off North Harvard Street.
5. Fred Allen, *Much Ado about Me* (Boston, 1956), pp. 3-7, 211-213.
6. Allen, *About Me*, pp. 9-10.
7. Grandmother's house was on Emmons Place, a short half-street off Roberts Road, near Cambridge and Kirkland streets and the Harvard campus.
8. Allen, *About Me*, pp. 12-13.
9. Allen, *About Me*, pp. 18, 23-24, 26-27, 29, 38.
10. Allen, *About Me*, p. 31.
11. The three-decker that Fred Allen purchased for his aunt was off Dorchester Avenue at 7 Grafton Street, at the corner of Buttonwood Street. It is still standing. Allen, *About Me*, pp. 21, 37.
12. Allen, *About Me*, p. 27.
13. Allen, *About Me*, pp. 29-32, 37-38.
14. Allen, *About Me*, pp. 40-41.
15. Allen, *About Me*, pp. 42-50.
16. Allen, *About Me*, pp. 51-52.
17. Elliot Norton, *Broadway Down East* (Boston, 1978), pp. 20, 78-79.
18. Allen, *About Me*, p. 81.
19. Allen, *About Me*, pp. 80-93.
20. Allen, *About Me*, pp. 53-56.
21. Allen, *About Me*, pp. 54-59, 62-67, 99.
22. Allen, *About Me*, pp. 67-77.
23. Allen, *About Me*, pp. 103-118.
24. Allen, *About Me*, p. 203.
25. Allen, *About Me*, pp. 213-214, 314-319; *Boston Globe*, Aug. 17, 1976. The Hotel Clarendon was at 523 Tremont Street, near the National Theater, which has since been incorporated into the Boston Center for the Arts. The Clarendon, however, was torn down for urban renewal, and now the land serves as a parking lot.
26. Allen, *About Me*, p. 212.
27. Allen, *About Me*, p. 226.
28. Allen, *About Me*, pp. 275, 336; Allen, *Treadmill to Oblivion* (Boston, 1954), pp. 15-17.
29. During the thirties the Allens's address in New York City was 180 West 58th Street, and they vacationed at Old Orchard Beach, Maine. Joe McCarthy, ed., *Fred Allen's Letters* (New York, 1965).
30. Allen, *Treadmill*, pp. 154-159.
31. Allen, *Treadmill*, p. 5.
32. Allen, *Treadmill*, pp. 30-35. Hodge White's variety store stood at 891 Dor-

chester Avenue, on the corner of Edison Street. *Boston Globe*, Nov. 23, 1942.
33. Allen, *Treadmill*, pp. 6–8.
34. Allen, *Treadmill*, pp. 27, 210–211.
35. Allen, *Treadmill*, p. 212.

INTRODUCTION TO PART TWO

1. Barbara Miller Solomon, *Ancestors and Immigrants, A Changing New England Tradition* (Cambridge, Mass., 1956).
2. Edwin O'Connor, *The Last Hurrah* (Boston, 1956).
3. Robert O. Preyer, "The Romantic Tide Reaches Trinity," in *Victorian Science and Victorian Values*, ed. James Paradis and Thomas Postlewait, Annals of the New York Academy of Science, 360 (New York, 1981), pp. 49–53.
4. Alfred North Whitehead, *Science and the Modern World* (New York, 1925), pp. 129–132, 274–279; Edmund Wilson, *Axel's Castle; a Study in the Imaginative Literature of 1870–1930* (New York, 1931), pp. 4–10.

4. CHARLES A. STONE AND EDWIN S. WEBSTER

1. Thomas A. Watson, *Exploring Life* (New York, 1926), pp. 52–54.
2. *The Boston Directory for the Year Commencing July 1, 1889* (Boston, 1889; microfilm ed., Research Publications, New Haven, 1968).
3. Robert V. Bruce, *Bell: Alexander Graham Bell and the Conquest of Solitude* (Boston, 1973), pp. 83–86, 92, 98, 163, 234.
4. William H. Blood, Jr., "The First Generation of Electricity," *Stone & Webster Public Service Journal*, 11 (November 1912), 321–323; Percy Dunsheath, *A History of Electrical Power Engineering* (Cambridge, Mass., 1962), pp. 183–186; John P. McKay, *Tramways and Trolleys: The Rise of Modern Transit in Europe* (Princeton, 1976), pp. 36–51.
5. *Who's Who in New England, 1909; The Story of Stone & Webster, 1888–1932*, company pamphlet (Boston, 1932); *Dictionary of American Biography*, Supplement Three.
6. Russell Robb, "Early History of the Firm," *S & W Public Service Journal*, 1 (August 1907), 4–5; L. B. Buchanan, "Stone & Webster's Laboratory," *S & W Public Service Journal*, 1 (September 1907), 145–149.
7. Robb, "Early History of the Firm," p. 6.
8. "The Stone & Webster Organization," *Street Railway Journal*, 28 (July 1906), 27–31.
9. "Stone & Webster," *Fortune*, 11 (November 1930), 94.
10. L. B. Buchanan, "Stone & Webster in the Field of Electro-Chemistry," *S & W Public Service Journal*, 1 (September 1907), 150–153; Arthur D. Little letter, *S & W Public Service Journal*, 49 (July 1932), 473; "Arthur Dehon Little," *Who's Who in New England, 1916*.

11. "Chandler Hovey," *Who's Who in Massachusetts, 1940–1941* (Boston, 1940), vol. I.

12. *Who's Who along the North Shore . . . for the Summer of 1911* (Salem, 1911); *Who's Who in New England, 1916; The Boston Street Directory for the Year Commencing August 1, 1924;* Bainbridge Bunting, *Houses of Boston's Back Bay* (Cambridge, Mass., 1967), pp. 260–265; *Fortune,* 11 (November 1930), 92; obituary of Edwin S. Webster, *New York Times,* May 11, 1950; obituary, *Technology Review,* 52 (July 1950), 523.

13. *Who's Who in New England, 1916;* "House of Charles A. Stone, Esq.," *American Architect—Architectural Review,* 120 (Dec. 21, 1921), photographs; *Fortune,* 11 (November 1930), 92; obituary of Mrs. Mary Stone, *New York Times,* Oct. 8, 1940; obituary of Charles Stone, *New York Times,* Feb. 25, 1941; obituary, *Technology Review,* 43 (Apr. 1, 1941), 263.

14. Stone & Webster advertisement, *S & W Public Service Journal,* 44 (March 1929), inside cover; Memorandum, Sept. 15, 1929, "Informative Data, 1927–31," typescript, black looseleaf book, Stone & Webster Technical Information Center, Boston, Mass; letters of W. Cameron Forbes and Eliot Wadsworth, *S & W Public Service Journal,* 49 (July 1932), 461, 469.

15. "News from the Companies," *S & W Public Service Journal,* 8 (April 1911), 287.

16. *Electric Railway and Lighting Properties Managed by Stone & Webster, 1906* (Stone & Webster, Boston, 1906); *Electric Railway and . . . , 1929;* Memorandum, July 1, 1929, Tabulation of the Fifteen Largest Public Utility Operators in the Country, "Informative Data, 1927–31;" "Stone & Webster Scope is Broad," *Wall Street Journal,* Feb. 19, 1930.

17. Howard L. Rogers, "Stone & Webster Engineering Corporation," *S & W Public Service Journal,* 1 (August 1907), 57–59.

18. A. J. Farnsworth, "Big Creek Power Development," *S & W Public Service Journal,* 11 (September 1912), 170–175.

19. George K. Hutchins, "Water Power Development of the Chattahoochee River," *S & W Public Service Journal,* 11 (July 1912), 7–11.

20. "News from the Companies," *S & W Public Service Journal,* 8 (April 1911), 287; Hugh L. Cooper, "Hydro-Electric Development on the Mississippi River at Keokuk," *S & W Public Service Journal,* 8 (June 1911), 401–420.

21. *Fortune,* 11 (November 1930), 96.

22. William H. Blood, Jr., "The Hog Island Shipyard," *S & W Public Service Journal,* 23 (July 1918), 9–13; "Industrial Buildings," small black book, labeled "copyright 1918" with completion dates and final costs of projects added April 3, 1919, S & W Technical Information Center, Boston; Memorandum, Dec. 1, 1927, List of Building Work Done under Supervisory Form of Contract, "Informative Data, 1927–31;" *Stone & Webster Incorporated, Annual Report, 1931,* p. 9.

23. "Stone & Webster," *Dictionary of American Biography,* Supplement

Three; "News from the Companies," *S & W Public Service Journal,* 10 (February 1912), 83–86; Chart of Stone & Webster Organization in 1903, *S & W Public Service Journal,* 44 (January 1929), 12.

24. "News from the Companies," *S & W Public Service Journal,* 26 (January 1920), 60.

25. *Stone & Webster, Annual Report, 1932; Wall Street Journal,* Feb. 19, 1930.

26. Memorandum, Sept. 1, 1927, Size of the Engineering Department, "Informative Data 1927–31."

27. National Civic Federation, *Municipal and Private Operation of Utilities* (New York, 1907), 3 vols.; "Editorial," *S & W Public Service Journal,* 1 (August 1907), 52–56; Frederick P. Royce, "A Consideration of the Commissioner of Corporations on Water Power Development in the United States," *S & W Public Service Journal,* 10 (May 1912), 335–344; "Editorial," *S & W Public Service Journal,* 12 (January 1913), 1–4.

28. Philip Selznick, *TVA and the Grass Roots* (Berkeley, 1949); William E. Leuchtenburg, "Roosevelt, Norris and the 'Seven Little TVAs,'" *Journal of Politics,* 14 (August 1952), 418–441; Donald N. Rothblatt, *Regional Planning: The Appalachian Experience* (Lexington, Mass., 1971); Peter Barnes, "A Mixed Blessing, TVA after 40 Years," *New Republic,* 169 (Nov. 10, 1973), 15–18.

29. Memorandum, January 1, 1929, Why Stone & Webster Does No Lump Sum Work, "Informative Data 1927–31."

30. "The Stone & Webster Organization," *Street Railway Journal,* 28 (July 1906), 27–29.

31. "Editorial," *S & W Public Service Journal,* 11 (October 1912), 235; *Stone & Webster Annual Report, 1933,* p. 10.

32. Gifford Pinchot, "Giant Power," *Survey,* 51 (Mar. 1, 1924), 561–562.

33. *Survey Graphic,* May 1925, reprinted as *Planning the Fourth Migration: The Neglected Vision of the Regional Planning Association of America,* ed. Carl Sussman (Cambridge, Mass., 1976).

34. Arthur A. Shurtleff, "The Metropolitan Plan," in *Report; Public Improvements for the Metropolitan District,* ed. Massachusetts Commission on Metropolitan Improvements (Boston, 1909), pp. 188–199; Charles Sumner Bird, Jr., *Report of the Governor's Committee on the Needs and Uses of Open Space* (Boston, 1929); Robert Whitten, *Report on a Thoroughfare Plan for Boston* (Boston, 1930), pp. 28–34, 148.

35. *Stone & Webster Annual Report, 1937.*

36. Stone & Webster Engineering Corporation, *A Report to the People* (Boston, 1946).

37. *Stone & Webster Annual Report, 1982,* pp. 4–11.

38. *Stone & Webster Annual Report, 1982,* p. 45.

5. LAURA ELIZABETH RICHARDS

1. Laura E. Richards, *Stepping Westward* (New York, 1931), p. 10.

2. Henry Richards, *Ninety Years On* (Augusta, Me., 1940), p. 294.

3. Charles Dickens, *American Notes for General Circulation* (1842; reprint, Gloucester, Mass., 1968), pp. 44–61.

4. John Greenleaf Whittier, "The Hero," in *The Complete Poetical Works of John Greenleaf Whittier*, ed. Horace E. Scudder (Boston, 1894), p. 192: Laura E. Richards, *When I Was Your Age* (Boston, 1894), pp. 77–106.

5. Richards, *Your Age*, p. 87.

6. Richards, *Your Age*, pp. 91–94.

7. Richards, *Your Age*, p. 87.

8. Richards, *Your Age*, pp. 29–30. This family ritual bears a striking resemblance to the spirit of the contemporary poem "The Children's Hour," Henry Wadsworth Longfellow, *The Complete Poetical Works of Longfellow* (Boston, 1893; reprint ed., 1922), p. 201.

9. Richards, *Westward*, pp. 1–35.

10. Quoted in Louise Hall Tharp, *Three Saints and a Sinner* (Boston, 1956), p. 296.

11. Henry Richards, *Ninety*, pp. 301–303.

12. Henry Richards, *Ninety*, p. 300.

13. Richards, *Westward*, p. 304.

14. Richards, *Westward*, pp. 17–18, 73.

15. Richards, *Westward*, pp. 57–67.

16. Richards, *Westward*, pp. 122–123. Papanti's school was at 23 Tremont Street. The building has been replaced by the Center Plaza Building, which follows the arc of Cambridge, Court, and Tremont streets.

17. Henry Richards, *Ninety*, p. 263.

18. Henry Richards, *Ninety*, pp. 262–263; Laura Richards, *Westward*, pp. 120–126.

19. Henry Richards, *Ninety*, pp. 275, 277.

20. Henry Richards, *Ninety*, pp. 287–299, 307–308.

21. Richards, *Westward*, pp. 155–161.

22. Henry Richards, *Ninety*, p. 300.

23. Laura E. Richards, *Tirra Lirra, Rhymes Old and New* (Boston, 1932), p. 9.

24. Ruth Hill Viguers, "Laura E. Richards, Joyous Companion," *Horn Book*, 32 (December 1956), 477–478.

25. George J. Varney, *A Gazetteer of the State of Maine* (Boston, 1882), pp. 248–249.

26. Henry Richards, *Ninety*, pp. 337, 353–368.

27. Richards, *Westward*, pp. 209–217; Henry Richards, *Ninety*, pp. 320, 333–335, 381–382.

28. Richards, *Westward*, pp. 252–253; Henry Richards, *Ninety*, p. 354.

29. Richards, *Westward*, pp. 276–280; Henry Richards, *Ninety*, p. 381.

30. Quoted in Hoyt C. Franchere, *Edwin Arlington Robinson* (New York, 1968), p. 38.

31. Richards, *Tirra Lirra*, p. 31.

32. Richards, *Westward*, p. 324.

33. Viguers, *Horn Book*, 32 (April 1956), 90; Henry Richards, *Ninety*, p. 378.
34. Henry Richards, *Ninety*, pp. 348, 374–375.
35. Viguers, "Laura Richards," *Horn Book*, 32 (June 1956), 171.
36. Gardiner Public Library Association, *Laura E. Richards and Gardiner* (Gardiner, Me., 1940), pp. 19–63.
37. Ralph Waldo Emerson, "Nature," *Essays, Second Series* (1844), in *Complete Works*, vol. 3, ed. Edward Waldo Emerson (Boston, 1904), p. 191.
38. Quoted in Gardiner Public Library Assoc., *Richards*, p. 56.
39. Laura E. Richards, *The Social Possibilities of a Country Town*, publications of the Christian Social Union 44 (Boston, Dec. 15, 1897), p. 3.
40. Richards, *Possibilities*, pp. 3–5.
41. Richards, *Possibilities*, p. 9.
42. Richards, *Possibilities*, p. 11.
43. Richards, *Possibilities*, p. 6.
44. Richards, *Possibilities*, p. 12.
45. Henry David Thoreau, *Walden* (1854), ed. J. Lyndon Shanley (Princeton, 1971), p. 96.
46. Richards, *Possibilities*, p. 16.
47. Richards, *Possibilities*, p. 12.
48. Richards, *Possibilities*, pp. 15–17.
49. Henry Richards, *Ninety*, pp. 381–382.
50. Thoreau, *Walden*, pp. 78–79.
51. Edwin Arlington Robinson, "The Torrent" (1896), in *Collected Poems of Edwin Arlington Robinson* (New York, 1937), p. 108.
52. Louis Coxe, *Edwin Arlington Robinson: The Life of Poetry* (New York, 1969), pp. 47–49.
53. Franchere, *Robinson*, pp. 38–43; Laura E. Richards, *E.A.R.* (Cambridge, 1936), pp. 32–59.
54. Franchere, *Robinson*, pp. 46–47.
55. Edwin S. Fussell, *Edwin Arlington Robinson; The Literary Background of a Traditional Poet* (1954; reprint, New York, 1970), p. 175.
56. Laura E. Richards, *Mrs. Tree* (Boston, 1902), *Mrs. Tree's Will* (Boston, 1905), *The Wedding of Calvin Parks* (Boston, 1908), "*Up to Calvin's*" (Boston, 1923).
57. In addition to the Robinson contrast, there is an interesting measure of Laura Richards's place in the Boston tradition offered by her fable "The Golden Windows," which appeared in a book of the same name (1903). Herman Melville told an alternative version of the same tale, "The Piazza," *Selected Writings of Herman Melville* (New York, 1952), pp. 437–453.
58. Henry Richards, *Ninety*, pp. 417–418.
59. Emerson, "Nature," pp. 169–170.
60. Richards, *Westward*, pp. 298–303; Henry Richards, *Ninety*, pp. 452–453.
61. Ernest B. Balch, quoted in Porter Sargent, *A Handbook of Summer Camps* (Boston, 1924), p. 24.
62. Dr. C. Hanford Henderson, "The Boy's Summer," in Sargent, *Handbook*, p. 44. The separation of sons from mothers and the fear of city boys being

sissies long remained central themes of summer camps. Mary Harrod, "How to Choose a Summer Camp for Boys and Girls," *The Outlook*, 109 (Apr. 28, 1915), pp. 1001–1007.

63. Henderson, "Boy's Summer," *Handbook*, p. 45. A parallel camp movement for charitable and religious purposes was undertaken by settlement houses, city YMCA's, and the like, but the care of the well-to-do always dominated the summer camp movement. Henry Drummond, "Manliness in Boys—By a New Process," *McClure's Magazine*, 2 (December 1893), 68–77; Robert A. Woods, "The All-summer Boy's Camp," *The Survey*, 27 (October 1911), 926–927; "The State of Summer Camps," *School Review*, 39 (October 1931), 565–567.

64. Henry Richards, *Ninety*, p. 459.

65. Richards, *Westward*, p. 302.

66. Viguers, "Laura Richards," *Horn Book*, 32 (June 1956), 177; Richards, *Westward*, pp. 304–322; Henry Richards, *Ninety*, pp. 452–497.

67. Sargent, *Handbook*, pp. 159–160.

68. Richards, *Westward*, pp. 390–391; Richards, *Possibilities*, p. 8.

69. Richards, *Westward*, pp. 314–317.

70. Richards, *Westward*, pp. 314–316.

71. Robert Stevenson Smyth Baden-Powell, *Aids to Scouting for N.- Cos. and Men*, Gale and Polden's Military Series 188 (London, 1899); Henry Richards, *Ninety*, pp. 493–497.

6. EMILY GREENE BALCH

1. Mercedes M. Randall, *Improper Bostonian, Emily Greene Balch* (New York, 1964), pp. 40–41. The house at 130 Prince Street has been torn down, and the lot subdivided and rebuilt with a cluster of colonial-style houses.

2. Charles Fletcher Dole, *My Eighty Years* (New York, 1927), p. 198.

3. Randall, *Improper*, pp. 40, 54.

4. Quoted in Randall, *Improper*, p. 57.

5. Barbara Miller Solomon, Emily Greene Balch and the Tradition for Peace: New England Brahmin and Convinced Quaker," paper for the Interdisciplinary Symposium on Quaker Women as Shapers of Human Space, March 16–18, 1979, Guilford College, Greensboro, N.C., p. 5.

6. George Santayana, *The Middle Span*, vol. 2 of *Persons and Places* (New York, 1945), pp. 166–171.

7. Dole, *My Eighty Years*, pp. 416–417; Dole, *The Spirit of Democracy* (New York, 1906), pp. 344–348, 399–409.

8. Randall, *Improper*, p. 55.

9. Ralph Waldo Emerson, "The Over-Soul," *Essays* (1841), in *Complete Works*, vol. 2, ed. Edward Waldo Emerson (Boston, 1904), p. 268.

10. "Erin Go Bragh Club," Randall, *Improper*, pp. 55–56.

11. Randall, *Improper*, pp. 50–52, 62.

12. Randall, *Improper*, pp. 69–70.

13. Emily Greene Balch, "Public Assistance of the Poor in France," *Publica-*

tions of the American Economic Association, 8 (July and September 1893), pp. 178–179; Randall, *Improper*, pp. 79–80.

14. Quoted in Randall, *Improper*, pp. 80–81.

15. *Manual for Use in Cases of Juvenile Offenders*, Conference of Child-Helping Societies, Publication no. 2 (Boston, July 1895).

16. Randall, *Improper*, pp. 79–80.

17. Denison House was situated at 93 Tyler Street, opposite the old Quincy School (1847). It has been torn down to make room for a parking lot in the middle of the Tufts Medical School complex.

18. "Mary Morton Kimball Kehew," *Notable American Woman*, vol. 2 (Cambridge, Mass., 1972); Randall, *Improper*, pp. 82–86, 113–115.

19. Randall, *Improper*, pp. 86–87.

20. Emily Balch succeeded Professor Coman as chairman of the Department of Economics and Sociology in 1913; Randall, *Improper*, pp. 86–92, 100.

21. Herbert George Wells, *The Future in America* (1906; reprint, New York, 1974), pp. 227, 231; "Emily Greene Balch," *Notable American Women*, vol. 1 (Cambridge, Mass., 1971); Randall, *Improper*, pp. 123–125.

22. Barbara Miller Solomon, *Ancestors and Immigrants* (Cambridge, Mass., 1956), pp. 56–65, 89–90, 98–102, 136–137; Daniel Aaron, *Men of Good Hope: A Story of American Progressives* (New York, 1951), pp. 252–280; Constance Burns, "The Irony of Progressive Reform in Boston, 1898–1910," typescript, John T. Kennedy Library, Boston, 1982.

23. Mary K. Simkovitch, "Introduction," in Emily Greene Balch, *The Miracle of Living* (New York, 1941), p. vi.

24. Emily Greene Balch, "A Shepherd of Immigrants," *Charities*, 13 (December 1904), 193.

25. Emily Greene Balch, "A Week in Hercegovnia and Bosnia," *Bryn Mawr Alumnae Quarterly*, 2 (October 1908), 5–22.

26. Emily Greene Balch, *Our Slavic Fellow Citizens* (New York, 1910), pp. 47–58. The book was first published as a series of illustrated articles in the New York Charity Organization Society's magazine, *Charities and Commons*. Part One of the book, entitled "Conditions in the Old Country," appeared from February through September 1906; Part Two, the studies of American Slavs, was published under the title "Our Slavic Fellow Citizens," from April through December 1907.

27. Balch, *Fellow Citizens*, p. 5.

28. *Beyond Nationalism, The Social Thought of Emily Greene Balch*, ed. Mercedes Randall (New York, 1972), pp. 57–58.

29. Balch, *Fellow Citizens*, p. 406.

30. Balch, *Fellow Citizens*, p. 404.

31. Balch, *Fellow Citizens*, p. 355.

32. Balch, *Fellow Citizens*, p. 372.

33. Balch, *Fellow Citizens*, p. 328.

34. Quoted in Randall, *Improper*, p. 134.

35. Merle Curti, *Peace or War, The American Struggle 1636–1936* (New

York, 1936), pp. 37–43, 75–77, 178–179, 202–203; Peter Brock, *Pacifism in the United States from the Colonial Era to the First World War* (Princeton, 1968), chaps. 11, 13–14, 22.

36. Curti, *Peace or War*, p. 238.

37. Quoted in Randall, *Improper*, p. 140.

38. Solomon, "New England Brahmin and Convinced Quaker," pp. 13–17; Randall, *Improper*, pp. 138–141, 220–223; Arthur A. Goren, *Dissenter in Zion* (Cambridge, Mass., 1982), pp. 24–26.

39. Emily Greene Balch, "Working for Peace," *Bryn Mawr Alumnae Bulletin*, 13 (May 1933), 12.

40. Immanuel Kant, *Eternal Peace and Other Essays* (1784), ed. Edwin D. Mead (Boston, 1914), pp. 9–11.

41. Kant, *Eternal Peace*, pp. xii–xiii, 9–11.

42. Journal of Miss Emily Greene Balch, 1915, p. 7, Swarthmore College Peace Collection, Swarthmore, Pa.

43. Kant, *Eternal Peace*, p. x.

44. Jane Addams, Emily G. Balch, and Alice Hamilton, *Women at the Hague* (New York, 1915), p. 122.

45. Randall, *Improper*, pp. 141, 149, 156–164.

46. Randall, *Improper*, pp. 180–192.

47. Randall, *Improper*, pp. 193–212.

48. Theodore Roosevelt, "Social Values and National Existence," in *War and Militarism in Their Sociological Aspects*, American Sociological Society Meeting, Washington, December 28–31, 1915, pp. 18–21.

49. Emily Greene Balch, "Effects of War and Militarism on the Status of Women," in *War and Militarism*, pp. 46–50.

50. Brooks Adams, "Can War Be Done Away With?" in *War and Militarism*, pp. 108–109, 112, 122–123.

51. Adams, "Can War Be Done Away With?" p. 123.

52. Adams, "Can War Be Done Away With?" p. 103.

53. Adams, "Can War Be Done Away With?" pp. 109–112.

54. Adams, "Can War Be Done Away With?" p. 123.

55. Emily Greene Balch, *Approaches to the Great Settlement*, introduction by Norman Angell (New York, 1918).

56. Randall, *Improper*, pp. 242–245.

57. Quoted in Randall, *Improper*, p. 248.

58. Balch, "Working for Peace," 13–14; Randall, *Improper*, p. 246.

59. Randall, *Improper*, pp. 246–257. From 1925 until a few years before her death she lived on the edge of the campus at 17 Roanoke Road.

60. Randall, *Improper*, pp. 267–269; Gertrude Bussey and Margaret Tims, *Women's International League for Peace and Freedom 1915–1965* (London, 1965), p. 37.

61. Emily Greene Balch, "Home," in *The Miracle of Living* (New York, 1941), pp. 4–5.

62. Randall, *Improper*, p. 373.
63. *Beyond Nationalism*, p. 110; Busey and Tims, *WILPF*, pp. 58–59; Randall, *Improper*, pp. 303–307, 316–319, 323.
64. Rudyard Kipling, "With the Night Mail, A Story of A.D. 2000," (1909), in *Actions and Reactions* (reprint, London, 1951), pp. 113–171.
65. Randall, *Improper*, p. 321; Lawrence S. Wittner, *Rebels Against War: The American Peace Movement 1941–1960* (New York, 1969), pp. 3–37; Charles Chatfield, *For Peace and Justice, Pacifism in America 1914–1941* (Knoxville, Tenn., 1971).
66. Emily Greene Balch, *The Women's International League for Peace and Freedom* (Geneva, 1938), p. 29; Simkovitch, "Introduction," in *The Miracle of Living*, pp. vii–viii.
67. Jane Addams, *The Second Twenty Years at Hull House* (New York, 1930), pp. 154–155; Judith Papachristou, *Women Together* (New York, 1976), pp. 197–200.
68. Randall, *Improper*, p. 319.
69. Chatfield, *For Peace and Justice*, pp. 326–327; Randall, *Improper*, pp. 348–363.
70. Emily Greene Balch, *Refugees as Assets*, (Women's International League for Peace and Freedom pamphlet, April 1939).
71. Randall, *Improper*, p. 365.
72. Quoted in Randall, *Improper*, p. 366.
73. Emily Greene Balch, "Toward a Planetary Civilization" *Four Lights*, 2, Women's International League for Peace and Freedom (Philadelphia, June 1942), n.p.
74. *Boston Globe*, Mar. 6, 1947.

INTRODUCTION TO PART THREE

1. Seymour E. Harris, *The Economics of New England, A Case Study of an Older Area* (Cambridge, Mass., 1952); John T. Cumbler, *Working Class Community in Industrial America* (Westport, Conn., 1979); Sam Bass Warner, Jr, and the Boston Public Library Staff, "Jobs," in *Boston An Urban Community, Annotated Reading List for The Way We Really Live: Social Change In Metropolitan Boston Since 1920* (Boston, 1977), pp. 8–13.
2. Robert W. Eisenmenger, *The Dynamics of Growth in New England's Economy* (Middletown, Conn., 1967).
3. "Marlborough," in *George D. Hall's Directory of Massachusetts Manufacturers 1981–1982* (Boston, 1982).
4. "Marlborough," in Rev. Elias Nason, *Gazetteer of the State of Massachusetts* (Boston, 1890); Federal Writers' Project of the W.P.A., *Massachusetts*, American Guide series (Boston, 1937); Ray Bearse, *Massachusetts*, new American Guide series, 2nd ed. (Boston, 1971).
5. Max Evans, "Boots for Suits," *Esquire*, 89 (May 9, 1978), 83–84.
6. Foy Spencer Baldwin, Emily G. Balch, and William L. Rutan, *The Strike of the Shoe Workers in Marlboro, Mass.* (Boston, 1899), pp. 1–7.

7. Baldwin, Balch, and Rutan, *Strike of Shoe Workers*, pp. 8, 11, 19.
8. Baldwin, Balch, and Rutan, *Strike of Shoe Workers*, p. 8; *Who's Who in New England, 1909*, ed. Albert Nelson Marquis (Chicago, 1909).
9. Baldwin, Balch, and Rutan, *Strike of Shoe Workers*, pp. 9, 13–14.

7. WILLIAM MADISON WOOD

1. "William Madison Wood," *National Cyclopedia of American Biography*, 15 (1916; reprint, Ann Arbor, 1967), 320–321; Edward G. Roddy, *Mills, Mansions, and Mergers, The Life of William M. Wood* (No. Andover, Mass.: 1982).
2. *Boston Globe*, Feb. 3, 1926.
3. American Woolen Company, *A Sketch of the Mills of the American Woolen Company* (Boston, 1901), p. 12.
4. "Frederick Ayer," *National Cyclopedia of American Biography*, 15 (1916), 320.
5. "American Woolen Company," *Fortune*, 3 (April 1931), 72; American Woolen Company, *Sketch of the Mills*, p. 12.
6. Arthur Harrison Cole, *The American Woolen Manufacture*, vol. 2 (Cambridge, 1926), pp. 110, 122, 221.
7. "Charles Ranlett Flint," *Dictionary of American Biography*, 3:305–306.
8. American Woolen Company, *Sketch of the Mills*, p. 7.
9. Cole, *Woolen Manufacture*, 2:236.
10. Cole, *Woolen Manufacture*, 2:231–236.
11. "Centralization," from the first annual report of the American Woolen Company, quoted in "The Story of a Quarter Century," *A. W. Employees Booster*, 9 (April 1924), 8.
12. Alfred D. Chandler, Jr., *The Visible Hand: The Managerial Revolution in American Business* (Cambridge, Mass., 1977), pp. 337–339; Shaw Livermore, "The Success of Industrial Mergers," *Quarterly Journal of Economics*, 50 (November 1935), 68–96.
13. Cole, *Woolen Manufacture*, 2:247–249.
14. *Fortune* (April 1931), 95.
15. Cole, *Woolen Manufacture*, 2:250.
16. *Fortune* (April 1931), 72.
17. Steve Dunwell, *The Run of the Mill* (Boston, 1978), p. 155.
18. Fred E. Beal, *Proletarian Journey* (New York, 1937), p. 32.
19. Donald B. Cole, *Immigrant City, Lawrence, Massachusetts 1845–1921* (Chapel Hill, 1963), p. 115.
20. Donald B. Cole, *Lawrence*, p. 120.
21. Cole, *Woolen Manufacture*, 2:248.
22. *A. W. Employees Booster*, 8 (July 1932), inside cover.
23. The Boston house, at 21 Fairfield Street, corner of Commonwealth Avenue, has been converted to condominiums. Bainbridge Bunting, *The Houses of Boston's Back Bay* (Cambridge, Mass., 1967), pp. 216–217.
24. *A. W. Employees Booster*, 8 (May and November 1923).

25. *A. W. Employees Booster*, 9 (April 1924), 11; *Fortune* (April 1931), 73, 94.
26. Ralph Waldo Emerson, "Self-Reliance," *Essays, First Series* (1841), in *Complete Works*, vol. 2, ed. Edward Waldo Emerson (Boston, 1904), p. 61.
27. American Woolen Company, *Shawsheen. The Model Community ...*, pamphlet, company print (Andover, Mass., 1924); "American Woolen,"*Fortune*, 11 (June 1935), 67–68.
28. Cole, *Woolen Manufacture*, 2:221–224, 239.
29. *Fortune* (June 1935), 68, 72.
30. *Boston Globe*, Feb. 3, 1926.
31. Dero A. Saunders, "The Twilight of American Woolen," *Fortune*, 49 (March 1951), 92–96, 198–204; and his "The Stormiest Merger Yet," *Fortune*, 52 (April 1955), 136–139, 162–171.
32. Edward A. Filene, "Unemployment in New England: Some Fundamental Factors," *New England's Prospect: 1933*, American Geographical Society, Special Publication no. 10 (New York, 1933), pp. 65–95.
33. *Boston Globe*, Feb. 3, 1926.
34. *Boston Globe*, Feb. 3, 1926.

8. FRED ERWIN BEAL

1. Steve Dunwell, *The Run of the Mill* (Boston, 1978), pp. 82–107.
2. Maurice B. Dorgan, *History of Lawrence* (Lawrence, Mass., 1924), pp. 113–120; Donald B. Cole, *Immigrant City, Lawrence, Massachusetts 1845–1921* (Chapel Hill, 1963), pp. 17–67.
3. Fred E. Beal, *Proletarian Journey, New England, Gastonia, Moscow* (New York, 1937), p. 30.
4. Beal, *Journey*, pp. 30–31.
5. Beal, *Journey*, p. 28.
6. Beal, *Journey*, p. 27.
7. Beal, *Journey*, p. 32.
8. Beal, *Journey*, pp. 33–34.
9. Beal, *Journey*, p. 34.
10. Cole, *Immigrant City*, p. 179.
11. Beal, *Journey*, p. 38.
12. Beal, *Journey*, p. 41.
13. Beal, *Journey*, p. 41.
14. *The Essays of A. J. Muste*, ed. Nat Hentoff (Indianapolis, 1967), pp. 43–44.
15. This theme is the focus of Cole's study of Lawrence, *Immigrant City*.
16. Robert E. Todd and Frank B. Sandborn, *The Report of the Lawrence Survey* (Lawrence, Mass., 1912).
17. Cole, *Immigrant City*, pp. 4–9.
18. *The Strike at Lawrence, Mass. Hearings Before the Committee on Rules of the House of Representatives ... 1912*, House Document no. 671, 62nd Cong., 2nd Sess. (Washington, 1912); Charles P. Neill, *Report on Strike of Textile Workers in Lawrence, Mass. in 1912*, Senate Doc. no. 870, 62nd Cong., 2nd Sess. (Washington, 1912).

19. Cole, *Immigrant City*, pp. 181, 184.
20. Beal, *Journey*, pp. 42–44.
21. Beal, *Journey*, pp. 46–47; Cole, *Immigrant City*, pp. 181–182.
22. Beal, *Journey*, p. 47.
23. Dorgan, *Lawrence*, pp. 150–151.
24. Beal, *Journey*, p. 74.
25. Beal, *Journey*, pp. 61–67.
26. Robert K. Murray, *Red Scare 1919–1920* (Minneapolis, 1955); William Preston, Jr., *Aliens and Dissenters: Federal Suppression of Radicals 1903–1933* (Cambridge, Mass., 1963); Francis Russell, *A City in Terror: 1919 Boston Police Strike* (New York, 1975).
27. *Boston Globe*, July 2–6, 1918.
28. *New York Times*, Jan. 26, 1919.
29. *New York Times*, Feb. 1, 1919.
30. *New York Times*, Feb. 5, 1919.
31. *New York Times*, Feb. 8, Apr. 19, 29, 1919.
32. The ministers had their collective in Boston's South End, at 99 Appleton Street. The building still stands, much refurbished.
33. *Essays of A. J. Muste*, pp. 58–62. George E. Roewar later served as Beal's attorney in his arrest and extradition in 1938.
34. *New York Times*, May 20, 1919.
35. *New York Times*, Feb. 17, 1919.
36. *New York Times*, May 25, 1919.
37. *Essays of A. J. Muste*, pp. 62–83; *New York Times*, May 7, 8, 1919.
38. Quoted in *New York Times*, May 23, 1919.
39. Beal, *Journey*, pp. 72–77.
40. Beal, *Journey*, pp. 75–76.
41. Bramhall appeared in the newspapers, *New York Times*, Aug. 3, 1932, as a leader of the Communist party free speech delegation before Governor Ely.
42. *Boston Globe*, Feb. 13, 14, 22, 1922.
43. *Boston Globe*, Feb. 22, 1922.
44. Beal, *Journey*, p. 72.
45. Beal, *Journey*, p. 76.
46. Beal, *Journey*, pp. 76–78.
47. *Lawrence Evening Tribune*, Dec. 15, 1923.
48. Beal, *Journey*, pp. 79–81.
49. Beal, *Journey*, pp. 81–86; Fred Beal, *The Red Fraud, An Exposé of Stalinism* (New York, 1949), p. 72.
50. *A. W. Employees Booster*, 9 (January 1924), 2.
51. *A. W. Employees Booster*, 9 (July 1924), cover.
52. *A. W. Employees Booster*, 9 (December 1924), 2.
53. *Boston Herald*, July 8, 1926.
54. Beal, *Journey*, p. 87.
55. Beal, *Journey*, p. 91.
56. Beal, *Journey*, p. 97.

57. Beal, *Journey*, p. 98.

58. Beal, *Journey*, pp. 98–99.

59. A good general description of these southern Massachusetts and Rhode Island mill towns is John T. Cumbler, *Workingclass Community in Industrial America: Work, Leisure, and Struggle in Two Industrial Cities 1880–1930* (Westport, Conn., 1979), pp. 194–217.

60. *Fall River Globe*, Apr. 16, 1928.

61. *Fall River Globe*, Apr. 18, 1928.

62. Beal, *Journey*, p. 99.

63. *New York Times*, June 2, 1928.

64. Beal, *Journey*, pp. 100–101.

65. *Fall River Globe*, June 29, Aug. 7, 1928.

66. *Fall River Globe*, July 13, 1928.

67. *Fall River Globe*, June 30, July 23, 1928; Beal, *Journey*, pp. 101–104.

68. *Fall River Globe*, July 13, 1928.

69. *New York Times*, Oct. 7, 1928.

70. *New York Times*, Nov. 20, 1928.

71. Beal, *Journey*, pp. 129, 139–142.

72. Beal, *Journey*, pp. 109–122.

73. Beal, *Journey*, pp. 131, 144–145. The Manville-Jenckes company descended from a merger of two Rhode Island firms. There is one of today's typical nostalgic pictures of the Manville mills in Dunwell, *Run of the Mill*, p. 162.

74. Mary Heaton Vorse, who had covered the Lawrence strike of 1912 wrote a novel about the Gastonia situation, *Strike* (New York, 1930); another was Fielding Burke [Olive T. Dargan], *A Stone Came Rolling* (New York, 1935); Grace Lumpkin, *To Make My Bread* (New York, 1932) was later adapted for a play, *Let Freedom Ring*, by Albert Bien in 1936. A very thorough, and very reactionary, study of Gastonia and its strike is Liston Pope, *Millhands and Preachers: A Study of Gastonia*, Yale Studies in Religious Education, 15 (1942; reprint, New Haven, 1973).

75. Beal, *Journey*, pp. 209–221.

76. Beal, *Journey*, pp. 275–327; *Boston Herald*, Oct. 19, 1939.

77. Beal, *Journey*, pp. 328–344; Beal, *Red Fraud*, pp. 45–70.

78. *Jewish Daily Forward*, June 17–July 2, 1935.

79. *Boston Herald*, Sept. 4, 14, 15, 1937; *New York Times*, Sept. 5, 1937.

80. *New York Times*, Jan. 22, 26, Feb. 15, 17, 21, 1938.

81. Beal, *Red Fraud*, pp. 74–80.

82. Pope, *Millhands and Preachers*, p. 309.

83. *Boston Herald*, Oct. 19, 1939.

84. Beal, *Red Fraud*, p. 80.

85. *Time*, 51 (May 31, 1948), 19; *Life* (June 7, 1948), 63–64.

86. *Boston Herald*, Mar. 22, 1951; *New York Times*, Nov. 16, 1954.

87. Ralph Waldo Emerson, "History," *Essays, First Series* (1841), in *Complete Works*, vol. 2, ed. Edward Waldo Emerson (Boston, 1904), p. 36.

INTRODUCTION TO PART FOUR

1. Steve Dunwell, *The Run of the Mill* (Boston, 1978), p. 165.
2. Emily Greene Balch, "Effects of War and Militarism upon the Status of Women," in *War and Militarism in Their Sociological Aspects*, American Sociological Society meeting, Washington, Dec. 18–21, 1915, p. 55.
3. Sheila M. Rothman, *Woman's Proper Place, A History of Changing Ideals and Practice* (New York, 1978), pp. 97–132.
4. Words by Rida Johnson Young, music by Chauncey Olcott and Ernest Ball, Aug. 18, 1910. James J. Fuld, *The Book of World-Famous Music*, rev. ed. (New York, 1971), p. 377.
5. Page Smith, *Daughters of the Promised Land* (Boston, 1970), pp. 210–214.
6. Jennie June Croly, *The History of the Woman's Club Movement in America* (New York, 1898); Maine, pp. 523–572; Massachusetts, pp. 588–674; New Hampshire, pp. 795–824; Rhode Island, pp. 1057–1072. Karen J. Blair, *The Clubwoman as Feminist, True Womanhood Redefined 1868–1914* (New York, 1980).
7. Croly, *Woman's Club Movement:* Somerville, Heptorian Club, p. 626; Newton clubs, pp. 643–651.
8. Reed Ueda, "Suburban Social Change and Educational Reform, the Case of Somerville, Mass. 1912–1924," *Social Science History*, 3 (October 1979), 167–203.
9. Henry K. Rowe, *Tercentenary History of Newton, 1630–1930* (Newton, 1930), pp. 240–427, 458–513; Robert L. Church and Michael W. Sedlak, *Education in the United States* (New York, 1976), pp. 268–315.
10. Joseph Lee, "Play as Landscape," *Charities and Commons*, 16 (July 7, 1906), 427–432.
11. Charles Eliot, Sr., *Charles Eliot, Landscape Architect* (Boston, 1902), p. 317.
12. Charles Eliot, Sr., *Charles Eliot* chaps. 17 and 18; Sylvester Baxter, "A Trust to Protect Nature's Beauty," *Review of Reviews*, 23 (January 1901), 42–48.
13. Charles E. Fay, "Our Quarter-Century," *Appalachia*, 9 (March 1901), 231–237; John Ritchie, "Fifty Years of Progress," *Appalachia*, 19 (February 1926), 323–346; C. Francis Belcher, "A Century of the Appalachian Mountain Club," *Appalachia*, 41 (June 1976), 5–45. R. Stuart Wallace, "A Social History of the White Mountains," in Donald Keyes, ed., *The White Mountains, Place and Perceptions* (Hanover, N.H., 1980), pp. 36–38; Carlton S. Van Doren and Louis Hodges, *America's Park and Recreation Heritage, A Chronology* (Washington, 1975).
14. Woman's Educational Association, *Annual Report for 1888* (Boston, 1888), pp. 7–9; Frank R. Lillie, *The Woods Hole Marine Biological Laboratory* (Chicago, 1944), pp. 20–37.
15. Jane Addams, *The Second Twenty Years at Hull House* (New York, 1930), pp. 153–156.

16. Sheila Rothman, *Woman's Proper Place*, pp. 177–188.
17. Those living along the Brookline-Newton-Wellesley suburban axis in 1925 could place their children in the town's up-to-date public schools or choose among four coeducational private schools, five boys' day and boarding schools, seven girls' nonsectarian Protestant schools, and three Catholic girls' schools. Porter Sargent, *A Handbook of American Private Schools, 1925–1926* (Boston, 1926).
18. Vannevar Bush, *Pieces of the Action* (New York, 1970), p. 172.

9. LOUISE ANDREWS KENT

1. The firm was Charles Storrow & Co., 53 State Street, Room 601. His partner was Edward C. Storrow of 47 Hereford Street, Boston, *Boston Street Directory, 1901.*
2. Louise Andrews Kent, *Mrs. Appleyard and I* (Boston, 1968), p. 49.
3. Kent, *Mrs. Appleyard*, pp. 39, 77, 80. The Edge Hill Road house is still extant.
4. Kent, *Mrs. Appleyard*, p. 23.
5. Kent was able to construct a lively autobiography in her old age because she was rewriting material she had been using throughout her lifetime. For instance, the chapter in her autobiography on seeing the Great White Fleet in Bar Harbor, chapter 5 of *Mrs. Appleyard, and I,* was a reworking of a column in the *Boston Herald,* "Better Battleships," Feb. 15, 1930.
6. Kent, *Mrs. Appleyard*, p. 25.
7. Kent, *Mrs. Appleyard*, pp. 28–29.
8. Kent, *Mrs. Appleyard*, p. 30.
9. Kent, *Mrs. Appleyard*, p. 50.
10. Kent, *Mrs. Appleyard*, pp. 50, 54–56.
11. Kent, *Mrs. Appleyard*, pp. 78–99. Miss Haskell's School was at 314 Marlborough Street, one of a pair of large houses built in 1879 on the south side of the street, near Gloucester Street. It is still standing, now converted to apartments.
12. Kent, *Mrs. Appleyard*, p. 81.
13. Kent, *Mrs. Appleyard*, pp. 80–81.
14. Kent, *Mrs. Appleyard*, pp. 102–119.
15. Kent, *Mrs. Appleyard*, pp. 115–118; Obituary, *Boston Globe*, Aug. 7, 1969.
16. Kent, *Mrs. Appleyard*, pp. 122–134. The house at 66 Chestnut Street, near Charles, is still standing.
17. Ira Rich Kent worked for *The Youth's Companion* from 1912 until 1925, when he moved to Houghton Mifflin; Obituary, *New York Times*, Nov. 11, 1945.
18. Kent, *Mrs. Appleyard*, p. 133.
19. Kent, *Mrs. Appleyard*, pp. 160, 167. Her first house in South Brookline was at 25 Waverly Street.
20. Kent lived at 17 Hawthorne Road from 1920 until 1959 when she retired to Vermont. The Hawthorne Road house is still standing.

21. Kent, *Mrs. Appleyard*, p. 170.

22. Kent *Mrs. Appleyard*, pp. 185–186, 191–197, 293. Much of the material for the first Appleyard book was drawn from a series of occasional columns she wrote for the editorial page of the *Boston Herald* during the 1930s. For example, "Shelling Peas," *Boston Herald*, July 23, 1930, reappeared as the July chapter in *Mrs. Appleyard's Year*.

23. Louise Andrews Kent, *Mrs. Appleyard's Year* (Boston, 1941), pp. 10–15.

24. Kent, *Mrs. Appleyard*, p. 241.

25. Dorothy Canfield Fisher, *A Montessori Mother* (New York, 1912); "About the Montessori Method," *Outlook*, 104 (Aug. 30, 1913), 1012–1013; Kent, *Mrs. Appleyard*, pp. 182, 216.

26. Kent, *Mrs. Appleyard*, pp. 228–229.

27. Kent, *Mrs. Appleyard*, pp. 240–241.

28. Kent, *Mrs. Appleyard*, pp. 259–265.

29. Charles B. Hosmer, Jr., *Preservation Comes of Age, From Williamsburg to the National Trust 1926–1949*, vol. 1 (Charlottesville, Va., 1981), pp. 133–144.

30. Kent, *Mrs. Appleyard*, pp. 219, 222–223.

31. Kent, *Mrs. Appleyard*, pp. 230, 240–253, 265–266.

32. Louise Andrews Kent, "Mrs. Appleyard Originates a System of Cool Cooking," *House Beautiful*, 85 (July 1943), 22–23; "Mrs. Appleyard Masterminds a Service Wedding," *House Beautiful*, 86 (March 1944), 60–61, 92–93, 126; Elizabeth Kent Gay, "Appleyard Open House," *Ladies Home Journal*, 74 (December 1957), 62–63, 123; "Barn Dance at Appleyard Center," *Ladies Home Journal*, 75 (September 1958), 72–74.

33. Kent, *Mrs. Appleyard*, pp. 271–275.

34. Kent, *Mrs. Appleyard's Year*, p. 16.

35. Jane Addams, *The Second Twenty Years at Hull House* (New York, 1930), pp. 144–146.

36. Kent, *Mrs. Appleyard*, p. 313.

37. Kent, *Mrs. Appleyard*, pp. 401–404.

10. VANNEVAR BUSH AND LAURENCE K. MARSHALL

1. Christopher Rand, "Center of a New World," *New Yorker* (Apr. 11, 18, 25, 1964), reprinted as *Cambridge, U.S.A., Hub of a World* (New York, 1964); Gene Bylinsky, *The Innovation Millionaires, How They Succeed* (New York, 1976).

2. Otto J. Scott, *The Creative Ordeal, the Story of Raytheon* (New York, 1974).

3. Eric Hodgins, Oral History of Vannevar Bush, Archives of the Massachusetts Institute of Technology, typescript, reel 1, pp. 1–11.

4. The church, built at Clark and Cary Avenues after the fire of 1908, is gone, replaced now by a four-story brick apartment house. The parsonage next door at 24 Clark Avenue still stands.

5. Rev. R. Perry Bush, *Boston Evening Transcript*, Apr. 3, 1926.

6. Vannevar Bush, *Pieces of the Action* (New York, 1970), p. 239.

7. Hodgins, Oral History, reel 2, pp. 100–101.

8. Bush, *Action*, pp. 162, 250–251; Hodgins, Oral History, reel 1 p. 12.

9. Bush, *Action*, p. 163.

10. Bush, *Action*, pp. 163, 199, 230, 247; Hodgins, Oral History, reel 10B, pp. 658–660.

11. *Current Biography, 1940*, ed. Maxine Block (New York, 1940), pp. 129–130.

12. Author's interview with Edward L. Bowles, professor emeritus, Massachusetts Institute of Technology, July 29, 1982; Vannevar Bush, "A Tribute to Dugald C. Jackson," *Electrical Engineering*, 70 (December 1951), 1063–1064.

13. Obituary, *New York Times*, June 30, 1974.

14. Bush, *Action*, p. 164; Hodgins, Oral History, reel 9, p. 558.

15. Bush, *Action*, p. 155.

16. Interview with Bowles, July 29, 1982.

17. Author's interview with Lorna Marshall, May 22, 1982; Scott, *Creative Ordeal*, pp. 7–9.

18. *Who's Who in New England, 1938*, ed. Albert Nelson Marquis (Chicago, 1938); William Gammell, Sr., *New York Times*, Nov. 13, 1943.

19. Inteview with Bowles, July 29, 1982.

20. Bush, *Action*, pp. 163–167; Hodgins, Oral History, reel 9, pp. 607–608; Scott, *Creative Ordeal*, pp. 14–22.

21. Bush, *Action*, pp. 168, 197; Hodgins, Oral History, reel 1, p. 26A; reel 9, pp. 557A–558; reel 13, p. 790; Scott, *Creative Ordeal*, pp. 21–22.

22. Scott, *Creative Ordeal*, pp. 23–26.

23. Scott, *Creative Ordeal*, pp. 28–31, 68, 91–92; Bush, *Action*, pp. 168, 198.

24. Bush, *Action*, p. 172.

25. Scott, *Creative Ordeal*, pp. 30–36.

26. Interview with Lorna Marshall, May 22, 1982; Bush, *Action*, pp. 176–180.

27. Noobar Retheos Danielian, *A.T. & T., The Story of Industrial Conquest* (New York, 1939), pp. 99–109.

28. Danielian, *A. T. & T.*, pp. 108–133.

29. Scott, *Creative Ordeal*, pp. 39–40, 45–48.

30. Scott, *Creative Ordeal*, p. 89; interview with Bowles, July 29, 1982.

31. Josephine Young Case and Everett Needham Case, *Owen D. Young and American Enterprise* (Boston, 1982), pp. 586–588, 591–594.

32. Scott, *Creative Ordeal*, pp. 48–49.

33. Scott, *Creative Ordeal*, pp. 38, 73, 97.

34. Vannevar Bush, "The Key to Accomplishment," *Textile Research*, 3 (November 1932), 7–13.

35. James B. Conant, *Modern Science and Modern Man* (New York, 1952), p. 17.

36. *Current Biography, 1947*, ed. Anna Rothe (New York, 1947); Daniel J. Kevles, *The Physicists, The History of a Scientific Community in Modern America* (New York, 1978), pp. 83, 109–111.

37. Bush, *Action*, pp. 30–42, 315; Kevles, *Physicists*, pp. 296–301.
38. The official history of Bush's Office of Scientific Research and Development is James P. Baxter, *Scientists Against Time* (Boston, 1946).
39. Scott, *Creative Ordeal*, p. 90.
40. Scott, *Creative Ordeal*, pp. 87, 91, 98–113; Bush, *Action*, pp. 89, 327–328.
41. Scott, *Creative Ordeal*, pp. 33–34; *Who Was Who in America, 1969–1973; Who Was Who in American History*, vol. 5 (Chicago, 1973), p. 682.
42. Interview with Bowles, July 29, 1982; Scott, *Creative Ordeal*, pp. 123–127.
43. Scott, *Creative Ordeal*, pp. 162–163, 182.
44. Interviews with Bowles, July 29 and Oct. 14, 1982: Scott, *Creative Ordeal*, pp. 162–163, 176–177, 184–185, 187–189, 214–219.
45. Scott, *Creative Ordeal*, pp. 152, 174–175.
46. Scott, *Creative Ordeal*, pp. 174–175, 254–257; Raytheon Company, *Annual Report, 1981*.
47. Raytheon Company, *Annual Report, 1981;* employment information furnished by the firm's public relations department.
48. Hodgins, Oral History, reel 9, pp. 573–575A.
49. Sir James Percy Fitzpatrick, *Jock of the Bushveld* (1907; reprint, London, 1957).
50. John Marshall, *The Hunters* (1958), *N!ai* (1980); Lorna J. Marshall, *The !Kung of Nyae Nyae* (Cambridge, Mass., 1976).
51. Bush, *Action*, pp. 23, 245–246.
52. Bush, *Action*, pp. 94–95; Vannevar Bush, *Science Is Not Enough* (New York, 1967), pp. 100, 178–179.
53. Bush, *Science Is Not Enough*, p. 139.
54. Vannevar Bush, *Science the Endless Frontier, A Report to the President* (Washington, 1945), pp. 131–132; Bush, *Science Is Not Enough*, pp. 39–44, 135.
55. Bush, *Science Is Not Enough*, pp. 140–141.
56. Sam Bass Warner, Jr., *The Way We Really Live* (Boston, 1977), p. 37.
57. Bush, *Science Is Not Enough*, pp. 100, 141.
58. Bush, *Science Is Not Enough*, pp. 11–13.
59. Henry David Thoreau, *Journal*, May 9, 1852, ed. Bradford Torrey and Francis H. Allen, vol. 4 (Boston, 1949), p. 42.
60. Bush, *Science Is Not Enough*, pp. 172, 176, 178.

INTRODUCTION TO PART FIVE

1. Joseph Huthmacher, *Massachusetts People and Politics, 1919–1933* (Cambridge, 1959).

11. JAMES BRYANT CONANT

1. James Bryant Conant, *My Several Lives, Memoirs of a Social Inventor* (New York, 1970), p. 8.
2. Conant, *Lives*, pp. 7–8.

3. Conant, *Lives*, p. 15.

4. Conant, *Lives*, p. 7. The Conant family lived at 1937 Dorchester Avenue, near Bailey Street, opposite the Ashmont station of the MBTA. The house may still be standing in much altered form between a row of early twentieth-century three-deckers.

5. Conant, *Lives*, p. 8.

6. The Swedenborgian Church stood at St. James Street, near Regent Street. A handsome small church, it is now the Bethel Baptist Church.

7. Conant, *Lives*, pp. 11–12; James Bryant Conant, "Wanted: American Radicals," *Atlantic Monthly*, 171 (May 1943), 41–45.

8. James Bryant Conant, *Education in a Divided World, The Function of the Public Schools in Our Unique Society* (Cambridge, Mass., 1948), pp. 80–82, 89–90.

9. Conant, *Lives*, pp. 13–19; Black later became a Harvard instructor in elementary physics and scientific methods: Arthur G. Powell, *The Uncertain Profession, Harvard and the Search for Educational Authority* (Cambridge, Mass., 1980), pp. 138, 193, 315 n. 14.

10. Millicent Bell, *Marquand, An American Life* (Boston, 1979), pp. 60–61.

11. Conant, *Lives*, pp. 29–31, 72–76.

12. Conant, *Lives*, pp. 20–39.

13. Conant, *Lives*, pp. 52, 82.

14. Conant, *Lives*, pp. 39–40.

15. Conant, *Lives*, pp. 43–44.

16. Conant, *Lives*, pp. 72–76.

17. Conant, *Lives*, 84–86.

18. The gas seems to have been named for Captain W. Lee Lewis of the Chemical Warfare Service. The first shipment stood at the dock at the time of the 1918 armistice: Alden H. Watt, *Gas Warfare* (New York, 1942), pp. 55–56. Paul F. Douglas, *Six Upon the World, Toward an American Culture for an Industrial Age* (Boston, 1954), p. 337; Conant, *Lives*, pp. 48–49.

19. Conant was a member of a distinguished citizens' group that supported President Lyndon Johnson's policy on Vietnam in 1967 and 1968: Committee for Peace with Freedom in Vietnam, *New York Times*, May 24, 1968; Conant, *Lives*, pp. 640–642.

20. Conant, *Lives*, pp. 49–50. The gas, dichloro (2-chlorovinyl)arsine, is still regarded as highly toxic, even lethal. Morris B. Jacobs, *War Gasses, Their Identification and Decontamination* (New York, 1942), pp. 33–34; *The Merck Index*, 9th ed., ed. Martha Windhoz (Rahway, N.J., 1976), p. 3035.

21. Conant, *Lives*, p. 50.

22. Conant, *Lives*, pp. 50–51.

23. The young couple's house at 20 Oxford Street, Cambridge, has been torn down and replaced by Harvard's Hofmann Laboratories.

24. Conant, *Lives*, 54–90.

25. Conant, *Lives*, pp. 170–176.

26. Conant, *Lives*, in order of listed items: pp. 412–416, 399, 128, 417–419, 374–383, 367–369.

27. Letter of Marshall Cohen et al., *New York Review of Books*, 24 (July 14, 1977), 40.

28. James Bryant Conant, "Oration at the Solemn Observance of the Tercentenary of Harvard College, Sept. 18, 1936," reprinted in Conant, *Lives*, p. 656.

29. Conant, *Lives*, pp. 120–137, 417–419.

30. As a new college president giving speeches on education Conant discovered his affinity for Jefferson, especially for Jefferson's writings against hereditary aristocracy and in favor of a "natural aristoi": in *Works of Thomas Jefferson*, ed. Paul Leicester Ford (New York, 1904), "Autobiography," vol. 1, p. 58, and letter to John Adams, Oct. 28, 1813, vol. 11, p. 343; Conant, *Lives*, pp. 137–138.

31. Francis Trow Spaulding (1896–1950) was the son of Frank E. Spaulding, who had been superintendent of the Newton schools from 1904 through 1914 and had attained a national reputation as the organizer of the Yale Graduate School of Education: *New York Times*, June 8, 1960. Francis Spaulding's reputation rested on his report on the condition of the schools of New York, *High School and Life, The Regent's Inquiry* (New York, 1938).

32. Powell, *Uncertain Profession*, pp. 188–205.

33. Conant, *Lives*, p. 191.

34. William M. Tuttle, Jr., "James B. Conant, Pressure Groups and the National Defense 1933–1945," Ph.D. dissertation, University of Wisconsin, 1967 (University Microfilms, 1970), pp. 86–91; "Aid-to-the-Allies Short-of-War," *Journal of American History*, 56 (March 1970), 840–858.

35. Conant, *Lives*, p. 213.

36. Conant, *Lives*, p. 209.

37. Conant, *Lives*, p. 248.

38. Conant, *Lives*, pp. 272–280.

39. Len Giovannitti and Fred Freed, *The Decision to Drop the Bomb* (New York, 1965), p. 105.

40. Conant, *Lives*, p. 303.

41. Giovannitti and Freed, *Decision*, pp. 98–108; Richard G. Hewlett and Oscar E. Anderson, Jr., *The New World, 1939/1946*, History of the United States Atomic Energy Commission, vol. 1 (University Park, Penna., 1962), pp. 344–346, 392–407.

42. Advisory Committee report quoted in, Richard G. Hewlett and Francis Duncan, *Atomic Shield, 1947/1952*, v. 2. A History of the United States Atomic Energy Commission (University Park, Pa., 1969), p. 384; Gregg Herken, *The Winning Weapon, The Atomic Bomb in the Cold War* (New York, 1980), pp. 307–308; Conant, *Lives*, pp. 492–502.

43. James Bryant Conant, *On Understanding Science, An Historical Approach* (New Haven, 1947), p. xiii.

44. Conant, *Understanding Science*, pp. xi–xiii; Conant quoted Ralph Waldo Emerson, "Compensation," *Essays, First Series* (1841), in *Complete Works*, vol. 2, ed. Edward Waldo Emerson (Boston, 1904), pp. 99, 107.

45. Conant, *Lives*, p. 302.

46. Louis F. Fieser, *The Scientific Method, A Personal Account of Unusual Projects in War and Peace* (New York, 1964), pp. 9–33; Watt, *Gas Warfare*, pp. 78–83; *New York Times*, July 27, 1977.

47. U.S. Office of Air Force History, *The Pacific: Matterhorn to Nagasaki*, ed. Wesley F. Craven and James L. Crate, The Army Air Force in World War II, vol. 5 (Chicago, 1953), pp. 614–618.

48. Henry L. Stimson, Diary, June 6, 1945, quoted in Giovannitti and Freed, *Decision*, p. 110.

49. Emerson, "Compensation," in *Works*, vol. 2, p. 109.

50. Conant, *Lives*, pp. 475–489.

51. Conant, *Lives*, pp. 501–502.

52. Harvard's official position was one of strict opposition to Senator McCarthy; Conant also testified in behalf of J. Robert Oppenheimer in 1954 when he was charged with disloyalty, Conant, *Lives*, pp. 501–504. Controversy, however, lingers over Harvard University's internal management of staff who had had associations with the Communist Party: letters by Robert N. Bellah, McGeorge Bundy, Clark Kerr, and Sigmund Diamond, " 'Veritas' at Harvard: Another Exchange," *New York Review of Books*, 24 (July 14, 1977), 38–41.

53. Conant, *Lives*, p. 304.

54. Conant, *Lives*, p. 506.

55. Conant, *Lives*, pp. 505–506.

56. During World War II Conant had supported the idea of exemptions for training for some students: William M. Tuttle, Jr., "Higher Education and the Federal Government: The Lean Years, 1940–42," *The Record—Teachers College*, 71 (December 1969), 299, 301.

57. Conant, *Lives*, 514–524, 528–531.

58. James Bryant Conant, *Slums and Suburbs* (New York, 1961).

59. Conant, *Lives*, p. 656.

60. Conant, *Lives*, pp. 368–370.

61. Paul Buck, ed., *Report of the Harvard Committee, General Education in a Free Society* (Cambridge, Mass., 1945), pp. 39, 46–49.

62. James Bryant Conant, "Introduction," in *General Education*, p. vii.

63. Conant, *Lives*, pp. 372–373; James Bryant Conant, *Science and Common Sense* (New Haven, 1951), chap. 10.

64. J. Robert Oppenheimer, "Physics in the Contemporary World," *second annual Arthur Dehon Little memorial lecture*, Cambridge, Mass., Nov. 25, 1947, pp. 20–21.

65. Philip W. Jackson, "The Reform of Science Education: a Cautionary Tale," *Daedalus*, 112 (Spring 1983), 147–150; Robert L. Church and Michael W. Sedlak, *Education in the United States* (New York, 1976), pp. 406–412.

66. James Bryant Conant, *On Understanding Science, An Historical Approach* (New Haven, 1947), pp. 1–2, 11–12; Jon D. Miller, "Scientific Literacy: A Conceptual and Empirical Review," *Daedalus*, 112 (Spring 1983), 29–48.

67. Conant, *Lives*, pp. 191, 506.

68. James Bryant Conant, *Education in a Divided World, The Function of the Public Schools in Our Unique Society* (Cambridge, Mass., 1948), pp. viii–xi.

69. Conant, *Divided*, pp. 22, 24, 57, 217.

70. Conant, *Divided*, pp. 54–55.

71. Conant, *Understanding Science*, p. 4.

72. Conant, *Divided*, p. 65.

73. Tuttle, "Conant, Pressure Groups, and the National Defense 1933–1945," pp. 25–34.

74. Conant, *Divided*, p. 74.

75. Conant, *Divided*, p. 85.

76. Conant, *Divided*, p. 48.

77. Conant, *Divided*, pp. 65–67, 71–72, 81, 85, 89, 91.

78. James Bryant Conant, *The American High School Today* (New York, 1959); *The Comprehensive High School* (New York, 1967).

79. Conant, *Divided*, pp. 47–52, 67.

80. Conant, *Divided*, p. 108.

81. Conant, *Divided*, pp. 64–65, 108–110; James Bryant Conant and Francis T. Spaulding, *Education for a Classless Society* (Cambridge, Mass., 1940).

82. Conant, *Divided*, p. 82.

83. Conant, *Divided*, p. 91.

84. Conant, *Divided*, pp. 103, 106–108, 126–127.

85. Conant, *Divided*, pp. 126–127, 130–131.

86. Conant, *Divided*, pp. 140–141.

87. Conant, *Lives*, p. 366.

88. C. P. Snow, *Science and Government* (Cambridge, Mass., 1961).

89. Gerald Holton, "Where Is Science Taking Us?" National Endowment for the Humanities, tenth Jefferson Lecture, Boston Public Library, Boston, Mass., May 13, 1981, typescript, p. 8. Holton referred to a similar observation by literary critic Lionel Trilling in the first Jefferson Lecture, *Mind in the Modern World* (New York, 1972), p. 14.

90. James Bryant Conant, *Modern Science and Modern Man* (New York, 1952) pp. 54–58.

91. Conant, *Modern Science*, pp. 50–54.

92. Conant, *Modern Science*, pp. 59, 63.

93. Conant, *Modern Science*, p. 21.

94. Conant, *Modern Science*, p. 80.

95. Holton, "Where Is Science Taking Us?" p. 35.

96. Conant, *Modern Science*, p. 92.

12. RACHEL CARSON

1. Philip Sterling, *Sea and Earth, The Life of Rachel Carson* (New York, 1970), pp. 147–148; Rachel Carson, *Silent Spring* (Boston, 1962), p. ix.
2. Sterling, *Sea and Earth*, p. 73.
3. Paul Brooks, *The House of Life, Rachel Carson at Work* (Boston, 1972), p. 88.
4. Brooks, *House of Life*, p. 159.
5. Sterling, *Sea and Earth*, pp. 4–5, 30–31.
6. Sterling, *Sea and Earth*, pp. 16, 24.
7. Sterling, *Sea and Earth*, pp. 52–53, 65.
8. Brooks, *House of Life*, p. 18; Sterling, *Sea and Earth*, pp. 80, 86.
9. In 1939 the Bureau of Fisheries was transferred from the Commerce Department to the Department of Interior, and in 1940 it was merged with the Biological Survey to become the present Fish and Wildlife Service of the U.S. Department of Interior; Sterling, *Sea and Earth*, p. 91.
10. Sterling, *Sea and Earth*, pp. 105–106.
11. Sterling, *Sea and Earth*, pp. 95, 146. As a young child Roger inspired a charming picture book: Rachel Carson, *The Sense of Wonder* (New York, 1956).
12. Stephen Jay Gould, *The Mismeasure of Man* (New York, 1981).
13. Samuel P. Hays, *Conservation and the Gospel of Efficiency: The Progressive Conservative Movement 1890–1920* (Cambridge, Mass., 1959); Roderick Nash, *Wilderness and the American Mind* (New Haven, 1967), pp. 108–181.
14. Donald Fleming, "Roots of the New Conservation Movement," *Perspectives in American History*, 6 (1972), 24–27; Nash, *Wilderness*, pp. 182–199.
15. Aldo Leopold, *Sand County Almanac* (New York, 1949), p. 210. The desirability of the steady state would be, of course, a value choice of man, not a rule of nature: essay on the Cambrian population explosion and the Permian extinctions, Stephen Jay Gould, *Ever Since Darwin* (New York, 1977), pp. 126–138.
16. Sterling, *Sea and Earth*, p. 95.
17. Rachel L. Carson, "Undersea," *Atlantic Monthly*, 160 (September 1937), 322–325.
18. Henry Beston, *The Outermost House, A Year of Life on the Great Beach of Cape Cod* (Garden City, N.Y., 1928), p. 10.
19. Rachel Carson, "Our Ever-Changing Shore," *Holiday*, 24 (July 1958), 117; *Under the Sea-Wind*, pp. 119–120.
20. Rachel Carson, *The Sea Around Us* (New York, 1950), pp. 7–15.
21. Carson, *Sea Around Us*, pp. 124–133.
22. Rachel Carson, *The Edge of the Sea* (1955; reprint, New York, 1959), p. 14; "Undersea," p. 325; "Our Ever-Changing Shore," p. 117.
23. Carson, *Edge of the Sea*, p. 15.

24. Arthur Lovejoy, *The Great Chain of Being* (Cambridge, Mass., 1936), pp. 315–316.
25. Albert Schweitzer, *Out of My Life and Thought, An Autobiography*, trans. C. T. Campion (London, 1933), pp. 185–190.
26. Brooks, *House of Life*, pp. 315–316.
27. Frank Graham, Jr., *Since Silent Spring* (Boston, 1970).

CREDITS

INDEX